International Educational Development and Learning
through Sustainable Partnerships

International Educational Development and Learning through Sustainable Partnerships

Living Global Citizenship

Steven Coombs
University of the South Pacific, Fiji

Mark Potts
Educational Consultant, UK

Jack Whitehead
University of Cumbria, UK

First published 2014 by
PALGRAVE MACMILLAN

Palgrave Macmillan in the UK is an imprint of Macmillan Publishers Limited, registered in England, company number 785998, of Houndmills, Basingstoke, Hampshire RG21 6XS.

Palgrave Macmillan in the US is a division of St Martin's Press LLC, 175 Fifth Avenue, New York, NY 10010.

Palgrave Macmillan is the global academic imprint of the above companies and has companies and representatives throughout the world.

Palgrave® and Macmillan® are registered trademarks in the United States, the United Kingdom, Europe and other countries.

ISBN 978–1–137–34997–2

This book is printed on paper suitable for recycling and made from fully managed and sustained forest sources. Logging, pulping and manufacturing processes are expected to conform to the environmental regulations of the country of origin.

A catalogue record for this book is available from the British Library.

A catalog record for this book is available from the Library of Congress.

Contents

Tables and Figures

Tables

Figures

Foreword

I am very happy and honoured to be asked to write this foreword for *International Educational Development and Learning through Sustainable Partnerships*, an important and timely publication that successfully and meaningfully brings together two very significant concepts: international education and global citizenship. Congratulations and thanks are due to the authors. As a graduate student in the International Education (IE) programme at the University of California at Santa Barbara (UCSB) in the early 1970s, I was intrigued by the type of conversations that were common among staff and students about what IE was and/or should be. I had registered for the programme accidentally since IE was offered only to doctoral students, but the Head of the Program, Professor Murray Thomas, welcomed me and supervised my Master's research study, perhaps because of the different perspectives I would bring to the IE cohort of mainly US citizens. That the rest of my co-learners did not know where Tonga was did not matter to me; they knew of the state of Hawaii and had seen the movie *South Pacific* and that was good enough for me.

There was a lot of talk about global citizenship among my colleagues, about assisting nations in their quest for freedom and democracy and of course there was the Vietnam War. I heard about the importance of becoming a global citizen but wondered how I could do this, especially given what I knew of the Pacific Island contexts in general and of Tonga in particular, where civic and/or citizenship education was about learning to be a good, obedient citizen, often in a colonised setting. At that time, only Fiji and Samoa were independent states, the rest were still colonies of France, United States, Australia or New Zealand. My own country, Tonga, although never directly colonised, was probably even more British than Fiji (the Fijians were under British rule until 1970) perhaps because of the huge influence of British missionaries and advisors since the early nineteenth century. I would express my concern about global citizenship and how difficult this might be in my part of the world, but no one seemed interested. By the time I completed my studies and left UCSB, I came to the conclusion that global citizenship was really a notion more relevant to people living in wealthy and more developed countries; people in poorer countries, in the contexts of development aid and/or humanitarian assistance, seemed to be the poor relatives in the global partnership equation.

I have learnt a bit more about international education and global citizenship since those days at UCSB. At the University of the South Pacific, where I now work and study, I became an international education consultant, serving in a number of externally funded educational projects in many Pacific Island Countries (PICs) as part of my job as UNESCO Chair and my university's contribution to its 12 member states. In these contexts, I worked with many consultants, drawn mainly from donor nations such as Australia, New Zealand, United States and United Kingdom and later the European Union. Some of my experiences are reflected in stories and articles written over many years, including one on citizenship education. In this I suggested that because of the cultural and colonial histories of most PICs, citizenship education was/is often problematic because of the perceived tensions between recently independent governments (patterned after ex-colonial masters) and many of their 'citizens' whose allegiances are often to their immediate localities (such as villages and/or provinces) and not necessarily to a 'nation' as such (Thaman, 2005).

It is therefore fortuitous and timely to come across this book, which not only helps clarify and enlighten us about notions such as international education and global citizenship but actually provides a framework for those willing to make global citizenship a real, living and dynamic experience. Many people have written about global citizenship, but the authors of this book tell us what they think it means and how one might achieve it through collaborative, participatory and context-specific processes and partnerships, taking into account issues of justice, power relations and diverse contexts. In recognising the importance of life-long learning as well as global values espoused by UNESCO such as education for human rights, peace, international understanding, tolerance and sustainable development (to name a few), Living Global Citizenship (LGC) is a new form of international education development and also serves to assist us to better understand the goals of existing global educational instruments such as Millennium Development Goals (MDGs), the Education Funding Agency and the Decade of Education for Sustainable Development.

More importantly, readers will be interested to learn the different ways and 'transformations' necessary for achieving LGC where values education would play a prominent part.

The last goal of MDGs is forging international partnerships. The case studies contained in this book document successful and meaningful partnerships which help demonstrate the main principles and values underpinning the LGC approach; they are bound to enhance our knowledge and willingness to learn and become more engaged in partnerships and interactions that are mutually beneficial and coherent as well as philosophically and politically adequate.

As well as explaining and developing ideas associated with international education, global citizenship and inter-cultural understanding, this book also challenges readers to shift their gaze from focusing on themselves or their group to focusing on those with whom they interact. For international consultants, it may mean a shift from a neo-liberal approach that views the partner being assisted as needing development to a position that offers both partners an opportunity for sharing knowledge and experiences for mutual benefit. The book also offers readers solutions as well as practices that they might wish to try out in different contexts.

One of the most useful aspects of LGC as well as of the book itself is the possibility it raises, for those willing to change, to address power imbalances, especially in relation to the role of donor governments as well as NGOs and the neo-liberal notion of development. For example, by reconceptualising sustainable development as a means of distributing power to the less powerful in order to determine their own sustainable futures, a new hope for a more balanced perspective is forged. This provides for a mutually beneficial partnership in the areas of knowledge production and exchange, often involving diverse peoples and cultures, using the latest in Information and Communication Technologies (ICTs).

Finally, this book is not only about LGC; it is itself a learning tool for achieving and living global citizenship. The book is well organised and written. Stories, diagrams and links to Internet sites and social media provide the reader with not only useful academic and technical information but also a realistic and human dimension to the content of the book. Whether one is a teacher or student, a consultant in an aid-funded project, a member of an international organisation or a donor/development agency, a member of a government department or NGO, or anyone interested in making a difference in their lives as well as in the lives of others, this book is a must-read for one who wishes to move away from business-as-usual and take risks for the sake of improved global partnerships and relationships. Enjoy!

Konai Helu Thaman
UNESCO Chair in Teacher Education & Culture
University of the South Pacific

Acknowledgements

This book is a multimedia project that has involved the use of various forms of new technology. The ideas have been developed over a number of years through conversations between the authors. The conversations have been aided by technology, as geography has not always enabled us to meet face-to-face. Therefore, we acknowledge the value of new technology in enhancing communication.

There have been many people with whom we have discussed and developed the ideas contained in the book. In particular, we acknowledge the contribution that Fran Martin has made through participation in discussion and through her writings.

We are grateful to Konai Helu Thaman for writing the foreword to the book.

We thank the contributors to Chapter 4, in particular Je Kan Adler-Collins and Phil Tattersall, who have allowed us to share their living legacies to inspire others.

We also acknowledge the tremendous work of all of the participants in the partnership between Sarum Academy (formerly Salisbury High School) and Nqabakazulu School in Durban, South Africa, especially Rose MJiyakho, David Ngcobo, Thiris Arumugam and Vusumuzi Shezi of Nqabakazulu School. That partnership formed the foundation for the idea of Living Global Citizenship.

1
Transforming International Educational Development through Living Global Citizenship

In this first chapter we establish the origins of the idea of 'Living Global Citizenship' and we represent it as three transformations in thinking that have taken place over the past 12 years as we have engaged in discussions about the nature of international educational development and learning through partnerships. We set it in the context of the discourse regarding partnerships between the Global South and the Global North, arguing that it is consistent with a postcolonial perspective that seeks to address issues of injustice and unequal power relations. We also position it in terms of the debate regarding educational cosmopolitanism and universal values and suggest that such notions ignore the importance of learning from difference, whereby difference is to be celebrated as a cultural asset. Finally, we suggest that Living Global Citizenship, by putting values at the heart of partnerships, can be regarded as an antidote to the prevalent ideas of de-skilling, de-moralisation and de-valuation inherent in contemporary economic rationalism.

The reader should note the three conceptual assumptions we make regarding the distinctions of living global citizenship, cultural empathy and living cases as theoretical concepts as opposed to the interpretation of their inherent personal values as *acts-of-being*. Please therefore note the terminology and syntax used below to help separate these distinctions we use throughout the book:

> 1. Throughout the book we make a distinction between the general theoretical concept of **Living Global Citizenship** and the unique personal act of meaning that an individual is seeking to live as fully as possible in *living-global-citizenship*.
> 2. We make a similar distinction between **Cultural Empathy** as a social value and *cultural-empathy* as the unique embodied expression of personal meaning as an individual seeks to live their value of cultural-empathy as fully as possible.
> 3. We also refer to an individual who is generating evidence through participation in a Living Global Citizenship project as a **Living Case** and the personal act of participation and generation of evidence as a *living-case* in the same manner that the personal act of generating a project's **Video Case** evidence can be referred to as a *video-case*.

1.1   Three transformations in learning – the emergence of Living Global Citizenship

We have identified three transformations in learning that led us to write this book and to promote the idea of Living Global Citizenship as a new form of international educational development.

1.1.1   First transformation – recognising the possibility of influencing others

The first transformation was recognition that it is possible to conduct research into how an individual can influence others as practising professionals and that this research can make a wider contribution to the academy as new professional learning knowledge.

Mark writes: As a deputy head in a state school in the United Kingdom, I was responsible for developing the professional practice of colleagues. As I enquired into the way that I worked with colleagues, I reflected on how I was influencing both my own and their practice. I grew in confidence as a researcher into my own professional practice through engagement in educational enquiries of the sort that start with the question, 'How can I improve my educational practice?'

In Jack Whitehead's (1993) words, I began the process of developing my own Living Educational Theory.

The term 'Living Educational Theory' is used here in the way that Jack Whitehead used the term as stated in his address to the 12th International Conference of Teacher Research at McGill University in April 2005.

> I want to see if I can captivate your imaginations with the idea of your living educational theory. I see your accounts of your learning, to the extent that they are explaining your educational influence in this learning, as constituting your own living educational theory.
>
> (Whitehead, 2005)

Living Educational Theory provides recognition for practitioners as knowledge creators. Through studying their practice, teachers (and any other similar professionals) can generate their own theories of practice, which they then make available for public testing. The individual practitioner who undertakes the research is at the heart of their own educational enquiry. The practitioner researcher is responsible for holding themselves to account for their potential influence on the learning of others. In this approach the aim of the researcher is to hold themselves accountable for their learning and their influence in the learning of others (McNiff, 2006). This approach appealed to me as an educator as it seemed to provide the opportunity to be creative and for me to be methodologically inventive (Dadds & Hart, 2001).

In 2000 I established an international educational partnership between my own school in the United Kingdom and a black township school in Durban, South Africa. In deciding to conduct an enquiry into 'How can I improve the delivery of citizenship education through an international school partnership?', I was holding myself accountable for my own learning and the learning of others from the partnership activities. The motivation to conduct such an enquiry emerged from my experiences as I visited the black township school and began to engage in dialogue with educators at the school. I came to recognise that I was not fully living out my values as a professional educator, and I wanted to examine how I could improve my practice to overcome the contradiction between the values that I express and the values that I was living out in my practice. The values that emerged from the dialogue between participants were social justice, equal opportunities and Ubuntu (a Zulu phrase loosely translated as 'humanity'). Through participation in the partnership and reflection on my values in dialogue with the other participants, we were seeking to engage in activities that would influence the social formations in which we were operating. The living theory approach to action research best suits my perception of people as human beings who live in relation to each other and who are participants in educating themselves and creating their own lives. This enquiry was the next part of my living educational theory. It is living because it is active. Through engagement in this research project, I was embodying my own values as a person and as a professional educator. As I came to understand and appreciate my own values and to live them out more fully, I was furthering my own professional development and contributing to the social manifesto research agenda. The concept of a social manifesto linked to action research was first proposed by Steve Coombs (1995) as part of his doctoral thesis and later followed up by Gardner and Coombs (2010). The key idea was to differentiate between hypothesis-based research enquiry linked to a 'prove' type agenda and a more practical needs-based social change approach, or a shift towards an 'improve' type research agenda. Thus, the research methodology requires a paradigm shift from 'prove' based experimental research to a more practical 'improve' approach that suits projects linked to change through social inquiry and action. Action research is a suitable methodology that aligns itself to just such an 'improve' applied experimental research paradigm and the research questions, and social tasks that need to be achieved can be suitably described as befitting a social manifesto approach linked to the project's values, needs and actions. This represents a paradigm shift from hypothesis-based research questions towards a social manifesto of social enquiry tasks and actions that can be achieved through action research. This social research paradigm identifies a different type of research question that relates to achieving social inquiry action and goals as defined and measured as a form of success against the project's predetermined 'social manifesto'.

We acknowledge that this approach fits with recent moves in the international development sector that is considering moving the UNESCO Millennium Development Goals (MDGs) to a new agenda defined by Sustainable Development Goals (SDGs),[1] requiring social impact targets that require a new research methodology and agenda and something that all countries need to meet, not just developing nations. We would argue that the Living Global Citizenship methodology provides a new way of understanding and meeting this sustainable development agenda and approach.

In conclusion, the first transformation was the recognition that we as professional educators can, through the examination of our own practice, contribute to educational theory in an original, creative, valid and meaningful way. By doing so, we add our own living educational theories as valid professional learning experiences to the knowledgebase of the 'academy' and thereby create a shared living legacy. In many ways the sharing of experiential derived professional knowledge should become the new *common law code of practice* and working standard for all active professionals in the twenty-first century global societies.

1.1.2 Second transformation – living citizenship emerging from an international educational partnership

Mark writes: During my first visit to the South African school, I met and talked to the students about their own lives. I vividly recall the conversations held about their hopes and dreams for their own futures and for the future of their country.

> In the gaze of a South African student I saw the joy and optimism of his youth. I saw the humanity of the gaze as he shows his love for me with whom he is communicating. When I spoke with him and others like him about his hopes and dreams for the future they were full of ambition, yet they were also well aware of the likelihood that their ambitions will not be realised because of the tragic realities of their lives. They are living in communities that are decimated by AIDS and by poverty. Their time and energy is taken by providing enough food for their families to eat.
>
> (Potts, 2012)

A short video is available at: http://www.youtube.com/watch?v=5rY1e qHQP20.

There was human tragedy in this picture and in the stories that I heard that touched my inner being and urged me to act. These were the first stirrings of what we now recognise as Living Global Citizenship. I claim that my response to this student expresses my value of cultural-empathy. As a result of my visit to the black township of a South African school, I was experiencing a concern that my values were not being fully lived in my practice. I formulated a plan and data was gathered to consider how to address this concern. Analysis of the data and reflection on the findings led to actions being taken and the development of a sustained[2] and active relationship between participants at the UK and South African schools. (For further discussion of this partnership see Chapter 4.)

Thus, the 'Living Citizenship' conceptual framework emerged from this action enquiry project carried out over 12 years, studying this inter-cultural partnership between a school in Salisbury, United Kingdom, and a black township school in South Africa. In this book, we offer a reconceptualisation of international educational partnerships as a form of 'Living Citizenship'. Just as through the development of a living-educational-theory the researcher is active, in the present and engaged through the research in living out his/her own values more fully, so through 'living-citizenship', the participants in the partnership are actively engaged in living out their values more fully through the activities of the partnership. Through this engagement they develop opportunities for living out their values as active citizens. Within this process, there are transferable pedagogical protocols that both define and enable participants to live out their values more fully as active citizens, and these can be applied to other international educational partnerships implying a new socio-ethical blueprint for planning and implementing international education development projects.

Living citizenship recognises the contribution that can be made by educational partnerships to improving the lives of oneself and of others, focusing on the question, 'How am I contributing to improving the lives of others?' The importance of stressing the idea of a 'contribution' to the lives of others is to acknowledge that whatever I do, with the intention of helping others to improve their lives, is going to be mediated by the creative response of the *other* to what I do. In other words I do not believe that I have a 'causal' influence in the lives of others of the kind, 'If I do this, then that will happen'. I believe that I have an intentional relationship in which what I do must be mediated by the creative response of the other for me to recognise any learning as 'educational'. Living Citizenship projects are motivated by the desire to contribute to the improvement of our own lives and to the lives of others (Whitehead & Huxtable, 2013) and provide a key goal or statement in any emergent social manifesto (Coombs, 1995).

Yet, at this stage the transformation is incomplete. This second transformation is insufficient in that it contains a worldview that is consistent with the dominant neo-liberal discourse of development that roughly sees the Global North as providing solutions to the problems of the Global South. Hence, the importance of the third transformation from 'living-citizenship' to 'living-global-citizenship' with the incorporation of a postcolonial perspective on development that recognises that the focus of any partnership should not solely be on economic poverty, but should also examine and confront the issues of injustice and power relations. Thus, such transformed partnerships need to initially negotiate their terms of reference through jointly identifying and articulating the key *shared values* of importance to all participants. Such a 'values-led' agenda predicates the flow of all such actions that any project may take forward. It can also usefully underpin any social manifesto or bespoke 'charter agreement' that builds in the unique cultural contexts and needs of all the participants. In this way Living Global Citizenship-designed (and inspired) projects celebrate and put cultural difference and knowledge at the heart of any international partnership. Understanding different cultural contexts and celebrating such 'difference' as part of the essential design of any partnership project requires a core value we refer to as Cultural Empathy that we explore in the next section.

1.1.3 Third transformation – living citizenship as Cultural Empathy becomes Living Global Citizenship

What makes living-citizenship become living-global-citizenship? This is one of the central questions that this book seeks to explore and provide some answers to. We believe that the global perspective of citizenship occupies a description of humanity itself. We are describing humanity in terms of its rich cultural differences and contributions to a twenty-first century world. So a global citizen can be understood in terms of cultural origins, exchange and development. Moreover, the ability of an emerging global citizen to appreciate other cultures and societies and move towards a common shared set of values and understanding is a valuable goal. This global appreciation of other cultures, traditions and values is something we argue as 'cultural empathy'. Cultural empathy is both a social policy and an act of humanity, and when combined with our notion of living-citizenship, it helps us to define what we mean by 'living-global-citizenship'. Cultural empathy also helps us to celebrate and appreciate the richness of 'cultural difference' as promoted by Fran Martin and H. Griffiths (2012) and others (Andreotti, 2011; Todd, 2008). While cultural empathy is a human, indeed, 'living' human quality, it is also something that can be formulated into social and educational policy. Existing educational areas such as citizenship can become 'global-citizenship' where such a curriculum includes both content and activities that enable cultural empathy to take place. Clearly, cultural empathy goes beyond mere study. It is something that needs to be acted upon and experienced by all those engaged within such a curriculum. Going further, we can argue that the multidimensional social nature of cultural empathy, when extended into global-citizenship, has the potential to add genuine societal value to a problematic area of social policy such as multiculturalism that traditionally operates within national contexts. The social problems of global mobility and the consequent emerging multicultural societies have been largely responsible for the introduction of national citizenship education programmes in the first place:

> Citizenship education has arisen against a social backdrop of considerable social and political upheaval caused by the rise of nationalism and increased disregard for 'civic virtues'. Within this climate the nation state can no longer be viewed as the given natural order.
>
> (Simon, 2005, p. 1)

According to QCA (1999) citizenship education is further propelled by the 'increasingly complex nature of our society, the greater cultural diversity and the apparent loss of value consensus, combined with the collapse of traditional support mechanisms such as extended families' (p. 7).

According to UNESCO (2000) citizenship education is about 'education for human rights, peace, international understanding, tolerance and nonviolence. It also includes all aspects of education relating to the principles of democracy and multicultural and intercultural education' (p. 2).

In this sense a global citizenship programme has the potential to add greater social and educational value to an otherwise more limited national citizenship programme. When citizenship education was launched in UK secondary schools in 1999, Crick recognised its potential educational value: 'Citizenship is more than a statutory subject. If taught well and tailored to local needs, its skills and values will enhance democratic life for us all, both rights and responsibilities, beginning in school, and radiating out' (Crick, 1999).

Though Crick's vision for citizenship education may seem ambitious, it is one that we share and that we believe Living Global Citizenship can aspire to. A Living Global Citizenship education curriculum would be one in which its participants engage with and develop a real sense of cultural empathy through the 'living' activities and opportunities offered. These might include a new interpretation and delivery of international educational exchange visits; smart uses of technology and social networking sites to enable greater access to cultural experiences; and new types of professional development for the educational workforce through a reconceptualisation of international educational development and an introduction of a new form of international continuing professional development (ICPD). This book explores and develops all of these ideas and provides the reader with some interesting insights and solutions to try out in practice.

1.2   Living Global Citizenship and postcolonialism

The neo-liberal paradigm that currently appears to dominate education has a focus mainly on *top-down* International Development. That dominant educational discourse is one which focuses on what is lacking in other countries when judged against Western lifestyles and assumed standards. This is in accord with the dominant discourse about Africa portrayed through the media. From 'Live Aid' in 1987 to 'Live 8' in 2004, the focus has been on Africa as a poverty stricken continent dependent on the West to help it to raise its standard of living (Martin, 2012). Certainly there is poverty in Africa, but there is a danger in focusing solely on economic poverty, that we miss the richness of culture, history and society that is inherent in the Global

South. There is, as Chimamanda Adichie (2009) says, more than a 'single story' of Africa as a 'place of beautiful landscapes, beautiful animals, and incomprehensible people, fighting senseless wars and waiting to be saved, by a kind white foreigner'. On another level this dominant discourse masks the issues of power and control exerted by the North over the South. 'This matters to education because teachers' worldviews are informed by broader societal discourses and have a profound impact on how North-South intercultural experiences are interpreted within the context of global educational partnerships' (Martin, 2012). This discourse is prevalent in other fields as well. Adler-Collins (2013b) refers to the colonisation by the West of the medical practices in China and Japan.

> One of the major areas where this is evident is in nursing education where, through the influence of the World Bank, large sums of money are made available to developing countries to update their medical and social services. Such updates often include the purchase of modern diagnostic, investigative and treatment systems and equipment and the incorporation of Western values intrinsic within the nursing culture of the United States of America, England or Europe. This practice, I suggest is totally unsuitable to the social history and culture of the country where it is introduced. Unsuitable not in the sense of the biology, because we are only one species, rather in the required compliance with western values at the expense of indigenous forms of knowing and values. (p. 5)

In challenging this paradigm, Living Global Citizenship has clear links with postcolonialism. Postcolonialism emerged as a theory from the South and seeks to reveal and challenge the hegemonic discourses inherent in the relationship between the North and the South. It offers a critique of dominant discourses around development, recognising that this is a contested term and field, and drawing on sources that question international aid and the role of NGOs. NGOs such as Oxfam, UNICEF and CAFOD, as well as charitable organisations such as Comic Relief and Sport Relief, have educational wings that aim to influence pupils' learning. They offer one solution to the 'lack' of wealth, education, sanitation, which is 'aid'. This single solution, it is argued, has in some ways undermined African people's ability to emancipate themselves from oppression (Andreotti, 2008; Sharp, 2009). The causes of inequality and oppression are hidden under the concept of care. Active citizenship education in the United Kingdom in a global context too often means *to care*, and global-citizenship is about being benevolent towards the *Other* (Jefferess, 2008). Andreotti (2008) argues that educational policy documents in the United Kingdom, such as 'Developing a global dimension across the school curriculum' (DfEE, DfID, 2005), reflect the neo-liberal view that poverty is a purely economic phenomenon resulting from the lack of development, and it ignores the view that the problem emanates from injustice and unequal power relations that lead to impoverishment of many kinds. Living Global Citizenship brings a more equitable approach to international partnership work and attempts to restore a *cultural balance* and shared humanity despite any prior inequalities between the parties involved.

Martin (2012) observes that in international partnerships participants' attention is often drawn to the most obvious difference, that of inequality, without understanding the influence of former colonial relationships (usually) between Northern and Southern countries and thus lacking awareness of how the inequality came about. While there has been political, and to some extent, economic decolonisation with independence, Sharp (2009) talks about the need for decolonisation of the mind in both Northern and Southern countries. Andreotti (2011) questions whether development is a project that is about development in the Global South and argues that transformation is required in the Global North – transformations in worldviews. We are making a case that this transformation can be achieved through adopting the ontological principles, epistemology, philosophy and human practice of Living Global Citizenship.

1.3   Living Global Citizenship as a means of redressing power imbalances

Living Global Citizenship addresses the concerns expressed regarding the role of NGOs and the neo-liberal notion of development. It contains an important commitment to genuine interactive dialogue that values the voice of all of the participants and that also gives priority to the participants in the southern countries as a means of redressing the imbalance of power relations between North and South.[3] This needs to happen in such a way that the participants from southern nations are put in the position of driving the partnership forward to realise their own vision of progress and development.[4] This links to the key recommendation (See Chapter 5) of creating a space for learning that focuses on negotiation and discussion of common 'values' as the initial preparatory phase of any partnership and an important part of the agenda setting of any new international partnership. During the dialogue, the participants need to step out of their own cultural space into a 'Third Space' (Bhabha, 1994) allowing new meanings and understandings to emerge, thereby acting as a first step in bridging any prior *cultural divide* and working towards *cultural balance* and greater social equanimity. Social equanimity is something proposed by Carl Rogers (1961) who believed that developing positive 'helping relationships' between humans was an important prerequisite of generating mutual trust and understanding and also referred to this as an 'empathic relationship'. Rogers' (1961) ideas about the characteristics of helping relationships are applicable to all relationships, not just counselling relationships, and would therefore be applicable to dialogue situations where people were negotiating and identifying common values as part of preparing for an educational development partnership. Developing helping and empathic relationships in *any* social partnership is therefore a useful conversational learning procedure that lends itself towards achieving cultural-empathy between participants in a living-global-citizenship context.

In summary, we have clarified the process and nature of how human beings need to develop social relations so as to achieve trust and mutual cultural understanding and as such defined our underpinning assumptions of the term 'development' and how it connects to the framework of Living Global Citizenship. Our paradigm of 'sustainable development' therefore operates as a means of negotiating and distributing power to the less powerful and privileged in order to determine their own future in a lasting manner. Living-citizenship focuses attention on a process of accountability and individual empowerment that engages participant learners with issues of power and privilege in society.

Living Global Citizenship assumes a Kuhnian paradigm shift (Kuhn, 1962; 2012) and allows participants to transform their view of the world and role within it. We argue that a new balanced perspective is required, whereupon we have greater *cultural equity* of ideas, judgement and decision-making, that is, a kind of *global inclusion* that allows genuine two-way and multichannel knowledge exchange. Rather than assuming great shifts in power from the Atlantic to the Pacific, as described in Sir Michael Barber et al.'s (2012) recent report on Global Education policy and leadership initiative 'Oceans of Innovation', we offer an alternative and radical new notion of Global Enlightenment. We envisage an alternative paradigm of borderless creativity achieved through the cultural inclusivity of nations and their diverse people and scaffolded using the twenty-first century social networking technology. Living Global Citizenship is both the concept and vehicle through which we can achieve this goal by intentional partnership activities in which individuals can generate Rogerian 'climates of trust' and share their living-educational-theories. Outcomes from such prerequisite learning conversations[5] can take the form of 'common needs' projects that levers cultural-empathy via in situ experiential knowledge exchange and production.

1.4 Educational cosmopolitanism and universal values

We recognise the weaknesses of the notion of educational cosmopolitanism and the contested idea of universal values. Nussbaum (1997) argues for educational cosmopolitanism by saying that the accident of where one is born is just that, an accident; any human being might have been born in any nation. Recognising this, she says, we should not allow differences of nationality or class or ethnic membership or even gender to erect barriers between us and our fellow human beings. We should recognise humanity wherever it occurs and give that *community of humanity* our first allegiance (Nussbaum, 1997, pp. 58–59).

Todd (2008) argues that such appeals to humanity reveal, constructed as they are on the positive, universal ideals such as dignity, respect, reason and freedom, an admission that the present human condition is in crisis. When organisations such as UNESCO, or even cosmopolitan educationalists, appeal to humanity, they are hoping to counteract the very devastating realities of social dissolution that plague societies throughout the world and unite us under a banner of respect for what we share as human beings. There is a danger, he argues, to assume that humanity exists in the universal risks diminishing concrete forms of existing, in all their rich variety and diversity. In this, then, the cosmopolitan emphasis on a 'shared humanity' is not something that we should advocate if we are really concerned with relieving social injustice. This is not to say that we do not share anything with one another (we do indeed share values, love, suffering and joy). Nor is it to claim that people cannot forge alliances and friendships across these shared spaces, which is fundamental to Living Global Citizenship projects. To educate on the basis that we already know what humanity is, risks counting some persons 'in' while leaving others (those who express violence and hatred, for instance) 'out'. Humanity is not an ideal, but an orientation (a responsibility) that responds to human difference; it is here that dignity resides. So long as cosmopolitanism aims to mould, encourage or cultivate a humanity that is already seen as 'shared', it prevents us from confronting the far more difficult and much closer task at hand of facing the troublesome aspects of human interaction that emerge in specific times and places.

The importance of learning from difference as opposed to always looking for similarities and universalities is stated by Martin (2012). Writing about learning from difference, she emphasises the importance of understanding culture in a relational sense. Culture, she argues, exists in the interaction between people. Culture is not something that is static; rather it changes, evolves and modifies itself as it is challenged by people from other cultural backgrounds (by difference). Such a perspective leads to a more open-minded and positive disposition towards difference in building intercultural relationships.

Living Global Citizenship encourages a focus on friendship as a means of recognising and respecting differences and similarities. Rather than promoting the idea of a shared humanity that focuses on similarities and excludes aspects of humanity which do not conform to a shared ideal, living-global-citizenship instead seeks to respond positively to human difference and therefore to respect the dignity of the other and regard these as cultural assets for creative innovation. In the same way that living-global-citizenship is a result of transformations in thinking, it has the potential to lead to transformation of lives and the evolution of culture as participants in partnerships learn from difference. As participants discuss their values, they are likely to express different values. In a Living Global Citizenship project, it is important to provide the space for discussion of these different values and the possibility of evolution and modification of values as a way forward is found for the partnership. This enables cultural empathy through active participation in commonly determined projects, whereupon participatory action research is both suggested and recommended as a suitable methodology and change agency.

1.5   De-valuation and de-moralisation in the influence of economic rationalism

Economic Globalisation, with its emphasis on 'free markets', influences the conditions within which learning and education take place. The dominance of such economic forces can have a de-valuation and de-moralisation influence on educational practices that are seeking to live as fully as possible the values that carry hope for the future of humanity. McTaggart (1992) has expressed this tension as:

> De-valuation refers to diminishing or denying the relevance of all but one type of value to an issue; de-moralization denies the relevance of moral questions. The reduction of all values – intellectual, civic, health, among others – to a money value would be an example of de-valuation; the slogan 'business is business' is an example of de-moralization (Broudy, 1981, p. 99). (p. 50)

Living Global Citizenship puts the values that carry hope for the future of humanity at the heart of actions and encourages people to critically engage in their world and ask moral questions as they account for and explain their lives in terms of these values.

We do not want to be understood as denying the vital role that economies can play in supporting the resources needed for enhancing educational opportunities and improving their quality. Indeed, we support the meaning of promoting an 'entrepreneurial spirit' as developed by Yvonne Crotty (2012) in her doctoral research, where she integrates the creativity of an entrepreneurial spirit with the values that carry hope for the future of humanity. We integrate this creativity in our meanings of living-global-citizenship.

2
Pedagogy for Effective Citizenship Education

In this chapter we first deconstruct current notions of citizenship education and explore how it is regarded and delivered in various educational settings. We then go on to deconstruct contemporary UK ideas about the 'Big Society' and cultural education. From this position we then construct our own alternative pedagogy for the delivery of effective citizenship education within any cultural setting, thereby creating a new meaning for the term 'cultural education'.

2.1 Deconstructing citizenship education

2.1.1 Citizenship education in the United Kingdom

When citizenship education was launched in UK schools as part of the then national curriculum, Crick (1999) emphasised the deeper value of citizenship education. He indicated that it ought to be about more than just delivering a content-based curriculum.[1] It should also be about exploring values, developing human relationships and enhancing the democratic process. In order to be informed citizens, Crick maintains that pupils should be taught about:

> The opportunities for individuals and voluntary groups to bring about social change locally, nationally, in Europe and internationally.

This resonates with our idea of initiating Living Global Citizenship projects that seek to bring about social change locally, nationally and internationally. Living Global Citizenship projects provide a means for exploring values and inculcating a sense of responsibility, which we believe is the core responsibility of any educational citizenship programme for *any country* to promote as part of its educational policy, planning and implementation. The rhetoric behind the intentions of the UK citizenship curriculum was sound. However, as with many things in real life the practice has turned out to be somewhat different.

Garratt and Piper (2010) argued for a renewed commitment to Citizenship and Values Education to coincide with the problem that:

> Secondary schools in England are reported to be struggling to provide citizenship lessons, due to other pressures on the curriculum and the low status of the subject. (p. 18)

This negative picture of citizenship education provision in the United Kingdom is supported by OFSTED's 2010 report into Citizenship Education that in just under half of all cases provision is 'no better than satisfactory overall' and that a 'new direction and impetus are needed' (OFSTED, 2010, p. 5).

The Citizenship Education Longitudinal Study conducted by UK's National Foundation for Educational Research (NFER, 2010) reported that schools needed help with embedding citizenship education into their curriculum, school culture and wider community. Practice remains patchy and uneven, with some schools making better progress with citizenship education than others. The report highlighted that the most successful approach was one where citizenship education is embedded into the curriculum, has links to student participation across the school/college and encourages links with the wider community. The report called for an increase in the use of *active* teaching and learning methods.

Gove's ideas on the reform of the English public assessment system of A levels is to include encouragement of voluntary work for post-16 students, coupled with an extended piece of writing. This initiative provides a perfect opportunity to promote the notion of living-global-citizenship in which a student involved in a voluntary partnership with a community organisation critically reflects on his/her values with the participants in that organisation and develops a socially constructed meaningful narrative of how he/she is living out those values through the activities that they are engaged in. There is a danger that the young persons engaged in the partnerships may feel unable to freely express and explore their values with the participants of the organisation because of the evident unequal power relations. Therefore, it is imperative that the discussion around values is conducted in an open environment of mutual trust and Rogerian 'congruence' (Rogers, 1961) where the young person feels able to express themselves and where their ideas are given equal consideration to those of the other participants.[2] This social development provides a real opportunity for young people to actually experience the curriculum, to engage in the process of discussion and negotiation of shared values that ultimately lead to participation in activities that enable them to live out their values as citizens and for them to authentically become living global citizens, that is, the embedding and deep learning of long-term citizenship values rather than the surface learning of citizenship as a set of mere content topics.

Citizenship has been re-confirmed as a subject in the revised UK national curriculum from 2014. While this cements its place in the curriculum it fails to address questions about the effective delivery of citizenship education. Thus, we seek to contribute to the debate about *how to deliver* effective citizenship education in the United Kingdom and argue that it should be embedded into real life and authentic community action projects rather than be treated as a set of topics to be surface learnt within the confines of the school classroom.

2.1.2   Citizenship education in the United States

In the United States voluntary work is built into the curriculum in many schools. Voluntary work by students in the form of 'Service-Learning' is currently practiced in about a third of all public K-12 schools in the United States (National Service-Learning Clearing House, 2012). Kezar's (2002) review of multiple studies found consistent positive connections between service-learning and outcomes associated with cultural awareness, tolerance for diversity, altruistic attitudes, moral development, sensitivity and reasoning and self-esteem. Eyler et al. (2001) cite 32 studies and dissertations linking service-learning with 'reducing stereotypes and facilitating cultural and racial understanding'. Developing a Living Global Citizenship project can build on the gains made by service-learning to deliver deeper cultural awareness, greater respect for difference and reduced stereotyping and thereby achieve greater *cultural empathy* and overall understanding.

Finley (2011) questions whether service-learning *really* is civic engagement? A number of scholars have argued that most forms of service-learning (or other forms of apolitical community engagement) fail to intentionally engage students in the activities and processes central to democratic building (i.e. deliberative dialogue, collaborative work, problem-solving within diverse groups). In essence, these scholars argue it is not enough for students to just engage in the community. So we argue that it is necessary for them to develop specific social skills and knowledge and to be *equipped* so as to be able to reflect on their values as participants in a partnership, thereby leading to greater civic engagement and social stakeholding. Dialogue, collaboration and problem solving across cultures are all key elements in a Living Global Citizenship project and therefore this type of intended participation in such activities helps to enhance the democratic process and through such social design address Finley's concerns.

The Civic Mission of Schools report (2003) identifies some promising approaches towards citizenship education in US schools, such as:

- The design and implementation of programs that provide students with the opportunity to apply what they learn through performing community service that is linked to the formal curriculum and classroom instruction.
- Offering extracurricular activities that provide opportunities for young people to get involved in their schools or communities.
- The encouragement of students' participation in simulations of democratic processes and procedures. (p. 6)

Living Global Citizenship projects both applaud and build on these promising approaches to citizenship education by providing the opportunity for participants to apply their knowledge and use their skills to engage in dialogue and collaborate across cultural divides. This goes *beyond simulation* with students actively engaged in authentic, indeed living, democratic processes and procedures for shared purposes.

Pickerel (2006) says that teaching young people the specifics of civic engagement is the crucial component of creating a democratic self and society. In creating a democratic self, young people need to learn how to bring their fellow citizens together around common concerns; and how to articulate a critical but knowledgeable *voice* to their ideas, support and objections. Therefore, schools should provide opportunities for all students to be active, principled citizens through an 'engaged school,' a school that embraces its community, provides resources to its community, develops mutually beneficial collaborations with its community and in fact is considered a critical and crucial member of its community. Schools need to be able to create authentic engagement opportunities for students to address community issues. Living-global-citizenship links well with Pickerel's (2006) notion of an 'engaged school' as participants in community partnerships critically reflect on their values together and collaborate in activities that benefit members of all the communities involved. We argue that educational partnerships that are developed within a Living Global Citizenship framework offer an opportunity to embed citizenship education into the school culture and wider community as an authentic and participant-enabled form of living-global-citizenship.

The importance of dialogue is highlighted in a comprehensive review of the literature on intergroup dialogue from Zuniga Nagda, Chesler, and Cytron-Walker (2006). A range of positive effects related to civic outcomes were found to be consistently connected with intergroup dialogue activities. Among the outcomes cited as important preparation for democratic participation were engagement in diverse settings; development of perspective taking skills; ability to work in dissonant or unequal environments; and development of a sense of pluralism. As participants in Living Global Citizenship activities critically reflect on their values and engage in dialogue across cultures to move the partnership forward they are likely to confront notions of prejudice; include different viewpoints; and embrace issues linked to social justice.

The US Department of Education (2012) joined the National Task Force on Civic Learning and Democratic Engagement, the American Commonwealth Partnership and the Campaign for the Civic Mission of Schools in a new national call to action to infuse and enhance civic learning and democratic engagement for all students throughout the American education system.[3] The US Department of Education (2012) supports the following initiatives:

1. The advancement of civic learning and democratic engagement in both the US and global contexts by encouraging efforts to make them core expectations for elementary, secondary and postsecondary students – including undergraduate and graduate students;
2. Developing more robust evidence of civic and other student achievement outcomes of civic learning, and of the impact of school- and campus-community partnerships;
3. Strengthening school- and campus-community connections to address significant community problems and advance a local or regional vision and narrative for civic engagement;
4. Expanding research and the range of public scholarship, with a special emphasis on promoting knowledge creation for the good of society; and,
5. Deepening civic identity by sharing stories of civic work in social media and organising deliberative discussions about the roles of higher education in communities across the country.

We maintain that Living Global Citizenship projects fulfil all of these aims. Participants in Living Global Citizenship partnerships engage in activities that strengthen community connections and address community problems. They are encouraged to make their stories public through their living-educational-theories, thus sharing their success and learning in civic work. The critical reflection on values and the processes that make the community partnerships work promotes research with an emphasis on knowledge creation tied to social dissemination for the good of society and consequently builds up a considerable body of case study evidence of the impact of such community partnerships. Thus, personal acts of living-global-citizenship can contribute to the goal of enhancing civic learning and also leverage democratic engagement for *all* students throughout the American education system.

2.1.3   International citizenship education

UNESCO in 1995 recognised the importance of including an international dimension to citizenship education as follows:

We, the Ministers of Education (of the world) strive resolutely to pay special attention to improving curricula, the content of

textbooks, and other education materials including new technologies with a view to educating caring and responsible citizens
committed to peace, human rights, democracy and sustainable
development, open to other cultures, able to appreciate the value
of freedom, respectful of human dignity and differences, and able
to prevent conflicts or resolve them by non-violent means. It is
necessary to introduce, at all levels, true education for citizenship
which includes an international dimension.

UNESCO (1995) Declaration and Integrated Framework of Action
on Education for Peace, Human Rights and Democracy

In our view there are problems with this statement from UNESCO.
While it demonstrates a clear commitment to international citizenship education, it fails to provide any indication; apart from vague
references to improving textbooks and other educational materials,
as to how 'true education for citizenship' is to be delivered. There is
no consideration of effective pedagogy to help deliver such an aspiration of integrating the 'global' into otherwise 'national' citizenship
education systems. It also emphasises the notion of educating 'caring citizens', which as stated in the previous chapter (section 1.2)
is an aim which remains open to question in terms of the association of caring with philanthropy and the neo-liberal viewpoint and
associated policies governing many aid and development projects.

Kerr (1999) reflected UNESCO's concern about the attitudes of
young people in many countries and, in particular, with the signs
of their increasing lack of interest, apathy and non-participation in
public and political life. Effective citizenship education in schools
was seen as crucial towards addressing this social concern. However,
there remained considerable debate as to what was meant by the term
'effective' and how it could best be measured.

Thus, Kerr (1999) profoundly asked: What is meant by 'effective
citizenship education'?

He argues that some countries have developed specific curriculum
programmes which encourage a mixture of approaches to ensure
the goals of 'education FOR citizenship' are achieved. There is, he
argues, an urgent need to map those curriculum projects that lead
to effective practice and to make this practice more widely available,
both within and across countries. This would also include reference
to what is known from effective practice about how students learn

best in citizenship education. Sadly, Kerr found in 1999 that for most countries, citizenship education teaching still proceeded from the use of the textbook as the predominant teaching resource and adopting a didactic pedagogical knowledge-based learning assumption, that is, based upon the indirect experience of a teacher-disseminated content-based curriculum rather than actively student centred – *passivity* versus *activity*.

Living-global-citizenship learning activities can build on good practice and develop it further so that we can address the question: What is effective citizenship education? We can also build up significant case study evidence to demonstrate its effectiveness so that a new pedagogy for enabling citizenship education across cultural boundaries can be developed. Hence, UNESCO's insightful aim of introducing true education for citizenship with an international dimension can then be met.

More recently, the International Association for the Evaluation of Educational Achievement (IEA) (2010) study indicated that its participating countries are increasingly seeing civic and citizenship education as including not just knowledge and understanding but also activities that promote civic attitudes and values. This operates alongside opportunities for students to participate in activities in and beyond the school (Eurydice, 2005; Torney-Purta, Schwille & Amadeo, 1999). They identified a movement in some countries to broaden the role that civic and citizenship education plays in preparing young people as citizens by positioning this area of education in community-based activities.

All 38 countries involved in the study view civic and citizenship education as encompassing a rich variety of pedagogical processes, along with associated curriculum strategies. This area of education is designed to develop knowledge and understanding as well as skills of communication, analysis, observation and reflection, while providing opportunities for active student involvement in and beyond school. Tied up with this is the notion of developing positive attitudes towards national identity and promoting future participation in civic and civil society. Overall, although countries give greatest emphasis to developing knowledge and understanding of civics and citizenship, they still give credence to other processes that occur alongside. These other processes vary from country to country, but in general they focus on the Dewian concept of 'learning by doing' originally outlined in his seminal work 'Schools of Tomorrow' (Dewey, 1915) and provide opportunities for active student participation.

These findings suggest that although there is a move in most countries towards learning by doing and towards facilitating student participation in civic and citizenship activities, this approach is not always matched by opportunities for students to meaningfully reflect upon and analyse the learning they gain from such experiences. Living Global Citizenship goes beyond mere participation in activities and is critical of the type of civic engagement that legitimises existing power structures and processes (Bailee-Smith, 2011). It must make such power structures and processes transparent and recognise their limitations. Living Global Citizenship projects provide the opportunity for participants in different communities to engage in dialogue so as to explore what is different and what is similar between them, and to further develop a shared understanding of ways forward that are co-elicited and owned by them and that are not imposed by existing hierarchies and institutions with a fixed view of development. Living Global Citizenship activities are intended to provide the opportunity for participant reflection and analysis, a *critical learning space*, so that the learning is deep and sustained. Such a critical learning space helps transfer knowledge gained to new situations, thereby influencing future actions in tune with the Rousseauian philosophy of guided experiential learning. In this case the guide, or steer, coming from a mutually constructed and agreed agenda for action; much akin to Coombs' (1995) 'social manifesto' framework for defining and articulating social experimental questions in terms of defined goals and social change objectives. In this way the methodologies of living-global-citizenship projects can usefully deploy the social experimental process of participatory action research projects operating within an evolutionary Living Educational Theory paradigm (Whitehead, 2005). For further explanation of this paradigm see Chapter 3.

2.2   The lack of suitable pedagogy for citizenship education. The need to address Gearon's (2003) question: How do we become good citizens?

As shown above, governments around the world and international organisations have recognised the importance of citizenship education. Our analysis indicates that what is lacking is a clear pedagogy suitable for delivering the true educational objectives of citizenship education as defined by UNESCO and others; in other words, a means for delivering effective citizenship education that will have a lasting influence on pupils and other participants and that will enable them to become better citizens. This is not likely to emerge from the sole use of the textbook as the predominant teaching resource.

> The qualities of a good citizen must come from within the child; otherwise such qualities cannot be sustained and will not be genuine. Imparting citizenship is not just about teaching but 'touching' something that is real and has meaning to the children – living the life of a good citizen, teaching by example.
>
> (Sayers, 2002, p. 14)

The reference to good citizenship coming from *within the child* reflects the belief that one cannot claim to have educated anyone because education comes from *within the person* (Chomsky, 2003). However, one may make the claim to have influenced the learning of others through the intentional opportunities that are presented to students and participants in general, that is, the conceptual construct and epistemological assumption of the pre-designed learning environment and organisation.

Goleman (1998) agrees, arguing that one person can't develop other persons, but that they can create the conditions where they can develop themselves. The implication here is similar to Jack Whitehead's (2005) notion of influencing others. This has significance for the pedagogical relevance of Living Global Citizenship. The participants in a Living Global Citizenship community partnership cannot force the development of others, but they can facilitate their development through the design of opportunities for them to live out their values and empathise with others more fully, hence the 'Living' part of Living Global Citizenship. It is about developing socially relevant activities that touch people's hearts, influence their thinking and move them to initiate political and social change through their own actions. Through participation in a Living Global Citizenship project citizens learn from each other and develop new meanings and understandings, agreeing their own priorities and ways forward. This gives them ownership of the project and the problems that they face and facilitates a creative process of problem solving. Through engagement in the project the participants question their own values, learn about difference and similarity and develop transferable skills that they can use to make a fuller contribution to civic society.

Evidence of this social contribution and the change process through which it was achieved can also be seen as the project's *impact evidence* (Coombs & Harris, 2006; Flecknoe, 2003) and something which many governments (Coombs, 2007; Coombs, Lewis & Denning, 2007; Ofsted, 2004) are now keen to achieve through their various overseas development departments[4] and other funded national training agencies and global organisations (Baker, 2000). Indeed, we postulate the concept of an 'impact evaluation research methodology'[5] linked to participatory action research evidence and organisational knowledge production. Such a methodology is designed to both leverage and meaningfully report the social outcomes and gains from all practical capacity-building projects. This would include all practical community based projects that can increase capacities through mutual knowledge development in social infrastructure (people services); physical infrastructure (resources); social capital; regional knowledgebases; community relations; and cultural capital. Consequently, impact evidence is not so much a chance outcome from some project but designed intentionally through implementing the policy of an impact evaluation research methodology. Such a methodology provides the research instruments and processes to help deliver Living Global Citizenship projects in action. Given the needs of developing suitable activities based pedagogy for citizenship education located in authentic communities, it seems logical to further propose an *action research pedagogy* through which acts of living-global-citizenship can be pursued and assessed for their impact.

2.3   Citizenship education as a means of bringing about social change

Brian Simon (1991) argues that the teaching of citizenship needs to aim at the transformation of education and the social order. The notion that education can act as a lever of social change echoes Dewey (1915). This argument is also echoed by Whitehead (2005):

> Our influence in the education of the social formations in which
> we are living and working is significant in extending our influence
> beyond our classrooms into wider social contexts. (p. 7)

The significance of influencing social formations in the face of 'taken-
for-granted' ways of perceiving and acting has been highlighted by
Bourdieu (1990) in his idea of the 'habitus':

> Thus, paradoxically, social science makes greatest use of the lan-
> guage of rules precisely in the cases where it is most totally inade-
> quate, that is, in analysing social formations in which, because of
> the constancy of the objective conditions over time, rules have a
> particularly small part to play in the determination of practices,
> which is largely entrusted to the automatisms of the 'habitus'.
> (p. 145)

By emphasising the significance of the explicit awareness of the value
of living-global-citizenship in influencing social formations we are
seeking to move beyond the 'automatisms of the habitus' into forms
of social change and transformation that are motivated by values that
carry hope for the future of humanity.

Fountain (1995) also sees the potential of citizenship education
to deliver social change. She talks about the importance of students
moving beyond reactions of guilt, blame or resentment and instead
making an active commitment to promoting justice and equality on
all levels, whether personal, institutional, national or global. Fountain suggests that the development of pupils' attitudes and values
through citizenship education has a crucial part to play in bringing about the commitment to change, and we would certainly agree
with this!

We endeavour to explore how Living Global Citizenship community partnership activities can seek to influence the education of
social formations through the participants' actions in developing and
sustaining the partnership. Such work can be said to be part of a social
manifesto (Coombs, 1995) with the aim of both levering and validating social change, with the applied action research question/enquiry
now becoming the social goal and agenda for change. The results of
such change have an impact upon the community served.

The postcolonial view as expressed by Andreotti (2011) argues for transformation in worldviews so that issues of social injustice and unequal power relations are addressed.

Thus, there needs to be a change in perception of the relationship between the north and the south and a move away from reliance on aid. There needs to be a rethinking of the term 'development' as it is used in the predominant neo-liberal discourse. This transformation in worldviews can be achieved through Living Global Citizenship projects as participants in such a partnership engage in dialogue about their values and the context in which those values are expressed. There is critical reflection on those values and an intended recognition of prior cultural difference, as an understanding is reached on a way forward for the partnership. This leads to openness towards new possibilities.

Thus, in our authentic examples of living-global-citizenship projects as presented in Chapter 4 we see evidence of people's perceptions and views of the world changing through engagement in the various projects highlighted. We see participants challenging stereotypes and breaking down the traditional hierarchies. The projects demonstrate the possibilities that a living-global-citizenship approach can really open up.

Living-global-citizenship projects provide the means by which participants from different communities can be heard and their priorities both *valued* and *voiced*. Participants can share their concerns, their problems and their solutions, thus giving rise to their own priorities for development and taking ownership of the long-term transformation of their own communities.

2.4 Notions of citizenship: Passive, active and living

More passive notions of citizenship seek merely to embed national identity. Thus, the 'Life in the United Kingdom' test is a computer-based test constituting one of the requirements for anyone seeking leave to remain in the United Kingdom for naturalisation as a British citizen. It is designed to prove that the applicant has sufficient knowledge of British life and sufficient proficiency in the English language. The test is a requirement under the United Kingdom's Nationality, Immigration and Asylum Act, 2002. It consists of 24 questions covering topics such as British society, government, everyday life and employment. The test has been widely criticised (Glendinning, 2006; Hasan, 2012) for containing factual errors, not serving its stated purpose and expecting candidates to know information that would not be expected of native-born citizens. In 2008, Lord Goldsmith stated in a report on citizenship that the test 'is not seen typically as a stimulus for learning, though that was one of its stated aims.' In 2012, the New Statesman described the test as mocking Britishness since there was no general agreement among the population on what was or wasn't relevant to culture and history. The test was described as irrelevant in determining who will be a good citizen. From our Living Global Citizenship perspective of citizenship education there is a real danger that such forms of citizenship education lead to impersonal embedding of national values as cultural stereotypes and that this in turn leads to potential myth making and passive misconstruing of the 'citizenship' construct.

What would a Living Global Citizenship interpretation of the 'Life in the United Kingdom' test look like? How could this examination process be re-conceptualised? In Chapter 6 we make suggestions to potential policy makers as part of the readership. Thus, a personally constructed and authenticated 'living in the United Kingdom' presentation portfolio could be produced by prospective British citizenship 'applicants' to demonstrate a genuine attempt to become actively included within society and examined for authenticity. Examples of British culture and personal proficiency of language could be embedded within such a proposed 'Living in the United Kingdom' test.

We also have to review the concept of *active citizenship*. An active citizen is someone who takes a hands-on role in the community. The term has also been identified with voluntary service by writers such as Jonathan Tisch (2010), who advocated that busy Americans should try to help others. In the United States, writer Catherine Crier (2006) wondered about whether US citizens had lost sight of Thomas Jefferson's sense of *active citizenship*. Crier lamented how such 'Americans' have tended to neglect participating in voluntary associations and tend to live as 'strangers apart from the rest', quoting Tocqueville (1835). In contrast, writer Eboo Patel (2010) suggested that US President Obama had a somewhat different sense of active citizenship, meaning strong families, a vibrant civic center in which persons of different faiths and secular backgrounds work together, with government acting as a 'catalyst.'

While active citizenship recognises the importance of experiential participation in partnership work, living-global-citizenship accounts of community-based learning take the activity a step further. This is because the Living Global Citizenship approach encourages participation as a form of embedded critical engagement through cultural negotiation, analysis and critical dialogue with participants. Thus, the paradigm shift in moving from normal systems of active citizenship is one where living-global-citizenship can be seen as a 'values-added' experience linked to meaningful action. We believe that activity in itself is insufficient for a sustained form of participation as a citizen; and that a more meaningful citizenship experience is one where there is critical engagement between participants, as equals, in dialogue about values that lead to a common understanding on how the partnership develops. From this living-global-citizenship activity the identification and agreement of any resultant project's *social manifesto* for change emerges. Thus, living-global-citizenship becomes a way of living out one's values more fully through engagement in activities that contribute to improving the lives of oneself, others and the social formations in which we live. In turn, this type of social engagement develops a better understanding of diversity and cultural differences through personal acts of cultural-empathy within a climate of mutually generated trust associated with the core principles of Living Global Citizenship.

2.5   The Big Society and Living Global Citizenship

The Big Society was a flagship idea of the 2010 UK Conservative Party general election manifesto. It then formed part of the legislative programme of the Conservative – Liberal Democrat Coalition Government. In the government's own document[6] entitled 'Building the Big Society' one can find that the second principle of the policy is to: 'Encourage people to take an active role in their communities'. The document goes on to outline how this will be legislated for.

- We will take a range of measures to encourage volunteering and involvement in social action, including launching a national

'Big Society Day' and making regular community involvement a key element of civil service staff appraisals.

- We will take a range of measures to encourage charitable giving and philanthropy.
- We will introduce a National Citizen Service. The initial flagship project will provide a programme for 16 year olds to give them a chance to develop the skills needed to be active and responsible citizens, mix with people from different backgrounds, and start getting involved in their communities.

Active citizenship is thus promoted as part of the UK government's agenda. There is much to commend in such a proposal as outlined by the New Economics Foundation (2010) in their document entitled *'Ten Big Questions about the Big Society'* ... *'What's good about it?'*
The NEF (2010) maintains that:

When people are given the chance and treated as if they are capable, they tend to find they know what is best for them, and can work out how to fix any problems they have and realise their dreams. Bringing local knowledge based on everyday experience to bear on planning and decision-making usually leads to better results. Evidence shows that, when people feel they have control over what happens to them and can take action on their own behalf, their physical and mental well-being improves. When individuals and groups get together in their neighbourhoods, get to know each other, work together and help each other, there are usually lasting benefits for everyone involved: networks and groups grow stronger, so that people who belong to them tend to feel less isolated, more secure, more powerful and happier. It serves the well established principle of subsidiarity: that matters should be handled by the smallest, lowest or least centralised competent authority.

However, what is unclear is the nature of the problems it is supposed to fix or how it is supposed to fix them and the NEF (2010) further maintains that:

Getting people at local level to take more responsibility and do more to help themselves and their neighbours is seen as an alternative to action taken by state institutions and public services. Poverty, unemployment and inequalities are signs of social breakdown and these, according to the Prime Minister, are best addressed by shifting power, control and responsibility from the central state to families and communities. Increasing the volume of voluntary action is seen as a way to cut public spending. But that's as far as the Big Society vision goes to address the economic causes of poverty and inequality. It pays no attention to forces within modern capitalism that lead to accumulations of wealth and power in the hands of a few at the expense of others. Nor does it recognise that the current structure of the UK economy selectively restricts the ability of citizens to participate. A combination of social and economic forces, working across and between generations, result in some having much more and others much less. While these inequalities persist, people who have least will benefit least from the transfer of power and responsibility, while those with higher stocks of social and economic resources will be better placed to seize the new opportunities. Many of those who are currently poorest and least powerful are at risk of being systematically excluded from any benefits that arise, in spite of the Prime Minister's declared intention that no-one should be left behind.

There is nothing in the government's plans to encourage the inclusion of outsiders, to break down barriers created by wealth and privilege, to promote collaboration rather than competition between local organisations, or to prevent those that are already better off and more dominant from flourishing at the expense of others.

The Big Society idea is strong on empowerment but weak on equality. By equality, we mean everyone having an equal chance in life so that, regardless of background or circumstance, they can contribute to society, fulfil their potential and live a satisfying life.

Thus, promulgation of the Big Society as outlined by the UK government, while useful in igniting a debate about citizenship and the role of citizens as participants in society, falls well short of providing the sort of living-global-citizenship involvement that we are suggesting.

Engagement in Living Global Citizenship projects as part of a Big Society initiative would enable participants to critically assess the unequal distribution of resources between people and groups and to negotiate activities that are based on agreed values, such as social justice and equal opportunities, that are sustainable and make a lasting difference to people's lives. This in itself would strengthen democracy. The UK government's ideas on the Big Society ignore the global dimension and are focused on solving problems in the United Kingdom. Living Global Citizenship includes engagement in projects that extend across cultural settings and operates both within and beyond national boundaries.

As with notions of 'Active' citizenship, what is missing from the 'Big Society' is the focus on values and on how to overcome the existing unequal political, economic and social conditions.

2.6 Deconstructing cultural education

Let us start by examining some definitions of culture:

> Culture: learned and shared human patterns or models for living; day-to-day living patterns. These patterns and models pervade all aspects of human social interaction. Culture is mankind's primary adaptive mechanism.
>
> (Damen, 1987, p. 367)

> Culture is the shared knowledge and schemes created by a set of people for perceiving, interpreting, expressing, and responding to the social realities around them.
>
> (Lederach, 1995, p. 9)

> A culture is a configuration of learned behaviors and results of behavior whose component elements are shared and transmitted by the members of a particular society.
>
> (Linton, 1945, p. 32)

> Culture has been defined in a number of ways, but most simply, as the learned and shared behavior of a community of interacting human beings.
>
> (Useem & Useem, 1963, p. 169)

According to these definitions, culture would seem to be concerned with behaviours or activities of human beings as part of a community responding to the society in which they live. This type of definition would suggest that the study of cultural education should be a key part of any national education system. Understanding how communities respond to the society in which they live seems to us a fundamental element in a 'good' education. There is an economic rationale for this, as in an increasingly globalised world a global outlook is required to consider new opportunities and challenges. But more than this, there is a political and social rationale as well, as shown by Said's (1993) explanation of culture.

Edward Said develops an understanding of the idea of culture beyond a definition. In an article in the *Sunday Observer* in 2011,[7] Said is quoted as interpreting culture in his book *Culture and Imperialism* (1993) as follows:

> The word 'Culture' means two things in particular. First of all, it means all those practices like the arts of description, communication, and representation, that have relative autonomy from the economic, social, and political realms and that often exist in aesthetic forms, one of whose principal aims is pleasure. Included of course, are both the popular stock of lore about distant part of the world and specialized knowledge available in such learned disciplines as ethnography, historiography, philology, sociology and literary history.

The author of the article goes on to argue:

> In my view, Edward Said has opened up many pathways to us, including a new discipline called Postcolonial studies. This new discipline provides new ways of understanding global, national and local political and cultural concerns through a variety of tools and lenses by raising critical cultural questions. In a world engulfed with ethnic conflicts, wars and riots and demonstrations to overthrow dictators, it is important that our understandings of history, sense of place, race, culture and identity be examined with an open mind as practicable as possible.

> With regard to Edward Said's work on Culture and Imperialism, whether we are with him or opposing his views with our innate biases, his ideas would lead us to examine and understand the world around us.

This seems to us to reinforce the importance of cultural education and, indeed, of integrating this *human knowledge* into citizenship and other curriculum subjects. Examining and understanding the world around us through raising critical cultural questions and engaging in partnerships in a world of conflicts seems crucial to the resolution of conflict and the maintenance of peace. Approaching cultural questions with an open mind and being willing to engage in dialogue about values across cultures is a way forward. Critical engagement in partnerships and dialogue to develop a fuller understanding of the world around us and the ways that people live in that world are key elements in acts of living-global-citizenship.

Unfortunately, the UK government takes a very narrow view of cultural education. The UK government commissioned a review of cultural education in England that was published in 2012. This document, entitled 'Cultural Education in England',[8] interprets cultural education as follows:

> For the purposes of this Review, Cultural Education includes: archaeology, architecture and the built environment, archives, craft, dance, design, digital arts, drama and theatre, film and cinemas, galleries, heritage, libraries, literature, live performance, museums, music, poetry and the visual arts.

This artistic response, indeed skewing of the terms of reference, is only one aspect of how different communities of people respond to the social realities around them. What is left out of this review is consideration of cultural education as a means of learning about different human cultures and societies, learning from similarities and differences between how people in different communities respond to social realities both within and beyond national boundaries. Also left out is any exploration of shared and differing values between and across diverse communities.

The Review was followed by the announcement of £15 million of funding for cultural education in England and this was allocated to a range of national projects. In addition, in 2013 a 'Summary of Programmes and Opportunities in Cultural Education'[9] was published by the UK government. The document contains a summary of various existing cultural activities within the *scope* of culture as defined in the Review. This is all very well, but in terms of cultural education its value is limited. A review of cultural education in the United Kingdom in a broader sense would be much more helpful. Such a review needs to address a set of wider questions as follows:

- To what extent are students engaged in partnerships across cultures?
- What are the shared values of those partnerships?
- What was the process by which those negotiated values were arrived at?
- To what extent are the participants in those partnerships engaged in critical reflection of their roles and the activities?
- To what extent do all the participants have an equal voice and stakeholding in determining any shared project design, goals set and outcomes?

A summary of effective strategies for delivering the type of cultural education that studies how communities respond to the society in which they live should then be published together with a National Plan for implementation of proposals on how to improve such cultural education. Funding should then ideally be allocated to support the development of cross-cultural community partnerships that deliver effective cultural education.

A more complete perspective on cultural education is found in the Parliamentary Assembly Council of Europe (2008) report entitled 'Cultural education: The promotion of cultural knowledge, creativity and intercultural understanding through education.' This document takes a far broader view of cultural education. It makes the following statement:

> The ability to enter into intercultural dialogue and transcultural understanding will decide our future. When we speak of culture and education today, we have to take into account global migrations, worldwide communication networks, international business groups and the problem of poverty, which concerns all societies. Europe, both as a cultural area and as an economic area, needs qualified citizens with intercultural competence, interest in linguistic diversity, the willingness to partake in innovative lateral thinking, a vigorous sense of social awareness and the capacity to act with solidarity.

Cultural education thus implies opening up our society by means of art and culture. Open forms of learning and shared creative processes create space for encounters and for dealing constructively with differences. This space has physical, intellectual, sensual, emotional and social dimensions. Cultural education cannot simply be prescribed. It requires a new culture of teaching and learning, which:

- is open and cooperative both internally and externally,
- focuses on the needs of the pupils,
- is open to innovative, interdisciplinary work and,
- is project-oriented.

Quality in cultural education is achieved by means of exchange and partnerships; a major factor in achieving such quality is thus the ability to cooperate. It is necessary to initiate and extend networks and partnerships between culture and working life that also includes civil society and other stakeholders. Such partnerships require the proper supporting framework conditions and supervision. And they succeed best in cases where such activities become a part of the overall strategic orientation of an institution. Essential preconditions for good co-operation are:

- shared spaces for these types of learning,
- common visions,
- clear strategies,

Learning communities and educational policy measures need to be based on good practices, differentiated exchange and appropriate dissemination. Overstepping institutional boundaries, attempting to break out of clearly delimited systems, does not, as a rule, proceed without conflicts. And it always demands above-average commitment. Stretching boundaries always begins with taking an interest in others. It requires openness for new things and the courage to become involved in something that could develop in unforeseen ways. The European goals – equality of opportunity for all, cosmopolitanism and justice – have to lead the way. If we are aware of the challenges that life today presents for individuals and the community – namely, not merely to tolerate cultural differences but to analyse them and come to understand the reasons behind their ever new manifestations, not to confuse integration with assimilation, and to see participation as a constructive and active 'taking part' rather than only as something passive – then we have arrived at the core of cultural education.

Cultural education grows out of learning processes that take the inner differentiations and complexities of culture into account. It lets us experience the learning process with the senses and allows us to internally comprehend how people, under different conditions, have understood the world, interpreted it, acted in it and changed it in different ways and continue to do so.

This conception of cultural education is one that goes beyond the narrow focus on the arts and associated heritage in the United Kingdom. It is this form of cultural education that Living Global Citizenship projects can deliver. The opening statement that emphasises the role of intercultural dialogue and transcultural understanding in deciding our future gives an indication of the importance that should be attached to this form of education. Participation in living-global-citizenship projects can deliver the requirement that European citizens have: 'intercultural competence, a vigorous sense of social awareness and the capacity to act with solidarity' through a culture of learning that is open, cooperative, innovative, driven by the participants and is project based. As can be seen from the examples in Chapter 4 living-global-citizenship projects are based on the building of networks and partnerships between participants reaching out to a wide range of stakeholders. The projects have worked because of the shared vision and clear strategies that have been agreed through dialogue. There has been outstanding commitment from the participants as they have shown the courage to get involved in something that has developed in unforeseen ways. Thus, they have come to see participation as an active and reflective process and so have been the beneficiaries of cultural education in the sense that this report views it.

It would seem therefore that our current ideas for developing Living Global Citizenship as a form of cultural education appear more likely to find political acceptance in Europe than in the United Kingdom.

2.7   Living Global Citizenship – pedagogy for effective citizenship education in any cultural setting

Having deconstructed citizenship education, the Big Society and cultural education we now provide an alternative approach that offers a pedagogy for the delivery of effective citizenship education to include cultural education that is based on the following principles:

- The importance of Values in Education and a values-based education system.
- A pedagogy of 'touching' hearts rather than the usual teaching assumptions.
- The importance of developing local, national and international partnerships to enable students to experience participation with others and to critically engage in the process of discussion and negotiation of shared values; thus, leading to participation in activities that enable them to live out their values more fully as citizens.
- The incorporation of an *impact evaluation research methodology* with critical reflection as a cultural value to society in its own right; and as a means of transforming learning within communities.

Such an approach is capable of providing cultural education through cross cultural contact, which leads to what we call Cultural Empathy. Living Global Citizenship emphasises the participation by pupils in cross-community projects which enable a more 'Living' immersive educational experience that develops cultural-empathy within participants. Based on our research evidence this is what we believe can provide a meaningful form of effective citizenship education within any cultural setting. Here, we explore these principles in more depth.

2.7.1   The importance of values in education and a values-based education system

Shaver and Strong (1976) define values as:

> Our standards and principles for judging worth. They are the criteria by which we judge 'things' (people, objects, ideas, actions

and situations) to be good, worthwhile, desirable; or, on the other hand, bad, worthless, despicable. (p. 15)

These criteria affect our cultural, political, pedagogical and epistemological assumptions. The shared core values that a partnership espouses, for example, those of equal opportunities and social justice shapes the cultural, political, pedagogical and epistemological outlook that the participants have. Thus, it is important to define these values that underpin the partnership so that the influence on these assumptions is made clear.

Halstead (1996) identifies two ways in which values are central to education. Firstly, as a way of influencing the developing values of the students and, secondly, as a reflection and embodiment of the values held within society. Brighouse (2005) supports the crucial point that values are central to education:

It is essential not to separate values (as some lofty ideal) and practice: you have to address how you as a teacher walk the talk and empower learners to walk the talk as well by giving them the wherewithal to become effective citizens.

The importance of values in education is highlighted in Ginott's (1972) powerful poetic address to teachers in which he highlights the fact that the perpetrators of the holocaust were well-educated high school and college graduates and exhorts teachers to view education as more than just reading, writing and arithmetic, and to pay attention to the education of their students as human beings. Irrespective of government policy, educators in schools have it in their power to ensure that values remain at the heart of what is taught and that humanitarian values are communicated to the students.

Bernard Crick (1999) emphasised the importance of values as part of citizenship education in launching the new subject of citizenship as part of the UK National Curriculum:

Citizenship is more than a statutory subject. If taught well and tailored to local needs, its skills and values will enhance democratic life for us all, both rights and responsibilities, beginning in school, and radiating out. (p. 125)

Crick's comments about the value of citizenship education indicate that he believes that it ought to be about more than delivering a content curriculum. It should also be about exploring values, developing human relationships and enhancing the democratic process.

A pedagogical approach based on the principles of Living Global Citizenship puts values at the heart of education. As the participants engage in partnership they discuss their own values, identifying areas of similarity and difference. A learning space needs to be created where this discussion can take place in an open and democratic way, such that the participants are committed to sharing and learning. The participants need to come to a negotiated agreement about the group-identified values that underpin the partnership and devise activities that move the partnership forward. Thus, such predetermined *values* predicate not only the action itself but define the nature and purpose of the action and therefore the assumptions underpinning the design of all partnership activities. As the partnership develops and expands bringing in new participants, there is a need to engage in ongoing critical review, so as to reconsider and rearticulate the underpinning values of the partnership and the related activities that all are engaged in. This feedback dialogue needs to be ongoing throughout the life of the partnership. In this way values become central to the project and central to the education of the participants.

2.7.2   A pedagogy of 'touching' hearts not just teaching

Sayers (2002) use of the word 'touching' (hearts) in the context of teaching about citizenship is one that the authors find useful. The intention is for the activities of the partnership to touch the hearts of the participants. Images portrayed through video and photographs can give the values meaning to the participant students and teachers. Providing opportunities for individual contact between people of different cultures allows personal relationships and friendships to develop. Through organised activities participants are given the opportunity to explore, reflect upon, and experience their own qualities and to decide how to act in response to the issues that are raised. These are ways of 'touching' those involved and making the meaning of good citizenship real to the involved students and staff. We seek the development of these qualities within people and suggest using the term 'development' in the same way that it is used by Nick Maurice of United Kingdom One World Linking Association (UKOWLA) (2008). UKOWLA considers 'development' as opportunities for participants to develop their own self-confidence and activities helping them to reach their potential; or, in the words of McNiff (2006), live out their values more fully. Developing this pedagogical approach that touches the heart of the *other* and illustrating it through an outcome narrative of the project is a key aim of Living Global Citizenship (see section 5.2.3).

2.7.3   International educational partnerships

The dangers of international educational partnerships are well documented. They have been seen as problematic in terms of their potential for reinforcing negative prejudice and stereotypes (Martin and Griffiths, 2012) and have been heavily criticised by postcolonial theorists (Andreotti, 2011; Bailee-Smith, 2011) for unconsciously supporting the hegemonic nature of the neo-liberal paradigm in the discourse about international development. From a postcolonial perspective partnerships go wrong when they fail to challenge the dominant Western discourse of development and are then generally unable to provide the means for genuine social change. They also fail when they reinforce negative stereotypes and prejudices and Western notions of development, thus providing an unquestioning acquiescence to dominant power structures.

Living-global-citizenship projects provide a way of delivering authentic citizenship education through an international educational partnership that enables the participants to critically assess their own values and to develop meaningful relationships from which new meanings and understandings emerge that challenge the predominant view of development, negotiate a new inclusive development agenda of all the stakeholders involved and thereby allow *desirable* social change to take place. Participants in a living-global-citizenship project actively engage in cross-cultural dialogue, including critical reflection on their values, leading to an agreed partnership agenda in the form of a social manifesto (Coombs, 1995). This then serves as a meaningful 'declaration' of intent that is designed to contribute to improving the lives of the participants engaged in the partnership. Living-global-citizenship integrates social values with personal action and the generation of living-cases and living-theories which represents the authentic learning process of *becoming* a citizen.

2.7.4 Critical reflection as a cultural value

There is no doubt that participants engaged in living-global-citizenship-inspired partnership projects represent themselves as insider participant researchers engaged with generating evidence that can be used as a case study. Such authentic living-global-citizenship personal evidence from individuals engaged as both participant and insider action researcher is defined by us as operating as a Living Case. The acts of being engaged in such social change activity is further described as being a living-case and we cover this in more detail in sections 5.2.5 'Developing Activities That Bring About Social Change' and 5.2.7 'Participants as Living Cases'. Living Global Citizenship therefore implies a form of social democracy in action where its underlying purpose is to positively change people's lives through engaging them in their own critical reflection activities. The Living Global Citizenship research methodology and assumptions therefore operates within the humanistic social research paradigm that validates insider reflective researcher participants and is something that will be further explored in Chapter 3.

These pedagogical protocols also link to sections 5.2.4 'Developing Activities Which Tackle Stereotypes and Encourage Critical Reflection by Participants' and 5.2.6 'Developing Activities That Have Impact and Sustain the Partnership'.

Our definition of evaluation within such a humanistic and participant validated research paradigm is higher-order critical reflection. A willingness to engage in evaluation through critical reflection within a living context is a prerequisite of Living Global Citizenship. For Dewey (1933, p. 9), reflection is referred to as 'assessing the grounds (justification) of one's beliefs, the process of rationally examining the assumptions by which we have been justifying our convictions'. Questioning one's own beliefs, the reasons for those beliefs and the assumptions on which they are based is a key part of participation in a partnership as an enabled living-global-citizen. Engaging in the process of critical reflection, or the process of analysing, reconsidering and questioning experiences within a broad context of issues (Murray & Kujundzic, 2005) is an essential and ongoing aspect of a Living Global Citizenship project.

As illustrated in section 1.1, this can lead to transformations in learning and changes in the way that participants approach the partnership and influence the activities that are undertaken. As Mezirow (2011) says:

> To question the validity of a long taken-for-granted meaning perspective predicated on a presupposition about oneself can involve the negation of values that have been very close to the centre of one's self-concept. As we encounter new meaning perspectives that help us account for disturbing anomalies in the way we understand our reality, personal as well as scientific paradigm shifts can redirect the way we engage the world. (p. 8)

> Reflection on one's own premises can lead to transformative learning. Transformative learning involves a particular function of reflection: reassessing the presuppositions on which our beliefs are based and acting on insights derived from the transformed meaning perspective that results from such reassessments.
>
> (pp. 11–12)

When engaging in discussion about values and negotiating shared values, participants need to critically reflect on their own values and consider them in relation to the other persons. Thus, they will ask questions of themselves such as:

- What are my values?
- To what extent am I living out those values?
- What are the values of the other participants?
- To what extent are our values the same and different?
- Which values do we believe are crucial to the partnership?
- How can we develop partnership activities which reflect those values?

In Chapter 5 we emphasise the importance of using action reflection cycles which integrate evaluation as integral to the processes of improving practice and generating knowledge. Wallace (2000) has produced a particularly attractive version of an action reflection cycle known as the TASC (Thinking Actively in a Social Context) wheel within which you can see that evaluation is an integral part of the process (Figure 2.1):

Figure 2.1 TASC wheel

This process of critical reflection takes place as participants engage in intercultural dialogue that leads to a reassessment of one's beliefs and values, further leading to new perspectives and new ways of engaging with the world. This process of critical reflection therefore becomes a cultural value in its' own right and something that participants can live out through engagement in a Living Global Citizenship Project.

2.7.5 Developing cultural empathy

One of the key elements in Living Global Citizenship is the notion of Cultural Empathy. A key question that arises is: how do you develop Cultural Empathy through a partnership?

We argue that Cultural Empathy can be defined and developed through Living Global Citizenship partnerships. Understanding different cultural contexts and celebrating 'difference' as part of the essential design of any partnership project requires a value we refer to as Cultural Empathy. What makes Living Citizenship become Living Global Citizenship? We believe that the global perspective of citizenship occupies a description of humanity itself. Indeed, humanity described in terms of its rich cultural differences and contributions to a twenty-first century world. So a global citizen can be understood in terms of cultural origins, exchange and development. Moreover, the ability of an emerging global citizen to appreciate other cultures and societies and move towards a common shared set of values and understanding is a valuable goal. This global appreciation of other cultures, traditions and values is something we argue as Cultural Empathy. Cultural empathy is both a social policy and act of humanity and when combined with our notion of Living Citizenship helps us to define what we mean by Living Global Citizenship and can be simplified as given below:

Living Citizenship + Cultural Empathy => Living Global Citizenship

Cultural empathy also helps us to celebrate and appreciate the richness of 'cultural difference' as promoted by Fran Martin (2012) and others (Andreotti, 2011; Todd, 2008). Whilst Cultural Empathy is a human, indeed, 'living' human quality, it is also something that can be formulated into social and educational policy. And existing educational areas such as citizenship can become 'global citizenship' where such a curriculum includes both content and activities that enable Cultural Empathy to take place. Clearly, Cultural Empathy goes beyond mere study, it is something that needs to be acted upon and experienced by all those engaged within such a dynamic curriculum. Going further, we can argue that the multidimensional social nature of Cultural Empathy when extended into global citizenship has the potential to add genuine societal value to a problematic area of social policy such as multiculturalism that traditionally operates within national contexts. The social problems of global mobility and the consequent emerging multicultural societies have been largely responsible for the introduction of national citizenship education programmes. For many societies the problem of sudden multiple cultures emerging from immigration has caused a social backlash in the form of racial prejudice often engendered by the fear of extant communities to such 'difference'. Turning cultural differences into an asset that societies can come to terms and live with is the challenge of citizenship education as described by the excerpts from the following critical theorists:

> Citizenship education has arisen against a social backdrop of considerable social and political upheaval caused by the rise of nationalism and increased disregard for 'civic virtues'. Within this climate the nation state can no longer be viewed as the given natural order.
>
> (Simon, 2005, p. 1)

According to QCA (1999) citizenship education is further propelled by the

> increasingly complex nature of our society, the greater cultural diversity and the apparent loss of value consensus, combined with the collapse of traditional support mechanisms such as extended families. (p. 7)

According to UNESCO (2000) citizenship education is about

> education for human rights, peace, international understanding, tolerance and nonviolence. It also includes all aspects of education relating to the principles of democracy and multicultural and intercultural education. (p. 2)

In this sense a global citizenship programme has the potential to add greater social and educational value to an otherwise more limited national citizenship programme. When citizenship education was launched in UK secondary schools in 1999, Crick (1999) recognised its educational potential to enhance democratic life.

Ambitious though these visions for citizenship education may seem, they are ones that we share and that we believe living global citizenship can aspire to. A Living Global Citizenship education curriculum would be one in which its participants engage with and develop a real sense of *cultural-empathy* through personal engagement in the 'living' activities and opportunities offered. These might include a new interpretation and delivery of international educational exchange visits; smart uses of technology and Social Networking Sites to enable greater access to cultural experiences; and, new types of professional development for the educational workforce. On this latter point of professional development, we believe this can be achieved through a reconceptualisation of international educational development with the introduction of a new form of ICPD that also 'qualifies' the activities of teachers working in international education contexts and feeds back their working knowledge into the wider academy.

The development of Cultural Empathy (links to new ideas of development as inclusion of values) involves sharing and negotiating a common set of emergent values that drive the partnership forward. These unique *values* need to be negotiated without the existence of what we call *cultural blind spots*. Such cultural blind spots include ignorance of and misconceptions about each others' culture and ignorance of the power relations that exist between cultures, often as a past legacy of colonial relationships, and often unwitting! Awareness of these cultural blind spots and open discussion and elicitation of them between participants is an essential part of the process of negotiation of shared values. In this respect Martin Buber's (1947) notion of the special humility of the educator is helpful in making us aware of the dangers of imposing one's ideas, or constructs, on others. In seeking to allow the *other* to express their values and to avoid any such colonising or dominant influence in general, we hold in mind Buber's (1947) notion of the special humility of the educator:

> his selection remains suspended, under constant correction by the special humility of the educator for whom the life and particular being of all his pupils is the decisive factor to which his 'hierarchical' recognition is subordinated. (p. 122)

Cultural Empathy can develop through intercultural conversations which lead to learning from dialogue. This dialogue can take place in a *postcolonial space for learning* (Martin & Griffiths, 2012) where participants step out of their own cultural space into the space *between* and create a *Third Space* (Bhabha, 1994) in which new meanings and understandings can emerge. Participation in dialogue with partners needs to be followed by systematic critical reflection and a willingness to confront cultural blind spots. Conversational learning tools to support such critical reflection and scaffold/elicit new meanings and understandings have been developed by Harri-Augstein and Thomas (1991) and Coombs (1995) and are recommended as part of any supporting toolkit for ICPD programmes. Using such techniques along with any pedagogical protocols for developing partnership activities is intended to lever social and lasting impact – see Chapter 5 in general and sections 5.2 'The Pedagogical Protocols of a Living Global Citizenship Project' and 5.2.6 'Developing Activities That Have Impact and Sustain the Partnership'.

This process of negotiating shared values and developing *cultural-empathy* in action is illustrated in the partnership between Sarum Academy in Salisbury and Nqabakazulu School in Durban, South Africa. A video clip demonstrating the values of Living Global Citizenship and Cultural Empathy, together with responses to these values, is available at:

http://www.youtube.com/watch?v=H5U6LKhWzoo

The lead participant from the UK school was engaged in discussion with a range of participants from the South African School in order to establish the partnership. This was followed by reciprocal visits funded by the British Council. These supported visits were crucial in providing the opportunity for intercultural conversations between the participants. During the visits partners from both schools were able to meet and engage in discussion with a range of stakeholders in the organisations (students, teachers, school leaders, members of the community). Following the visits there was a period of reflection and discussion with participants in the home school. During this period of reflection in the home schools consideration was given to what the aims and purpose of the partnership were to be. Commitment to the partnership was also gauged. There was continued dialogue between the two schools so that mutually agreed values and activities were arrived at. What emerged from the ongoing dialogues between the various participants within and between the schools was an emphasis on the shared values of social justice and equal opportunities underpinned by an understanding of the notion of Ubuntu, a Zulu concept roughly translated as 'humanity'. These values informed the activities of the partnership, so that, for example, a fair trade business venture was started and continues to this day. (Further detail on this partnership can be found in Chapter 4.)

This short case study serves to illustrate how partnership values and activities were negotiated through engagement in dialogue. The space for learning was created through intercultural dialogue between participants in the two schools and equally important was the dialogue between the participants within the schools. This allowed for consideration of cultural blind spots such as addressing misconceptions and the legacy of colonialism. A map showing the network of dialogues that took place to shape the values and activities is shown here (Figure 2.2):

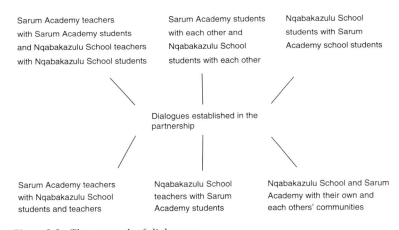

Sarum Academy teachers with Sarum Academy students and Nqabakazulu School teachers with Nqabakazulu School students

Sarum Academy students with each other and Nqabakazulu School students with each other

Nqabakazulu School students with Sarum Academy school students

Dialogues established in the partnership

Sarum Academy teachers with Nqabakazulu School students and teachers

Nqabakazulu School teachers with Sarum Academy students

Nqabakazulu School and Sarum Academy with their own and each others' communities

Figure 2.2   The network of dialogues

This network of dialogues facilitated decision making by the participants, with leveraging of the shared values determining the quality of the dialogue and being crucial to the success of the partnership. As the participants engaged in dialogue they learnt how to listen to each other. They learned from each other and they learned how they can support each other. A shared language was developed, for example, Ubuntu, which expressed the participants shared values in deepening the partnership. This shared language helped them to develop a common view of how the partnership was developing and how it was perceived by the participants and those outside the partnership.

Once these shared values were agreed then the activities that followed from them became a means for living out one's values. Thus, there was engagement in a Living Global Citizenship project, a more experiential 'Living' immersive educational experience that developed Cultural Empathy. Living Global Citizenship projects provide a form of intercultural learning, a means of living in other cultures, allowing us to compare and contrast and understand our own culture and transcending any prior cultural divide (Coombs & Potts, 2013).

2.7.6 Living Global Citizenship as a new form of cultural education

Cultural education can be seen as a form of *global etiquette*. Developing students (and anyone really) who can have an understanding and appreciation of the norms and behaviours of different communities and provide them with the skills to engage in activities with people from communities other than their own requires some form of global etiquette. We believe that this should be the main purpose of cultural education.

We therefore argue that all forms of cultural education also require the prerequisite of Cultural Empathy as a core social value, which also describes and underpins the socio-ethical basis of Living Global Citizenship and Living Educational Theory.

The importance of developing a global etiquette is supported by the Council for Industry and Higher Education (CIHE) in their report entitled 'Global Graduates into Global Leaders' (2011).

The report suggests that employers are seeking employees with a global mindset, which is:

the ability to see the world from a cosmopolitan viewpoint; to have an awareness of different cultures and values, and how one's own culture and values differ. (p. 8)

The CIHE also maintains the need for cultural agility:

the ability to understand the perspectives of individuals from different cultures and backgrounds and to empathise with these views, and respond to them. (p. 9)

According to the report the most highly ranked global competence and attribute was

> an ability to work collaboratively with teams of people from a range of backgrounds and countries. (p. 8)

There are some suggestions as to how students themselves, and businesses and universities, can develop these skills and competencies, but notably the following questions are posed for the reader:

> What more can UK schools and employers do together to inspire future global graduates and leaders? And how should they do this?
>
> How can higher education institutions develop students with a global outlook and employability competencies?
>
> How can employers go further to embed a global dimension in graduate programmes and nurture their graduates to become their future generation of global leaders? (p. 22)

Such questions provide a fertile breeding ground for Living Global Citizenship projects. A global mindset, cultural agility, the ability to work collaboratively with people from a range of backgrounds and countries is exactly what participation in such a project can deliver. The Global Graduates report signals the significance of this development for both our young people and for economic reasons, in order to deliver greater competitiveness in global markets. We would argue that there are other reasons for it as well. There is a need for more global etiquette in a world of conflict. Appreciation of cultural differences and similarities and engagement with people from different communities enhances the prospect of conflict resolution and peace. Therefore, cultural education in the form that we express it here, as the development of global etiquette, needs to be embedded into schools, universities and employers training programmes for economic, political and social reasons.

2.7.7 Applying the Living Global Citizenship approach to a variety of international cultural settings

There is no doubt that much educational and other international development has been made with the best of intentions. However, we have previously highlighted much criticism of the notion of development projects being 'done' to participants with little say or influence on the ground, This approach was usually led by the agendas of external agencies and charities with the best of intentions, however, things are changing. Globally and in the South Pacific Region the emphasis has recently shifted to make sure that development funds from donors operate through national governments and via recognised regional agencies. In the South Pacific one of the largest funding organisations is Australian Aid, affectionately known as AusAID, and was recently moved into Australia's Department of Foreign Affairs and Trade (See their website: http://aid. dfat.gov.au/Pages/home.aspx). Its mission is to make sure that their annual Aus$5B overseas aid budget provides as much impact as possible by using Performance Benchmarks: 'Performance benchmarks will improve the accountability of the aid program, link performance with funding, and ensure a stronger focus on results and alleviating poverty in the region'. At the same time much of that funding will be applied to projects via the appropriate ministries of the recipient countries. Their website declares: 'Australia looks for opportunities to use partner country processes and systems in aid program delivery'. A similar story can be reported for UNICEF and other large aid organisations throughout the South Pacific and similarly in other global regions. This ethical and culturally sensitive approach towards funding international development projects fits within the paradigm of Living Global Citizenship and we believe is one that should also be adopted by governments for citizenship projects linked to cultural education across a variety of national settings.

In the South Pacific one large funded project involves capacity building of teacher education across many island states. In particular, AusAID has funded something known as the Untrained Teachers Project. The funding has been provided by AusAID working through governments and the University of the South Pacific that operates as a regional university with campuses in 12 countries. In particular, a Memorandum of Understanding (MoU) was signed with the government of Vanuatu in May 2012 at the Forum of Education Ministers Meeting (FEdMM)[10] for USP to train up to 1,000 teachers in that country. From the USP website[11] we have an overview of the project:

> Under the agreement, USP will train about 1,000 untrained teachers over the next five years through support from the Australian Agency for International Development (AusAID). The project will

be funded by AusAID and the MOU is a requirement under the project. The MOU will see USP working in close collaboration with the Vanuatu Institute of Teacher Education (VITE) to provide teacher training in the country. With Quality of Education as the theme of the next phase of the Pacific Education Development Framework, and the focus on teacher education as a core requirement of quality education outcomes, it is believed that quality cannot be improved if a large number of untrained teachers teach students.

Given the cultural sensitivities of working on such a vast project across many countries and indeed many cultures within those countries the general protocols and operational assumptions of Living Global Citizenship would serve as a very useful platform for project management and delivery.

In order for such projects to be successful with genuine social impact, it therefore requires proper negotiation and planning on the ground; ideally, the sharing of shared identities through identified values that are ultimately linked to the project's goals. In the case of USP managing the UTP, a decentralised system of project co-ordination has been set up with local country coordinators. These coordinators are working with people in their local communities to set up meaningful training solutions that the project participants can identify with, take ownership of, and implement, resulting in impact evidence for donor *performance benchmarks*.

This *localism* and inclusive approach certainly works towards the proposed Living Global Citizenship agenda for action. For further examples of Living Global Citizenship in action see the various case studies reported and explored in Chapter 4 that provide a rich set of experiences from the viewpoint of each author.

In applying the Living Global Citizenship approach to a variety of cultural settings we also identify with the *way of being* that defines the African notion of Ubuntu and something that has influenced the life of major reformers such as Nelson Mandela:

http://www.youtube.com/watch?v=HED4h00xPPA

We identify with Mandela's Ubuntu way of being as expressing the values we use to characterise our meanings of Living Global Citizenship.

You can access the notes and video of Whitehead's inaugural Mandela Day Lecture at Durban University of Technology at:

www.actionresearch.net/writings/jack/jwmandeladay2011.
pdf

...and a video of Whitehead expressing his Ubuntu way of being in relation to a written text on Ubuntu, that he is suggesting needs visual data to be added so as to adequately communicate an Ubuntu way of being. This was delivered at the University of the Free State, South Africa:

http://www.youtube.com/watch?v=CkKyeT0osz8

What we are doing in our self-studies of our professional practices in education is to understand who we are and what we are doing with a view of ourselves as global citizens. Whether we are global citizens is of course open to question and challenge.

We also identify with Crompton's (2010) case for working with cultural values as we enhance our expressions of cultural-empathy. For example, Whitehead has accepted invitations to present keynotes and lead workshops on living theory action research in Thailand, Canada, United Kingdom, Belgium, Croatia, Mauritius, United States, Japan, Brazil, China, Holland, Norway, Mozambique, Ethiopia, Kenya, Nairobi, Israel, the Republic of Ireland and Montenegro. In each of his presentations and workshops he takes care to extend and deepen his understanding of the cultural influences that may affect people's perceptions of the gifts he is offering in the form of the living-theories of practitioner-researchers from around the world. For example, in the video tapes from a five-day workshop on action research in Thailand in 2013 (see http://www.actionresearch.net/writings/jack/thaischedulemay2013.pdf) to promote enquiry learning in science and technology, Whitehead can be seen enquiring into the way in which the cultural influences of Buddhism could be constraining the participant's willingness to question and challenge those older than themselves or in positions of greater authority; while at the same time the workshop was helping participants to move into collaborative groups to work together on the problem of encouraging enquiry learning in science and technology in Thai schools.

In the latest workshop at the International School of Brussels, Whitehead connected participants with the idea of Living Global Citizenship that he believes can emerge from the enduring goals of the International School of Brussels. In the statement of Mission and Enduring Goals of ISB there is the statement that

> The ISB experience is shaped by a spirit of community, characterised by students, parents, faculty and staff working together to achieve our goal of developing independent learners and international citizens.

While we prefer to stress the importance of both independent and interdependent learning, our preference is for the term 'global citizen' rather than 'international citizen'. This prompts us to suggest that applying the Living Global Citizenship approach in a variety of cultural settings requires each individual to accept the responsibility of exploring the implications of being global citizens in enquiries of the kind: How am I expressing my responsibility as a global citizen in living my values of global citizenship as fully as possible in my life, work and research?

3
Living Theory Transformed into Living Global Citizenship

3.1 Providing an academic framework for Living Global Citizenship as an evolutionary leap from notions of living theory

An academic framework for living-global-citizenship has emerged from the creation by individuals of their living-educational-theories as they engage with enquiries of the kind, 'How do I improve what I am doing?' and engage with the ideas of others. The evolution of living-global-citizenship from notions of living-theory has emerged from a 45-year research programme (1968–2013) into the nature of educational theories that can produce valid explanations for the educational influences of individuals in their own learning, in the learning of others and in the learning of the social formations in which we live, work and research.

Whitehead writes, I first coined the idea of a living-educational-theory (1989) as an explanation of an individual's educational influence in learning as a response to tensions in my research programme into the nature of educational theory. The most important tension was in my questioning the validity of the disciplines approach to educational theory. This approach held that educational theory was constituted by the philosophy, psychology, sociology and history of education. Having studied the conceptual frameworks and methods of validation of these disciplines and attempted to explain my educational influences in my own learning and in the learning of my pupils using these frameworks, I came to the conclusion that none of these frameworks, either individually or in any combination could produce a valid explanation of my educational influence that included the practical principles I used to explain what I was doing and my educational influence in my own learning and in the learning of my pupils.

In 1983, through the clarity of Hirst's (1983) point about the following mistake in the disciplines approach to educational theory, I came to see that this failure of the disciplines approach to educational theory, to include the practical principles I used to explain my educational influence, was based on the following assumption. The disciplines approach assumed that the practical principles I used to explain my educational influence in learning were at best pragmatic maxims that had a first crude and superficial justification in practice that in any rationally developed theory would *be replaced* by principles with more theoretical justification (p. 18). As I did not accept that my practical principles should be replaced I wanted to develop a view of educational theory that would include the practical principles used by individuals to explain their educational influences, while at the same time benefitting from insights from the traditional disciplines[1] and disciplines of education.

The idea of a living-educational-theory being an individual's explanation of their educational influences in learning emerged from two sources. The first was from Ilyenkov's (1977) question in his book on Dialectical Logic, 'If an object exists as a living contradiction what must the thought (statement about the object) be that expresses it?' (p. 313). Having experienced myself as a 'living contradiction' while watching video tapes of my classroom practice, I identified with this idea of existing 'as a living contradiction'. I liked the idea of being able to explain my educational influences through my enquiry, 'How do I improve what I am doing?' in which 'I' existed as a 'living contradiction'. Hence, I referred to these explanations as a living-educational-theory. My choice of the word 'theory' for such explanations came from my physical science degree. A theory in the empirical sciences was held to be a set of determinate relations between a set of variables in terms of which a fairly extensive set of empirically verifiable regularities could be explained. The view of theory I gained from my studies of the disciplines of education was that a theory was constituted by a conceptual framework with explicit methods of validation from which valid explanations for the behaviours or influences of individuals could be derived. In other words all theories in the physical and social sciences were explanations of some generality from which explanations for individual cases could be derived. The explanations moved from the general to the particular.

In my view of a living-educational-theory the theory was constituted by the explanations that an individual produced for their educational influences. A living-educational-theory is not derived from a more general theory.[2] A living-educational-theory is created as an explanation of educational influence in exploring the implications of asking, researching and answering a question of the kind, 'How do I improve what I am doing?'

My choice of the word 'influence' is also significant. My focus on explaining educational 'influences' in learning is to stress an intentional rather than a causal relationship in what constitutes learning as educational. No matter what an educator does with a student they cannot have a causal effect in the learning. This is because whatever an educator does must be mediated by the conscious responses of the learner for me to recognise the learning as educational. I also agree with Said's (1997) focus on the importance of 'influence' in the writings of Valéry:

> As a poet indebted to and friendly with Mallarme, Valéry was compelled to assess originality and derivation in a way that said something about a relationship between two poets that could not be reduced to a simple formula. As the actual circumstances were rich, so too had to be the attitude. Here is an example from the 'Letter About Mallarme'.

> No word comes easier or oftener to the critic's pen than the word influence, and no vaguer notion can be found among all the vague notions that compose the phantom armory of aesthetics. Yet there is nothing in the critical field that should be of greater philosophical interest or prove more rewarding to analysis than the progressive modification of one mind by the work of another. (p. 15)

The academic framework for living-global-citizenship as an evolutionary leap from a living-theory, is focused on the unit of appraisal, standards of judgement and logics of living-theories and the inclusion of living global citizenship as an explanatory principle in explanations of educational influence to which individuals hold themselves accountable; and as a living standard of judgement for judging the validity of a contribution to educational knowledge. The evolution from a living-theory to the inclusion of living-global-citizenship is intimately related to the third strand of the explanations that constitute a living-educational-theory. A living-educational-theory is constituted by the explanations that individual's produce to explain their educational influences in their own learning, in the learning of others and in the learning of the social formations in which we live, work and research. It is the third strand of a living-theory, the one that is focused on explaining educational influences in the learning of social formations that is particularly relevant to the inclusion of living-global-citizenship with a living-theory. The idea of living-global-citizenship includes Habermas' (2002) point that the private autonomy of equally entitled citizens can only be secured insofar as citizens actively exercise their civic autonomy:

> The dispute between the two received paradigms – whether the autonomy of legal persons is better secured through individual liberties for private competition or through publicly guaranteed entitlements for clients of welfare bureaucracies – is superseded by a proceduralist concept of law. According to this conception, the democratic process must secure private and public autonomy at the same time: the individual rights that are meant to guarantee to women the autonomy to pursue their lives in the private sphere cannot even be adequately formulated unless the affected persons themselves first articulate and justify in public debate those aspects that are relevant to equal or unequal treatment in typical cases. The private autonomy of equally entitled citizens can only be secured only insofar as citizens actively exercise their civic autonomy. (p. 264)

The academic framework for living-global-citizenship as an evolution of living-theory is distinguished by the following ontological, epistemological and methodological characteristics.

3.2 Ontological characteristics

In an enquiry of the kind, 'How do I improve what I am doing in my professional context?' the 'I' is ontological in the sense of seeking to live as fully as possible the values that the individual uses to give meaning and purpose to their lives.

In my own living-theory I include a flow of life-affirming energy with values that carry hope for the future of humanity. In relation to my ontological security I like the way Tillich (1962, p. 168) expresses the *state of being* grasped by the power of being – itself. While Tillich writes from a theological perspective and I have a humanistic rather than a theistic belief, I can recognise the experience of a cosmological energy that I identify as a flow of life-affirming and life-enhancing energy within which I feel at one with the cosmos. This flow of energy is vital in any explanation of why I do what I do and in explaining my educational influences.

In my theory of being, values play another vital role. I distinguish values from ethics as follows. In my studies of philosophy, especially Ethics and Education (Peters, 1966) Ethics formed a branch of philosophy. Ethical principles[3] such as freedom, justice, respect, consideration of interests and worthwhile activities would be used to distinguish the concept of education. I am using values in an embodied sense to mean what it is that motivates me to do what I do in my educational practices. I use the same value-words as the ethical principles of freedom, justice, respect, consideration of interests and worthwhile activities but the meanings are clarified in the course of their emergence in practice in the enquiry, 'How do I improve what I am doing?' These values constitute what I am meaning by 'improvement'. For example, early in my teaching career as a science teacher I valued 'enquiry learning'. Video tapes of my classroom showed me that I was giving my pupils the questions rather than eliciting the questions from them. Given that I valued enquiry learning, this recognition revealed to me that 'I' was a living contradiction. I valued enquiry learning yet negated this in my practice. Over time and interaction in my classroom with my pupils I produced evidence to show that my influence moved my classroom from an environment of denying enquiry learning to an environment where enquiry learning was being supported. My meaning of enquiry learning was clarified in the course of its emergence in practice.

A similar process can be seen in my clarification and communication of my value of academic freedom. In my 1993 text *The Growth of Educational Knowledge: Creating your Own Living Educational Theories* (Whitehead, 1993) I present an evidence-based narrative that shows how I clarified and communicated my embodied value of academic freedom in the face of pressures that could have constrained a less determined individual.

In emphasising the ontological nature of a living-theory in terms of its inclusion of the values that an individual uses to give meaning and purpose to their lives I want to stress the uniqueness of each individual's constellation of ontological values. We may use the same value-words such as love, hope, compassion, respect, justice, care, Ubuntu and freedom. The embodied expressions of these values as they are clarified, communicated and evolved in the course of their emergence in practice, form a distinct and unique constellation of meanings for each individual.[4] This is why each individual's living-theory is unique and this uniqueness shows in the epistemological characteristics that distinguish a living-theory.

3.3 Epistemological characteristics

In the theory of knowledge of a living-theory, the epistemological characteristics can be distinguished in the unit of appraisal, the standards of judgement and the logic used to validate and legitimate the knowledge-claim being put forward, usually in the form of an explanation.

The unit of appraisal is what is being judged as a contribution to knowledge. In a living-theory the unit is an individual's explanation of their educational influence in their own learning, in the learning of others and in the learning of the social formation in which we live, work and research.

The standards of judgement are how we judge the unit of appraisal as a contribution to knowledge.

For example, in conducting doctoral examinations in universities around the world I am asked to judge the contributions to knowledge with standards that always include a judgement on:

Is the thesis an original contribution to knowledge?

Has the candidate demonstrated sufficient critical engagement with the relevant literature – that is the ideas of others?

Does the thesis contain matter worthy of publication (it need not be in a form ready for publication)?

The living-theory doctorates at http://www.actionresearch.net/living/living.shtml have all had to satisfy an external and internal examiner in terms of the above standards of judgement.

Included within each original contribution to knowledge are the unique constellations of energy-flowing values that the individual researcher uses as explanatory principles in their explanation of educational influence and as the living standards of judgement they use to evaluate the validity and legitimacy of their own contribution to knowledge.

Here is an example of a unique constellation of values a living-theory researcher uses as explanatory principles and living standards of judgement in Crotty's (2012) abstract from her thesis 'How Am I Bringing An Educationally Entrepreneurial Spirit Into Higher Education?':

Abstract The originality of my research lies in clarifying and explaining what it means for me to have an educational entrepreneurial spirit and the values I hold that demonstrate this spirit in an explanation of educational influence in learning. This explanation includes a responsibility for students and acknowledging my values of passion and care ('love' of what I do), safety, creativity and excellence within my practice.

The unit of appraisal in a living theory methodology is the explanation of the influence in my own learning, the learning of others and in the learning of social formations. The methodological inventiveness, particular to the Living Educational Theory methodology, has afforded me an opportunity to express who I really am; body, mind and spirit. I use multimodal forms to communicate and express the nature of the knowledge that I am generating. I can now claim that my values have become living standards of judgement.

Music plays an integral part of my life and has been a source of enjoyment and inspiration for me over the years. I have shown its importance by embedding it within my doctoral research to express and represent the meaning of emotion.

I explain the importance of addressing emotion in education and the merits of reflecting on our experiences in order to become more educationally entrepreneurial, by taking risks, awakening our creativity and bringing ideas into action.

Within these safe educational spaces I connect the head with the heart, marry the 'sense and soul' (Wilber, 1988) to combine a constructivist, behaviourist, cognitive pedagogical approach that avoids a fragmented learning experience as I inspire others to bring their ideas to fruition.

Crotty also focuses on the importance of 'methodological inventiveness' in the creation of a living-theory and before I focus on the methodological characteristics of a living-theory I shall consider the living logic that distinguishes the rationality of a living-educational-theory.

3.3.1   Living logic

I follow Marcuse's (1964, p. 105) understanding of logic as a mode of thought that is appropriate for comprehending the real as rational. The 2,500-year struggle between formal and dialectical researchers for control over what counted as rational has been clearly demonstrated in the work of Popper (1963) and Marcuse (1964). Using Aristotelian Laws of Logic, Popper demonstrates that any theory that contains a contradiction is entirely useless as a theory and is based on nothing better than a loose and woolly way of speaking (p. 313). In contrast to this Marcuse points out:

> In the classical logic, the judgement which constituted the original core of dialectical thought was formalized in the propositional form, 'S is p.' But this form conceals rather than reveals the basic dialectical proposition, which states the negative character of the empirical reality.
>
> (Marcuse, 1964, p. 111)

In the living logic of an explanation of educational influence that constitutes a living-educational-theory, individuals can integrate insights from both propositional and dialectical theories without denying the rationality of either of these ways of thinking.

My texts on the growth of educational knowledge (Whitehead, 1993), on a discipline of educational enquiry (1999) and on an epistemological transformation of educational knowledge through S-STEP research (Whitehead, 2013), integrate insights from both propositional and dialectical theories without denying the rationality of my living-theory that is distinguished by my living logic. The characteristic that distinguishes my living logic from my use of propositional and dialectical logics in my explanations of educational influence is the living form of my evolving explanations that include my energy-flowing values as explanatory principles and living standards of judgement. The meanings of propositional and dialectical logics are usually communicated through symbols and words. The meanings of a living logic include the embodied expressions of energy-flowing values in explanations of influence in enquiries of the kind, 'How do I improve what I am doing?' The process of clarifying and communicating these meanings in the course of their emergence in practice can be understood in relation to the methodological characteristics in the production of a living-educational-theory.

3.4   Methodological characteristics

In my doctoral thesis (Whitehead, 1999) I outlined the methodology that emerged from the creation of my living educational theory as follows. The references in the text below refer to the original references in the thesis which can be accessed from: http://www.actionresearch.net/living/jackwhitehead2.shtml.

The question is whether there is an 'educational' research methodology, which can be distinguished from social science methodologies, for enquiries of the kind, 'How do I improve this process of education here?'

In my initiation into the disciplines approach to educational theory with Richard Peters in 1968 at the University of London, it was held that the first step in answering a practical educational question was to break it down into its component parts. These separate components were to be informed by contributions from the disciplines of education and integrated back into the solution of the practical problem. Educational research methodology, like educational theory, was seen to be derivative in that it was constituted by the methods and conceptual frameworks of the philosophy, psychology, sociology and history of education.

My rejection of this approach to educational research methodology was based on an analysis of nine research reports I produced between 1970 and 1980. I analysed my own education as my learning moved on through the reports (2.3, 80). I gave the following explanation for my own educational development:

1. I experience a problem because some of my educational values are negated
2. I imagine a solution to my problem.
3. I act in the direction of this solution.
4. I evaluate the outcomes of my action.
5. I modify my problems, ideas and actions in the light of my evaluations.

I was clear about the existence of 'I' as a living contradiction (2.3, 75–76) in my question and answer. The originality of mind which distinguished this basis for an 'educational' methodology from social science methodologies emerged from an initial satisfaction and then a tension as I applied Mitroff's and Kilman's (1978) classification of social science methodologies to my enquiry. In his autobiography of research in four world views, Allender (1991) uses the Mitroff and Kilman classification in a similar way to myself and states:

> A model of scientific worldviews that has received little attention but is probably the most comprehensive, is based on the Jungian framework (Mitroff and Kilman, 1978). Two dimensions – one ranging from sensing to intuition and the other from thinking to feeling – are used to form a four-quadrant typology: (1) the analytic scientist, (2) the conceptual theorist, (3) the conceptual humanist, and (4) the particular humanist. The typology is proposed as a complete universe into which all research orientations can fit. (p. 14)

The typology can be represented as follows (Figure 3.1):

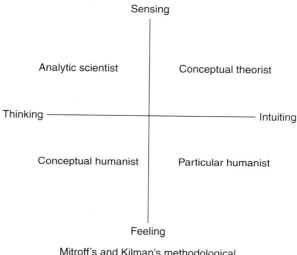

Mitroff's and Kilman's methodological
approaches to the social sciences

Figure 3.1   Typology of methodologies

Each methodology was distinguished by differences between its preferred logic and method of enquiry. The full details of my analysis are in 'A Dialectician's Guide for Educational Researchers' (3.2, pp. 61–67).

As I applied the above typology to the nine reports in my enquiry (2.3, p. 80), I felt a similar kind of satisfaction to the one I felt in 1968–1970, when studying and accepting the disciplines approach to educational theory. I felt that I had a comprehensive model for understanding my methodological approaches to my enquiry. I could understand my 'educational' enquiry within the preferred logics and methods of enquiry of an analytic scientist, a conceptual theorist, a conceptual humanist and a particular humanist (3.2, pp. 62–63).

I then began to feel uneasy because one of my reports appeared to fall outside the classification. This report was a story of my educational development as I moved through the four methodological approaches to the social sciences. While using these methodologies I was still taking the first step of the disciplines approach and breaking my question up into component parts. I was not seeing that

I could hold my enquiry together with an 'educational' methodology which had its own preferred logic and method of enquiry.

It may be helpful if I represent the emergence of my 'educational' methodology in terms of a spiral. This stresses it's living and dynamic nature. I have drawn this freehand to stress that the development is 'ragged', sometimes fragmented and anything but 'smooth'!

I move through the four methodological approaches to the social sciences into the creation of the fifth 'educational' methodology (EM) for enquiries of the form, 'How do I improve my practice?' (Figure 3.2).

(i)   I experience a problem because some of my educational values are negated
(ii) I imagine a solution to my problem.
(iii) I act in the direction of this solution.
(iv) I evaluate the outcomes of my action.
(v)   I modify my problems, ideas and actions in the light of my evaluations.

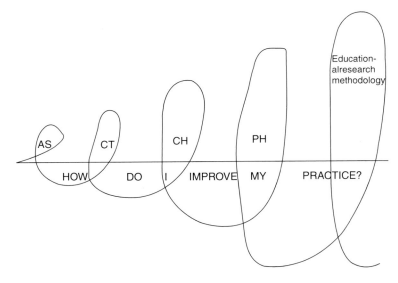

Figure 3.2   My educational methodology

Looking back some 20 years I can recall with some humour the responses by other scholars to my insistence that the personal pronoun, my 'I', could be included in a question worthy of research. Yet, I know of a recent case where a university research committee have asked for the personal pronoun to be removed from an action researcher's question! From the basis of the above answer to my question I began to focus on my practice as an educational researcher whose primary focus was the reconstruction of educational theory.

The paper 'An analysis of an individual's educational development' (2.4) marks the redefinition of my view of educational theory:

> My purpose is to draw your attention to the development of a living form of educational theory. The theory is grounded in the lives of professional educators and their pupils and has the power to integrate within itself the traditional disciplines of education.
>
> (2.4, p. 97)

Rather than being constituted by the philosophy, sociology, psychology and history of education, I now see that it can be constituted by the claims of professional educators to know their own educational development. The epistemological enquiries into my claims to know are focused on the nature of the critical standards which can be used to test the validity of the claims to knowledge:

> Questions concerning the academic legitimacy of a claim to knowledge are often focused upon the criticism of a particular piece of work. The work being criticised can be a single hypothesis or theory (Popper, 1963) or a research programme (Lakatos, 1972). Whatever is being criticised is known as the unit of appraisal. In criticising a claim to knowledge it is important to be clear about the unit and the standards of judgement which can legitimately be used in the criticism. There is some dispute amongst philosophers about the nature of the standards which can be used to criticise a claim to knowledge.

> The unit of appraisal in my conception of educational theory is the individual's claim to know his or her own educational development. Although this unit may appear strange to most educational

researchers I think that it is clearly comprehensible. The standards of judgement are however more difficult to communicate. I use both personal and social standards in justifying my own claims to know my own educational development.

(2.4, p. 99)

My enquiry then moves on in the paper 'Creating a Living Educational Theory' (2.5) into a fuller exposition of the central concerns of my thesis as a whole:

> In a living educational theory the logic of the propositional forms, whilst existing within the explanations given by practitioners in making sense of their practice, does not characterise the explanation. Rather the explanation is characterised by the logic of question and answer used in the exploration of questions of the form, 'How do I improve my practice?'
>
> In developing such an approach I have had to come to terms with questions concerning an appropriate methodology for enquiries such as 'How do I improve this process of education here?' In looking at video tapes of my practice I have had to confront questions which arise on recognising the 'I' in the question as existing as a living contradiction. In the production of an explanation for my practice I have had to question how to include and present values whose meaning can only be clarified in the course of their emergence in practice. I have had to face questions related to validity and generalisability. I have also had to question the power relations which influence the academic legitimacy of a living educational theory. In such a short article all I can do is outline the present state of my thinking in relation to these questions.

(2.5, p. 43)

The four papers which follow are:

- (1977) Improving Learning in Schools – An In-service problem.
- (1983) Assessing and Evaluating an Individual's Higher Education.
- (1985) The Analysis of an Individual's Educational Development.
- (1989) Creating a Living Educational Theory from Questions of the Kind, 'How do I improve my Practice?' (Whitehead, 1999).

The emergence of my living-theory-methodology (Whitehead, 2008) in the course of creating my living-educational-theory highlighted for me the importance of recognising that each individual can create their own living-theory-methodology using their own 'methodological inventiveness' (Dadds & Hart, 2001). For Dadds and Hart methodological inventiveness related to the way in which some practitioner-researchers created their own unique way through their research, and that this may be as important as their self-chosen research focus (p. 166). Dadds and Hart say that more important than adhering to any specific methodological approach may be the willingness and courage of practitioners – and those who support them – to create enquiry approaches that enable new, valid understandings to develop, understandings that empower practitioners to improve their work for the beneficiaries in their care (p. 169).

Because of the importance of methodological inventiveness for each individual in creating their own living-theory-methodology I wish to emphasise that a practitioner-researcher can draw insights from the following range of methodological approaches in creating their own. In outlining some distinctions between a living-theory-methodology and narrative enquiry, case study, grounded theory, phenomenology and ethnography I am indebted to Cresswell's descriptions of these methodologies. I have also added autoethnography as a methodology as this is the closest to a living-theory-methodology. Here is my justification for the use of a living theory methodology in the creation of your living educational theory.

I am aware of the responses of some supervisors of master's dissertations and doctoral theses when they are presented with draft writings on an individual's living educational theory. They say that they want a fuller justification of the approach used in relation to narrative research, phenomenological research, grounded theory research, ethnographic research or case study research. In my experience this kind of justification is not often useful to the student but is very helpful in revealing the methodological and epistemological assumptions in the supervisor's thinking.

I have found Cresswell's (2007, pp. 53–58) descriptions of five qualitative research approaches to narrative research, phenomenology, grounded theory, ethnography and case studies to be one of the best introductory texts. For each of the five approaches Cresswell poses a definition, briefly traces the history of each approach, explores types of studies, introduces procedures involved in conducting a study and indicates potential challenges in using each approach. He also reviews some of the similarities and differences among the five approaches 'so that qualitative researchers can decide which approach is best to use for their particular study'. I'll emphasise the point below that one can draw insights from each of these approaches without choosing between them in the development of one's own living-theory-methodology. You can access a 2008 paper of mine 'Using a Living Theory Methodology in Improving Practice and Generating Educational Knowledge in Living Theories' in the *Educational Journal of Living Theories* (*EJOLTS*) at http://ejolts.net/node/80.

Here are the descriptions of the five approaches that you might draw on in explaining why you need to go beyond the individual approaches or a combination of approaches in generating your explanations of educational influences in learning, in enquiries of the kind, 'How do I improve what I am doing?' and in generating your own methodology.

Dadds and Hart (2001) put the need for methodological inventiveness very clearly and this is the inventiveness that is needed to go beyond the following five approaches while drawing insights from the approaches where appropriate:

> The importance of methodological inventiveness. Perhaps the most important new insight for both of us has been awareness that, for some practitioner researchers, creating their own unique way through their research may be as important as their self-chosen research focus. We had understood for many years that substantive choice was fundamental to the motivation and effectiveness of practitioner research (Dadds 1995); that what practitioners chose to research was important to their sense of engagement and purpose. But we had understood far less well that how practitioners chose to research, and their sense of control over this, could be equally important to their motivation, their sense of identity within the research and their research outcomes. (p. 166)

> If our aim is to create conditions that facilitate methodological inventiveness, we need to ensure as far as possible that our pedagogical approaches match the message that we seek

to communicate. More important than adhering to any specific methodological approach, be it that of traditional social science or traditional action research, may be the willingness and courage of practitioners – and those who support them – to create enquiry approaches that enable new, valid understandings to develop; understandings that empower practitioners to improve their work for the beneficiaries in their care. Practitioner research methodologies are with us to serve professional practices. So what genuinely matters are the purposes of practice which the research seeks to serve, and the integrity with which the practitioner researcher makes methodological choices about ways of achieving those purposes. No methodology is, or should, cast in stone, if we accept that professional intention should be informing research processes, not pre-set ideas about methods of techniques. (p. 169)

3.4.1 Narrative research

Cresswell (2007) describes narrative research as follows:

Narrative research has many forms, uses a variety of analytic practices, and is rooted in different social and humanities disciplines (Daiute & Lightfoot, 2004). 'Narrative' might be the term assigned to any text of discourse, or, it might be text used within the context of a mode of inquiry in qualitative research (Chase, 2005), with a specific focus on the stories told by individuals (Polkinghorne, 1995). As Pinnegar and Daynes (2006) suggest, narrative can be both a method and *the phenomenon* of study. As a method, it begins with the experiences as lived and told stories of individuals. Writers have provided ways for analyzing and understanding the stories lived and told. I will define it here as a specific type of qualitative design in which 'narrative is understood as a spoken or written text giving an account of an event/action or series of events/actions, chronologically connected' (Czarniawska, 2004, p. 17). The procedures for implementing this research consist of focusing on studying one or two individuals, gathering data through the collection of their stories, reporting individual experiences and chronologically ordering (or using life course stages) the meaning of these experiences.

(pp. 53–54)

Cresswell (2007) describes a biographical study as a form of narrative study in which the researcher writes and records the experiences of another person's life. He says that:

> Autobiography is written and recorded by the individuals who are the subject of the study (Ellis, 2004). A life history portrays an individual's entire life, while a personal experience story is a narrative study of an individual's personal experience found in single or multi episodes, private situations, or communal folklore (Denzin, 1989a). (p. 55)

A living-theory, as an explanation by an individual of their educational influences in their own learning and in the learning of others, can be understood as a form of narrative research in that it begins with the experiences as lived and told by the researcher. Within the narrative what distinguishes the story as a living theory is that it is an explanation of the educational influences of the individual in their own learning and in the learning of others. Not all narratives are living-theories, but all living-theories are narratives.[5]

3.4.2   Phenomenological research

Cresswell describes phenomenological research as follows:

> Whereas a narrative study reports the life of a *single individual*, a *phenomenological study* describes the meaning for several individuals of their *lived experiences* of a concept of a phenomenon. Phenomenologists focus on describing what all participants have in common as they experience a phenomenon (e.g., grief is universally experienced). The basic purpose of phenomenology is to reduce individual experiences within a phenomenon to a description of the universal essence (a 'grasp of the very nature of the thing', van Manen, 1990, p. 177). To this end, qualitative researchers identify a phenomenon (an 'object' of human experience; van Manen, 1990, p. 163). This human experience may be a phenomenon such as insomnia, being left out, anger, grief, or undergoing coronary artery bypass surgery (Moustakas, 1994). The inquirer then collects data from persons who have experienced the phenomenon, and develops a composite description of the essence of the experience for all individuals. This description

consists of 'what' they experience and 'how' they experienced it (Moustakas, 1994).

(pp. 57–58)

Living-theories are phenomenological in that they begin from the experience of the phenomenon the researcher is seeking to understand. The purpose of a living theory differs from the basic purpose of phenomenology in that the purpose of phenomenology is to produce a description of a universal essence while the purpose of a living theory is to produce a unique explanation of the individual's educational influences in learning.

3.4.3 Grounded theory research

Cresswell (2007) describes grounded theory research as follows:

> Although a phenomenology emphasizes the meaning of an experience for a number of individuals, the intent of *grounded theory study* is to move beyond description and to *generate or discover a theory*, an abstract analytical scheme of a process (or action or interaction, Strauss & Corbin, 1998). Participants in the study would all have experienced the process, and the development of the theory might help explain practice or provide a framework for further research. A key idea is that this theory-development does not come 'off the shelf,' but rather is generated or 'grounded' in data from participants who have experienced the process (Strauss & Corbin, 1998). Thus, grounded theory is a qualitative research design in which the inquiry generates a general explanation (a theory) of a process, action, or interaction shaped by the views of a large number of participants (Strauss & Corbin, 1998).

(pp. 62–63)

A living-theory is similar to a grounded theory in that the intent of a living-theory is to move beyond description and to generate a valid explanation for an individual's educational influence in his or her own learning and in the learning of others. Living Theory differs from Grounded Theory in that the theory is not an abstract analytic scheme of a process. A living-theory is an explanation for an individual's educational influence in learning where the explanatory principles are not abstract generalisations. The explanatory principles are the energy flowing values and understandings the individual uses to give meaning and purpose to their life and to explain their educational influences in learning.

3.4.4 Ethnographic research

Cresswell (2007) describes ethnographic research as follows:

> Although a grounded theory researcher develops a theory from examining many individuals who share in the same process, action, or interaction, the study participants are not likely to be located in the same place or interacting on so frequent a basis that they develop shared patterns of behavior, beliefs, and *language*. An ethnographer is interested in examining these shared patterns, and the unit of analysis is larger than the 20 or so individuals involved in a grounded theory study.
>
> An *ethnography* focuses on an entire cultural group. Granted, sometimes this cultural group may be small (a few teachers, a few social workers), but typically it is large, involving many people who interact over time (teachers in an entire school, a community social work group). Ethnography is a qualitative design in which the researcher describes and interprets the shared and learned patterns of values, *behaviors*, beliefs and language of a *culture-sharing group* (Harris, 1968). As both a process and an outcome of research (Agar, 1980), ethnography is a way of studying a culture-sharing group as well as the final, written product of that research. As a process, ethnography involves extended observations of the group, most often through *participant observation*, in which the researcher is *immersed* in the day-to-day lives of the people and observes and interviews the group participants. Ethnographers study the meaning of the behaviour, the language, and the interaction among members of the culture-sharing group.
>
> (pp. 68–69)

A living-theory is similar to ethnographic research in paying attention to the cultural norms within which the researcher is acting and researching. It differs from ethnographic research in that it does not focus on an entire culture group. A living-theory is an explanation of an individual's educational influence in their own learning, in the learning of others and in the social formations in which the researcher is living and working. In engaging with the cultural influences in the individual's learning, especially in the learning of social formations, living-theorists include an understanding of cultural influences in the explanations of their educational influences in learning. These influences can be emphasised in the application of Habermas' (2002) four criteria of social validity, especially with the criterion of demonstrating an awareness of the normative background from within which the researcher is speaking and writing.

3.4.5 Case study research

Cresswell (2007) describes case study research as follows:

> The entire culture-sharing group in ethnography may be considered a case, but the intent in ethnography is to determine how the culture works rather than to understand an issue or problem using the case as a specific illustration. Thus, *case study* research involves the study of an issue explored through one or more cases within a bounded system (i.e., a setting, a context). Although Stake (1995) states that case study research is not a methodology but a choice of what is to be studied (i.e., a case within a *bounded system*), others present it as a strategy of inquiry, a methodology, or a comprehensive research strategy (Denzin & Lincoln, 2005; Marriam, 1998; Yin, 2003). I choose to view it as a methodology, a type of design in qualitative research, or an object of study, as well as a product of the inquiry. Case study research is a qualitative approach in which the investigator explores a bounded system (a *case*) or multiple bounded systems (cases) over time, through detailed, in-depth data collection involving *multiple sources of information* (e.g., observations, interviews, audiovisual material, and documents and reports), and reports a case *description* and case-based themes. For example, several programs (a *multi-site* study) or a single program (a *within-site* study) may be selected for study. (p. 73)

A living-theory may sometimes be mistaken as a case study. Stake (1995) refers to case study as a choice of what is to be studied within a bounded system. Living-theories, generated from a perspective of inclusionality, as a relationally dynamic awareness of space and boundaries, show an awareness of the experience and expression of a life-affirming and unbounded energy flowing through the cosmos. The main difference between a case study and a living theory is that a case study is a study of a bounded system while the explanatory principles of living theories are not constrained by a bounded system. They articulate explanatory principles in terms of flows of life-affirming energy, values and understandings that are transformatory and not contained within a bounded system.

The authors therefore recognise the conceptual importance of the individual 'case' and for an un-bounded learning system as proposed by a living-theory-methodology we propose the principle of the Living Case where participants become the *living-case* of their own study, not somebody else's. If you are conducting an enquiry of the kind 'How do I improve what I am doing?' with the intention of improving your practice and generating new personal knowledge in your living-educational-theory, we believe that as a *living-case* you will need to embrace Dadds' and Hart's (2001) idea of methodological inventiveness in the creation of both your living-educational-theory; and, your living-theory-methodology (Whitehead, 2009).

3.4.6 Autoethnography

Ellis and Bochner (2000) advocate autoethnography, a form of writing that 'make[s] the researcher's own experience a topic of investigation in its own right' (p. 733) rather than seeming 'as if they're written from nowhere by nobody' (p. 734). Autoethnography is 'an autobiographical genre of writing that displays multiple layers of consciousness, connecting the personal to the cultural' (p. 739); 'autoethnographers ask their readers to feel the truth of their stories and to become co participants, engaging the storyline morally, emotionally, aesthetically, and intellectually' (p. 745). (Porter, 2004, p. 1)

A living-educational-theory is autoethnographic in the sense that the explanations produced by the individual connect the personal to the cultural in explaining the individual's educational influence in the learning of social formations. A living-educational-theory also seeks to strengthen the integration of socio-historical and socio-cultural insights through the use of questions by a validation group that are derived from Habermas' four criteria of social validity. In particular the question: 'How can I strengthen the inclusion of socio-historical and socio-cultural insights into the explanation of educational influences in the learning of social formations?' helps to strengthen the autoethnographic quality of a living-educational-theory through strengthening the insights that relate the personal to the cultural.

The academic framework below is focused on inclusional meanings of living citizenship that can be included in living-global-citizenship as an explanatory principle and living standard of judgement. The inclusional meanings reveal limitations in traditional propositional and dialectical forms of understandings and draw insights from the meanings of embodied expressions of living citizenship that have been revealed in multimedia narratives or Living Case evidence.

3.5   Using living-global-citizenship as an explanatory principle and living standard of judgement in an individual's account of their influence in enquiries of the kind, 'How do I improve what I am doing?'

I was introduced to the idea of 'living citizenship' by Mark Potts (2012) during his doctoral research programme supervised by Dr. Steve Coombs at Bath Spa University, 'How can I Reconceptualise International Educational Partnerships as a Form of 'Living Citizenship'?

Abstract …. The project looks at how over a ten year period the partnership activities between Salisbury High School and Nqabakazulu School in the black township of Kwamashu in Durban, South Africa have influenced the education of the participants. Through a series of reciprocal visits, some funded by the British Council, and through curriculum activities, fundraising activities and personal contacts the partnership has developed to become a powerful influence on the lives of the participants. As it has developed certain underpinning values have emerged. These values have been articulated as social justice, equal opportunities and the African notion of Ubuntu, or humanity. The partnership between the schools has enabled the teaching of these values in a meaningful context.The research methodology is a participatory action research approach with the use of video, pictures and commentary to show the educational influence on the lives of the people in these communities. This has enabled the author to reflect on how the activities of the partnership have influenced the education of himself and his fellow participants. As a result of this study there will be three original contributions to knowledge:

1. The development of a transferable method for systematically analysing the large amount of qualitative data.
2. A range of transferable pedagogical protocols for citizenship education that can be derived from school international partnerships together with recommendations for government policy on how best to extend educational partnerships and implement international CPD between UK and South African schools.
3. An examination of the notion of 'Living Citizenship' and exemplification of it in practice through engagement in the activities of an international educational partnership.

Potts (2012, pp. ix–xxii) distinguishes 'living citizenship' with Ubuntu, Social Justice and Equal Opportunities. Coombs and Potts (2012) explain how living citizenship, as a living standard of judgement, has been brought into the academy through the legitimation of Potts' doctoral thesis:

This paper explores the conceptual framework of 'Living Citizenship' as a means for developing international continuing professional development (i-CPD) through action research projects. The research focuses on videocases that present findings from the development of an international educational partnership between two schools in England and South Africa. Adapting Whitehead's (2005) living educational theory approach to action research, 'Living Citizenship' supports and problematises international educational partnerships' through the influence of enabling participants' as critically active citizens. Such pro-active fieldwork links the values and objectives of social justice and knowledge exchange

to proffering educational change within authentic i-CPD professional learning environments. (p. 1)

Donald Schön (1995) called for the development of a new
epistemology from action research that would be appropriate for
comprehending new forms of scholarship. In creating this epistemology, living theory researchers have focused on new units of appraisal,
explanatory principles, living standards of judgement and living
logics in their explanations of educational influences in learning.

The importance of living citizenship as an explanatory principle
in living theories is that individuals are accounting for their lives and
influences in relation to living their value of living citizenship as fully
as possible. In Chapter 6 we, the authors, describe a move from a 'Life
in the UK test' to a 'Living in the UK' personal examination. We see
this move in terms of a paradigm shift towards an epistemology of
validating social inclusion through a demonstration of *becoming* a
living citizen and having the personal evidence to authenticate and
present one's case. Technical literacy and competency can report an
external viewpoint of 'Life in the UK', but only a personally validated account, reported via an experiential portfolio of evidence, can
authenticate actual 'living in the UK' and whether cultural inclusion
and understanding has been really achieved – the 'real' test!

The importance of living-global-citizenship as a living standard
of judgement is its epistemological significance in evaluating the
validity of contributions to knowledge that can fulfil both halves
of the core mission of the American Educational Research Association. That is, to advance knowledge about education, to encourage
scholarly enquiry related to education *and* to promote the use of
education to improve practice and serve the wider public good. It is
in relation to improving practice and serving the public good that
living-global-citizenship as a living standard of judgement is most
significant with the potential to leverage useful social impacts in the
community.

An Ubuntu way of being, doing and knowing can be used to
extend the idea of 'living-citizenship' into 'living-global-citizenship'.
The idea of 'living-global-citizenship' fluidises cultural and ethnic
boundaries that could otherwise limit 'living-citizenship' within
impermeable national and cultural boundaries. It can enhance flows

of communication within and between these boundaries with values that carry hope for the future of humanity and thereby enable greater social justice through challenging and mitigating cultural divisions (Coombs & Potts, 2013) within and across global societies.

For example, if you google Nelson Mandela and Ubuntu you can access a 1:37-minute video of Nelson Mandela talking about Ubuntu. In the following section we, the authors of this book, emphasise the importance of visual data in communicating the meanings of embodied expressions of values including 'living global citizenship'. Do please view the video and see and hear Mandela's embodied expressions of meaning as well as recognising the meanings in the words he uses. The subtitles on the video include:

> An icon of freedom in Africa and the world; an inspiring symbol of tolerance and humanity; the African tradition of 'ubuntu'; it is a universal truth; it is a way of life; Ubuntu – respect helpfulness, sharing, community, caring, trust, unselfishness, this is the spirit of Ubuntu.

Nelson Mandela expresses values of humanity that transcend national, cultural and ethnic boundaries. He is truly a citizen of the world and embodies in this video clip on Ubuntu what we mean by 'living-global-citizenship'. Jack Whitehead was privileged to accept an invitation to present the inaugural Nelson Mandela Day Lecture at Durban University of Technology in which he was able to focus on the personal values of *being* that constitute living-global-citizenship (Whitehead, 2011).

At the heart of this book is the belief that the more that individuals can be encouraged to account for themselves in learning to live their values of global-citizenship as fully as possible and to share these accounts with others, the more they are contributing to making the world a better place to be. This contribution rests on living and researching enquiries of the kind, 'How do I improve what I am doing?' in social contexts where the individual is seeking to live their value of living-global-citizenship as fully as possible. Researching one's own practice in this way requires the sharing of one's living-educational-theory with living-global-citizenship as an explanatory principle to which one holds oneself accountable. It requires others to use living-global-citizenship as a living standard of judgement to help to critically evaluate and strengthen the contribution to authentic knowledge.

3.6 Enhancing the influence of global citizens through living as fully as possible the values of living-global-citizenship

The United Nations designated 2012 as the Year of Co-operatives (Source – http://social.un.org/coopsyear/). We argue that the UN human values of co-operation are held within a personal concept of living-global-citizenship that has wide international significance in adopting the principles of Living Global Citizenship. In section 5.3 we present data from living-theory research in South Africa, Japan, India, China, Canada, Australia, the Republic of Ireland, the United Kingdom and the United States in relation to supporting the idea and practice of Living Global Citizenship. In this section we focus on an international continuing professional development project to show how it is enhancing the influence of global citizens through living as fully as possible the values of living-global-citizenship.

3.6.1 Living values and improving practice cooperatively: An international CPD project

The project is grounded in the assumption that each individual has talents that could be developed in learning that enhances the individual's well-being and the well-being of others through living loving and productive lives in enquiries of the kind, 'How do I improve what I am doing?' The project participants are committed to living as fully as possible, in the creation of their living-educational-theories, the personal and co-operative values and understandings that carry hope for the future of humanity.

Learners of all ages are capable of developing their ability to research as Living-Theory researchers and in the process contribute to their own learning, the learning of others and of the social formations they are part of.

Professional Masters programmes have been created as higher levels of training, over the years providing teachers and others with further qualifications. The traditional way of 'delivering' such academic training has been through lectures with pre-packaged content whereupon the learners 'surface learning' (West Burnham, 2006) has been assessed by the field 'knowledge' being reflected back to the coordinating lecturer in the form of module assignments. Evidence that the student might have gone to the higher levels of learning (Bloom, 1956) has been sought in the form of a dissertation, in which the student evidences they can analyse, evaluate and synthesise field knowledge benchmarked to relevant literature sources.

A Living-Theory Masters programme requires that the learner accept their responsibility for themselves as knowledge creators, thereby contributing to the knowledge base of educational and professional practice. Assignments require that the student critically and creatively draws on the knowledge created by others in their field as well as the Academy in the course of researching their practice, with an explanation of their educational influences) upon the encountered learning environment. Submitting their 'Assignments' and finally their dissertation as accounts of their explanations of their educational influence in learning for accreditation at Masters level helps keep the important events in focus among the urgent daily pressures they experience and also operates as a form of validation, working with Habermas' (1976, pp. 2–3) notion of validation including:

 (i) Does it communicate?
 (ii) Is there sufficient evidence to support the claims I am making?
 (iii) Have I given sufficient to show the complex ecology (Lee & Rochon, 2009) which includes the field and academic knowledge, practice, self etc as the normative background of my research?
 (iv) Is there sufficient evidence for you to know whether I have been authentic in my claims to be living my ontological and social values in practice (i.e.; do my values, clarified in their emergence through my research, form my living standards of judgement in explaining my educational influences in learning)?

Living-Theory research is therefore a transformational practice as embodied knowledge of; field, practice and self, and is indeed the subject of research to create new knowledge of improved practice.

Previously, Masters programmes were less constrained by models of 'education' that are now driven by economic rationalism. Currently, however, there is an overwhelming financial concern with numbers – the number of hours to 'deliver' content, mark scripts and, respond to students; and for the student the number of hours of lectures they must attend, the number of words they must submit and the number of students that successfully pass. Hence, there is a 'cost-effective' managerialist procedure akin to Ford's production line approach to mass-producing the early motorcar. There is little regard paid to the quality and nature of learning and enhancing the educational influence of the student in their learning, despite the blooming of government quality agencies to help 'regulate' the system. To challenge this mass educational training approach we have moved from having standard cohorts of campus-based students starting and finishing a fixed course at the same time, towards an alternative Continuing Professional Development (CPD) system of managing individual work-based projects and student-led enquiries. This professional learning *living curriculum* approach towards CPD project management held within the professional community itself suits a more individual supervised caseload system; one that attempts to improve personal access to field specific knowledge and expertise through enabling quality educational conversations and relationships. This professional learning strategy is also intended to support profound learning (West Burnham, 2006) by enabling participants to contribute to their own learning as field experts and practitioners. In this way professional learners create relevant knowledge which contributes to their field of practice and also supports a wider world within which humanity can potentially flourish. This is not to say that the quality of a Masters programme as a professional qualification should be 'reduced', quite the contrary.

By enabling practitioners to engage with researchers from different fields the knowledge base they draw on is inevitably widened. As they test the validity of their accounts as they are created through their research, it becomes more rigorous, and as they begin to recognise and clarify their ontological and social values through the course of their research, they progress their professional, academic and personal development.

This *in situ* work-based approach to accrediting masters level CPD (Gardner & Coombs, 2010, ch. 11) not only benefits students and their institutions through educational impact, but also points to an essential new role for universities in responding to and supporting the uniqueness of each student's community project's needs. This supervision support is catered through the diversity of the skills and embodied knowledge held within the available faculty of university staff. This new supervision role supports:

- Academic and field 'content' that is made available through access to online libraries, workshops, seminars, webinars, lectures and conferences.
- Access to educational conversations and relationships is made available through tutorials.
- Testing the validity and rigour of knowledge is through submitting accounts for accreditation.

Each of these support systems can be separately costed and offered as a useful CPD educational service to schools and colleges, thereby improving the academic quality and professional relevance of the degree awarded, and also improving the educational learning and field expertise of the student.

To date we have supported Masters students (registered with a university) with access to academic content by pointing them to references in libraries and developing web-based resources of papers and Masters and Doctoral enquiries offered as gifts by other Living-Theory researchers. To make the resources available on http://www.actionresearch.net more accessible to researchers who are beginning (as well as those who already have experience) as Living-Theory researchers we have set up: http://www.spanglefish.com/livingvaluesimprovingpracticecooperatively/resources.asp.

This is a virtual community of the Living Values Improving Practice Cooperatively CPD/research project. The project is intended for:

- professionals who, whatever their field of practice, are committed to improving the life-chances and well-being of individuals and communities;
- researchers developing understandings, quality and influence of Living-Theory research as contributions to a world where humanity can flourish; and,
- those who want to enquire co-operatively with others and who also want to express life-affirming and life-enhancing values in practice.

Through this project we will be engaged in research to create and make public our knowledge of how we are each, and together, enhancing our educational influence in our own learning, the learning of others and the learning of the social formations we live and work in, using a Living-Theory approach.

As we research to improve our individual daily practice we will be clarifying our values as they emerge in practice. In this way we research together to: learn how to improve how we learn; work and research cooperatively; and, collaboratively across professional and other social boundaries.

We want the content of this site to captivate imaginations, and researchers to feel supported and encouraged to not only to make public their embodied knowledge and their living-educational-theories, but also to engage in cooperative enquiries that can spread the influence of the values and understandings that carry wider hope for the future of humanity.

To facilitate access to references and resources on this website they are in the process of being organised into four strands:

- One generic for Living-Theory researchers developing their research, which will include subsections on, for instance, issues of:

  o Getting your Living-Theory research underway
  o Methodology, research methods
  o Validity, rigour
  o Standards of judgement
  o Explaining educational influences in learning
  o Dealing with data
  o Philisophical underpinnings
  o Issues, debates, critiques and allied methodologies
  o And – yet to be developed

- One of references and resources that have been of particular interest to researchers project's specific to their field of practice, for instance:

  o Health
  o School, FE, HE, Local Education Authorities etc.
  o Community

- o Business
- o Social and Public Services
- o Others yet to be identified

- One with resources and references concerned with the interest of practice-based researchers which transcend fields, for instance, the cross-cutting themes of:

- o values
- o mindfulness
- o developing talents as gifts
- o Social justice
- o Leadership
- o Educational (values-related) learning

- And one of things that might be really helpful and interesting, but we don't know yet where else to put them!

- o Interesting quotes (Huxtable & Whitehead, 2013)

The website http://actionresearch.net. gives free access to a huge range of resources and references concerning Living-Theory research. You will also find living-theory doctoral theses and Masters projects, which people have offered over the years as gifts of professional living legacies.

Living Global Citizenship is concerned with dialogue by participants in a partnership about their values and the context in which those values are expressed. It is important to recognise the danger that agreement on some values, such as care, represents a universalist view of morality as critiqued by Todd (2008). Therefore, recognition of difference in terms of values, understood contextually, can be just as important and serves as a basis for further learning. Souza (2008) argues that the goal should not be consensus, rather a pedagogy of *dissensus* as an alternative schema leading to an openness to new possibilities instead of universal certainties. Living Global Citizenship emphasises the importance of dialogue by participants with multiple perspectives and engages with Andreotti's (2008) question of how to develop an *'ethical relationship with the other'*, in other words a care ethics that is based on a contextualised approach.

The contribution of living-global-citizenship to making the world a better place to be rests on individuals and groups producing and

Table 3.1 Clarifying the terms living global citizenship, living-global-citizenship; Living educational theory, living-educational-theory; Cultural empathy, cultural-empathy & living case, living-case

General concept & framework theory	Term for adopted value and experiential construct
Living global citizenship This is the general term used to define the general concept and framework theory	Living-global-citizenship This is the personal term used to describe the unique meaning that an individual is seeking to live as fully as possible within a living-global-citizenship social learning environment
Living educational theory The general term living educational theory is a framework used to describe the general approach to professional development and to generating educational knowledge	Living-educational-theory This personal term describes the particular/unique living-educational-theories generated by individuals to explain their educational influences in their own learning, in the learning of others and in the learning of the social formations in which we live and work
Cultural empathy The general term cultural empathy can be understood as a core social value that both describes and underpins the socio-ethical basis of living global citizenship and living educational theory	Cultural-empathy The personal term of cultural-empathy is used to describe the unique embodied expression of meaning embraced by an individual seeking to understand the cultural positioning of others through experiential engagement. Such a person seeks to live their value of cultural-empathy as fully as possible and thereby represents an authentic living ethical paradigm
Living case The type of project evidence as a living educational methodology obtained from participants operating within a living educational theory or living global citizenship project	Living-case The personal experiential data derived by participants *engaged* in living-educational-theory or living-global-citizenship projects.

sharing their living-educational-theories in which they hold themselves to account for living their value of global citizenship as fully
as possible. We are committed to participating in the development
of a global community of living-theorists who are engaged in exploring the implications of asking, researching and answering questions
of the kind, 'How do I improve what I am doing?' in the context of
enhancing the flow of values that constitute living global citizenship
and something that carries hope for the future of humanity.

3.7   Summary of the key framework theories

In conclusion, we would like to synthesise the general concepts and
framework theories that make sense of Living Global Citizenship,
Living Educational Theory, Cultural Empathy and Living Case – see
Table 3.1. From these frameworks we have developed the separate
terms for their adopted value and the experiential construct for those
living participants engaged in such international cultural activity.

4

Living Legacies: Living Global Citizenship in Action

Each of the authors present their own living narrative of how they are engaged in a Living Global Citizenship project within which they are living out their values and contributing to improving their own lives and the lives of others. In addition, there are narratives of values-based activities from others that demonstrate the contribution that individuals are making as they live out their lives as global citizens and contribute to making a difference to the lives of others. These accounts exemplify difference and are personal statements of validity that validate the ideas of Living Global Citizenship and Cultural Empathy. They also reflect inter-cultural learning experiences. Individuals who are committed to holding themselves to account for living these values as fully as possible create a social movement that can contribute to transforming the world. We are claiming that our living legacies in the form of our living-educational-theories of our influences in living-global-citizenship can make a significant contribution towards social movements. This powerful approach towards professional learning can be applied to many different working cultural contexts within businesses and organisations, all educational sectors, across joint venture projects, government departments, NGOs and international projects in general.

4.1 Mark Potts – the international educational partnership between Sarum Academy and Nqabakazulu School, South Africa

4.1.1 Establishing the partnership

In 2000 I, along with 15 other Head and Deputy Head teachers, was fortunate enough to be funded by the UK government to visit South

Africa as a professional development opportunity to focus on leadership in education. One of the purposes of the visit was to establish links between our own schools in the United Kingdom and the South African Schools. We visited several schools in the Durban area including privileged, predominantly white schools, mixed-race schools and black-township schools. I was drawn to Nqabakazulu School in the black township of Kwamashu. There was vibrancy evident in the school, a feeling of joy and hope for the future which seemed to chime with the political tone as South Africa was at the beginning of the journey of black majority rule. As I spoke with staff and students at Nqabakazulu School I noticed the overwhelming sense of freedom that they were experiencing following the end of the apartheid era. I came to share the hopes and dreams of the staff and students of the school for their own futures and the future of their nation. It was for these reasons that I decided to establish a partnership between my own School, at that time Westwood St Thomas' School in Salisbury, UK (now Sarum Academy), and the black township school. As I reflected on the reasons for establishing the partnership with this school, I came to realise that it was the shared values that brought us together.

Regular dialogue followed between me and a colleague in the South African School and a teacher exchange funded by the British Council took place. This widened participation in the partnership as students and more staff from the two schools became involved. Fundraising activities followed and gifts were made from the UK School to the South African School.

4.1.2 The transformation from cultural imperialist to partners in learning

I now recognise that as a visitor from the dominant cultural milieu at the start of the partnership relationship I carried a sense of cultural imperialism. Like many teachers from the dominant culture I carried a view of South Africa as a country which compared unfavourably with the Western standard and as a result I gave insufficient recognition to the richness of culture, history and society that is also evident in the Global South. I was subject to the Western perspective of development that saw my own country as developed and assumed that black South African schools would want to adopt the same pattern of development. My attention was naturally drawn to the obvious difference in economic resources and therefore, like many others, my initial response was to consider how we could 'help' the school to become more like our UK school.

As the partnership developed I began to listen and question my own assumptions and preconceived notions of development. Thus, began the process of decolonisation of the mind (Sharp, 2009). I carried out a series of interviews with staff and students in Nqabakazulu School. A clip from one such interview is available at: http://www.youtube.com/watch?v=gVWYck2-SrM.

The more I listened the more I learnt about the aspirations of the members of the community and the more I was filled with optimism that we could work together in partnership for the benefit of our two communities. I came to recognise the potential for learning from the partnership for both communities.

Subsequent interviews with participants from both communities cemented my view that what was important was to encourage dialogue to find joint solutions to problems, not proposals imposed by the UK school. Continuing dialogue shaped the activities of the partnership. As I got to know the school and community better and as we began the process of *cross-cultural pollination*, a term used by the Head of Nqabakazulu School, our shared values emerged from this process and we developed activities to live out those values. These activities attracted more and more participants from both of our communities and there became a growing sense of optimism that together we could find a way forward that engaged participants in a learning process.

4.1.3   Clarification and communication of shared values to distinguish the partnership

Over a number of years as the partnership developed staff, students and members of both communities engaged in dialogue with each other. During this time the visual representations became integral to driving the partnership forward. I conducted a series of video interviews over a period of ten years with participants and reviewed and evaluated the data using two systematic methods for analysing qualitative data. One was an original method that I developed building on the work of Coombs (1995). Coombs and I built upon the model of self-organised learning of Harri-Augstein and Thomas (1991), Kelly's (1995) personal construct theory and Slater's (1976) laddering-up scaffolding procedure. This epistemological framework consisted of a series of experiential 'content-free' templates that provide a sequence of stages for eliciting findings from qualitative data. The second method was using ATLAS.ti© software (1993) which flexibly allows for a similar qualitative analysis process to be embedded within it.

One of the key findings that emerged from analysis of the data was the evidence of shared values between participants in the partnership and how they underpinned the activities that were developed. The three values that emerged were:

- Ubuntu
- Social Justice
- Equal Opportunities

These contested terms are explained as follows:

4.1.3.1   Ubuntu

For some writers Ubuntu is a way of recognising the humanity of others in its infinite variety of content and form (Van Der Merwe, 1996). This translation of Ubuntu emphasises a respect for particularity and individuality. But in Ubuntu the individual is defined in terms of his/her relationship with others (Shutte, 1993). Being an individual in this sense means 'being-with-others' (Louw, 1998). This is not the same as the Western concept of individuality as a solitary aspect of human life, where an individual exists independently from the rest of the community or society. In an Ubuntu sense the individual is not independent of others but is interdependent with others. Khoza (1994) argues that Ubuntu needs to broaden respect for the individual and tackle the negative elements of collectivism. Ndaba (1994) points out that Ubuntu describes how the individual can thrive in a situation where they have ongoing contact and interaction with each other. In this sense Ubuntu requires dialogue and this preserves the uniqueness of the other in his/her otherness. Ubuntu in the sense of the thriving individual describes very well the way that the participants came to behave in engaging in the activities of the international educational partnership between our schools. Through dialogue and interaction the individual participants in the partnership have thrived and been able to identify and live out their values more fully. Thus, this interpretation of Ubuntu which sees the individual participant as interdependent with others is the one that emerged as a key element in the partnership. When the Headteacher of the South African School said: 'You did Ubuntu by making them realise their dreams. It was an act of humanity' (Potts, 2012, p. 226), he is using the word Ubuntu to describe the sense of awareness of others that participants in the partnership have shown in providing financial support for pupils to further their education by attending university.

I came to an understanding of Ubuntu through participation in the partnership with Nqabakazulu School in South Africa, as an African way of being, that gives primacy to the idea of 'I am because we are' (Charles, 2007). It was through my participation in the partnership that Ubuntu provided a vision and framework for me for respectful engagement in my research of the partnership; one that permitted reflexivity, reciprocity, community connectedness, and cross-cultural understanding through a sense of humanity. It is in this sense that we use the term to emphasise it as a principle, concept and value that underpins the relationship between the participants in the partnership and our actions as living citizens. Living Citizenship carries with it a sense of responsibility towards the well-being of all and with it a message of hope for humanity. This is my understanding of Ubuntu and I think it is consistent with Nelson Mandela's meaning of the term as illustrated in this video clip: http://www.youtube.com/watch?v=HED4h00xPPA

4.1.3.2   Social justice

In the Rawlsian (1971) sense, social justice demands that people have equal rights and opportunities; everyone, from the poorest person on the margins of society to the wealthiest deserves an even playing field. This assertion gives rise to several questions such as, what do the words 'just' or 'fair' mean, and what defines equal? Who should be responsible for making sure society is a just and fair place? How do you implement policies regarding social justice?

According to those on the left of the political spectrum, the State must legislate to create a just society, and various mechanisms such as the Welfare State (Esping-Anderson, 1990; Rothstein, 1998) need to be put in place in order to transfer monies required to even out the otherwise naturally occurring inequalities. Beveridge (1942) proposed a series of measures to aid those who were in need of help or in poverty and argued that government should provide adequate income to people, adequate health care, adequate education, adequate housing and adequate employment. Equal rights can be defined as equal access to things that make it possible for people in any section of society to be successful. Therefore, leftist philosophy (Dworkin, 2000; Roemer, 1998) supports measures such as anti-discrimination laws and equal opportunity programmes, and favours progressive taxation to pay for programmes that help provide equality for all. They argue that there are certain basic needs that must be offered to all. Thus, there is a need for policies that promote equal education in all schools and policies that would help all children have the financial opportunity to attend further education.

Those with a more right wing political stance (D'Souza, 2000; Nozick, 1974) criticise those who make poor choices and feel that while equal opportunity should exist, a government should not legislate for this. In fact they argue that social justice is diminished when governments create programmes to deal with it, especially when these programmes call for greater taxation. Instead, those who have more money should be encouraged to be philanthropic, not by paying higher taxes, which is arguably unjust and an infringement of personal liberty (Nozick, 1974).

We use the term social justice in the sense that Rawls (1971) uses it to mean an increase in egalitarianism and equality of opportunity. This is the meaning of social justice shared by the participants in the partnership as shown by this statement by Siyabonga, the School Pupil President when commenting on the higher education bursaries: 'If two or three learners get successful or achieve their goals that will make a huge difference in their lives and in the life of South Africa, because they will be able to help other pupils' (Potts, 2012, p. 235). This idea of social justice is included in the notion of Living Global Citizenship. In practice this manifested as engagement by the participants in social acts to increase equity and fairness. These *acts* form part of the social improvement research goals and are defined by the partnership 'social manifesto' (Coombs, 1995; Coombs & Smith, 2003). The pursuit of social justice, along with Ubuntu, becomes another of the underpinning principles that distinguishes our meaning of Living Global Citizenship.

4.1.3.3   *Equal opportunities*

Substantive or fair equality of opportunity argues that there is a need to give those from less fortunate backgrounds a better initial chance in life and this usually happens through the creation of access policies to various societal resources, e.g. education, employment, health. This argument is summed up by Parekh (2000):

> All citizens should enjoy equal opportunities to acquire the capacities and skills needed to function in society and to pursue their self-chosen goals equally effectively. Equalising measures are justified on grounds of justice as well as social integration and harmony.
>
> (pp. 210–211)

Rawls' (1971) principle of Fair Equality of Opportunity was a variant of the substantive version described above. His view that individuals from different backgrounds should have the same prospects of success in life is supported by Marshall (1998) and Krugman (2011). Gardner (1984) criticises substantive equality of opportunity on the grounds that inequalities will always exist irrespective of any attempts to erase them and even if substantive equality is achieved there will inevitably be future inequalities as an outcome. Kekes (2001) asserts that other competing principles such as justice and property rights need to be balanced with equality of opportunity and that it is dangerous to promote equality of opportunity above the other principles. In a similar vein, Nozick (1974) argues against equal opportunities legislation as it interferes with an owner's right to do what he or she wants with their property. This view sees individual property rights as morally superior to equality of opportunity. Cavanagh (2003) argues against the state getting involved in equalising opportunity on the grounds that helping create a level playing field merely gives everyone an equal chance of becoming unequal.

While recognising the criticisms levelled at the notion of equal opportunity the way that we use the term in the partnership is in the substantive sense. Chomsky's (1976) reference to the need in a decent society to overcome inequality of condition in order to enable individuals to be accorded their intrinsic human rights in the sense of equality of rights echoes the arguments of Rawls and Parekh. I refer to the participants in the partnership as having a 'moral duty' (Potts,

2012, p. 60) to address the inequality of condition between the pupils at the two schools. When participants provide bursaries for pupils at Nqabakazulu School to attend University there is an attempt to address inequality of condition and create fairer equality of opportunity in the Rawlsian sense, as these pupils would not otherwise have access to the funds to enable them to pay the entry fees. When participants learn about fair trade through the partnership (See Example 2 in the next section) there is a recognition that fair trade can, if the money is spent by the recipients for example on education, lead to less inequality of condition and fairer equality of opportunity. The value of equality of opportunity becomes, alongside Ubuntu and social justice, another standard of judgement applied to the actions of the participants in the partnership and another core value that can be used to distinguish the meaning of Living Global Citizenship.

4.1.4 Living out the shared values

In living out the shared values participants must be vigilant about evaluating the impact of their actions. There may be unintended consequences of the actions and a change of course may be necessary. The impact of actions on the *Other* must be constantly evaluated. Consideration must be given to both the short-term and long-term effects of actions. Hence, the importance of an action reflection approach which puts evaluation of impact at the heart of the process.

Bearing the above in mind, what follows from the recognition of the shared values are actions to live them out. As a result, many participants engage in project activities for the partnership to provide social justice and more equal opportunities arising from their concern for individual and societal well-being. The following examples illustrate this response:

4.1.4.1 *Example 1 – Black Dust*

An internationally renowned author published a book to raise funds for bursaries to enable students from the South African school to attend Higher Education. This activity emanated from a colleague at Sarum Academy who became an active participant in the partnership and he persuaded his friend, the author, to become involved. He also worked hard in involving a number of other contacts: designers; proofreaders, printers to make the publication happen. He engaged his students at school in marketing the book. Many advance orders

were taken and Black Dust was published in 2005. It has raised sufficient funding to offer scholarships to Nqabakazulu students for eight
years and sales of the book continue to this day. This activity illustrates the humanity of these people. Their actions embody similar
values to the other participants. Their human spirit was touched to
react in this way to a problem. The giving of their time and creativity to help others in this way is a symbol of their humanity. Graham
Joyce (the author) shows that he was motivated by social justice to
engage in these activities to raise funds for the school as this quote
from his speech at the book launch indicates.

> When I was eighteen I wanted to change the world and everyone
> told me that you can't change this world. Well, maybe they are
> right, but what is true is that you can change the world for one
> person and you can change the world for ten people and projects
> like this are here to remind us about what you can do.
>
> (DVD – Black Dust, Roberts, 2005)

All of the contributors to this project have been touched by the activities of the partnership and motivated by a sense of Ubuntu to act to
increase social justice and equal opportunities, thus living out their
values as *active* citizens.

4.1.4.2   *Example 2 – Beautizulu jewellery*

This project was initiated by the South African partnership school.
Zulu jewellery made by the students and members of the South
African community at the school is sent to the UK school and sold,
with all the profits being returned to the South African community.
This joint business venture has engaged many participants.

Firstly, the Business Studies teacher at Sarum Academy encouraged the students to research the marketing of the jewellery and to
price each item up and make it ready for sale. Sales were made in
lunch times and at school events. Discussions continued between
the schools about the quality and content of the jewellery. There was
some high quality learning going on as the teachers and their students discussed the cultural differences between the South African
market and the UK market for jewellery. What might sell well in
a South African market does not necessarily sell well in the United
Kingdom for various reasons, such as fashion or tastes or climate. For

example, some Zulu jewellery is made from safety pins and this could not be sold in the United Kingdom for health and safety reasons. Lessons are being learnt as the business progresses and the South African suppliers have adapted their products to suit the UK market.

When the Sarum Academy students visited Nqabakazulu School they learnt about Zulu culture and part of this was how to make the jewellery, thus they learnt a traditional Zulu craft. This enhanced their understanding and appreciation of Zulu culture and developed their respect for the Zulu cultural heritage. It also gave them an understanding of the skills and time involved in producing the jewellery.

In a reciprocal visit to the United Kingdom the South African students learnt about marketing skills and studied the UK market, increasing their understanding of the UK consumer's requirements. This made them more aware of the needs of the UK consumer and better prepared for providing products which meet their needs. In addition, they learnt, alongside UK students, how to build a website for the business to promote their products. This is a technological skill that they took back with them to South Africa.

Geography teachers in the schools focus on the notion of fair trade and how this project promotes the tenets of fair trade with a fair share of the profits going to the suppliers of the products. The Beautizulu Jewellery project has led to the establishment of a Fair Trade group at Sarum Academy comprised of students, teachers, support staff, governors and members of the Salisbury community. This group is promoting fair trade within the school and the community and has successfully gained Fair-trade status for the School, a national award to mark the work of the school as a fair trade organisation. This is a good example of how the activities of the international partnership can lead to associated activities that broaden participants learning.

Again, this is an example of how participants in the partnership have lived out their values of social justice and equal opportunities by acts of Ubuntu as they seek to improve their own lives and the lives of others.

4.1.5   The emergence of Living Global Citizenship from the partnership

It was from the study of this international educational partnership over a period of 12 years that the notion of Living Global Citizenship emerged. The examples above show participants in the educational partnership as *living-cases*, acting to live out their values of social justice, equal opportunity and Ubuntu more fully. The participants in the partnership have recognised the reasons for the injustice of the situation in the black township and have advocated change. Participants have mobilised others to recognise the reasons for the lack of social justice and equality of opportunity and to take action to change the situation. In this sense the shared values have both defined and driven the activities of the international partnership.

Through the partnership activity, teachers, parents and adult members of the community are recognising and questioning their own values and attitudes. Their reflections are leading to actions to live out their values more fully. This is encouraging students to do the same.

The hearts of the participants were sufficiently touched by the activities of the partnership that they had an impact on their own lives and on their subsequent actions. The international partnership led to sustained long-term impact on learning over a period of 12 years and is something which still continues. The partnership has been sustained over a long period because of the negotiated values that underpin the activities. Thus, participants have come and gone, but the partnership lives on. The long-term impact has been to produce a response from the participants that improves the lives of citizens in both communities. Through the living-cases there is evidence of a change in worldviews of participants in the 'North' and an ownership of the priorities for development by participants in the 'South'. For these reasons this partnership exemplifies what we mean by a Living Global Citizenship project and provides the basis for articulating and, enabling future sustainable educational development.

4.2   Jack Whitehead – contributing to improving the lives of myself and others

Throughout my working life (1967–present) I have been influenced by Erich Fromm's (1960, p. 18) point from his *Fear of Freedom* where he says that if a person can face the truth without panic they will realise that there is no purpose to life other than that which they create for themselves through their loving relationships and productive work. In 1966 I chose a working life in education because I believed that it would be a worthwhile form of life in a process of continuous learning for myself and in contributing to the worthwhile learning of others. I continue to document my own learning and my influence in the learning of others on my web-site at http://www.actionresearch. net. My own learning is focused on my evolving understanding of the values that carry hope for the future of humanity and my practice in which I am seeking to live these values as fully as possible. My influence in the learning of others is acknowledged in the living-theory doctoral theses at:

http://www.actionresearch.net/living/living.shtml

and in the masters writings at:

http://www.actionresearch.net/writings/mastermod.shtml

For the past four years (2010–2014) I have supported research in the Centre for the Child Family and Society as an Adjunct Professor at Liverpool Hope University and supported the vision of the strategic map of the Faculty of Education to:

> develop educational thought and practices which promote education as a humanising influence on each person and on society locally, nationally and internationally and supported the purpose of the Faculty to: contribute to the development of knowledge and understanding in all fields of education, characterising all work with values arising from hope and love as well as living a concern for social justice.
>
> (Liverpool Hope University, 2011)

Recent evidence of my influence in the learning of others has been provided by Sonia Hutchison in her paper 'A living theory of caregiving' in the September 2013 issue of the *Educational Journal of Living Theories* at: http://ejolts.net/files/journal/6/1/Hutchison6(1).pdf:

> Love is a difficult thing to bring into research and practice; however I am trying to bring the concept of love into my research and practice. It has been a tricky thing for me to do because I am aware of the boundaries in work. I feel bringing the concept of love into research and practice is something we're not meant to do. I feel we are meant to keep those we work with separate and yet I love

what I do but I find it is difficult to talk about. I think it is difficult because in English there is only one word for love which covers everything from I love my partner to I love my phone. What does love mean? It has this huge range of meanings. In other languages there are lots of words for love some of which I have found helpful and I explore them below.

(Hutchison, 2013, p. 44)

Without in any way claiming to have influenced Hutchison's creativity in this paper, I appreciated her acknowledgement of my influence in the generation of her living-theory of care-giving. I do hope that you will access Hutchison's writings on 'love' as it seems to me that enhancing the flow of love in the world is one way in which we can contribute to making the world a better place to be. In doing this I claim that we are living productive lives.

4.3   Steven Coombs – developing open access resources and accessible pathways to learning technologies

The concept of 'open access' to education is an interesting one and clearly represents a deeper felt value by some people in society to bring about greater equality of access to a range of educational opportunities denied to *others*. My story is about the evolution of developing open access educational resources to adult education participants starting from the early 1980s in the United Kingdom and my personal engagement at the time. As a young lecturer working in a college of further education in the County of Cornwall, southwest England in 1983, I was involved in the early development of so-called *open access* education projects. In particular, the issue of *closed access* to educational opportunities was something prevalent in the public psyche of late 1970s and 1980s Britain and led to the development of new concepts and educational services linked to both open access and then open learning solutions (Dixon, 1987). This manifested in the educational systems and perceived lack of opportunities in 1980s Britain that had experienced a deep recession and period of unemployment under the then Thatcher government. One response was for the then Manpower Services Commission working with the departments for employment to increase educational training opportunities for both school leavers at 16 and unemployed adults in the community. As part of this initiative Colleges of Further Education (FECs) in the United Kingdom were given resources to set up targeted training courses for adult education, specifically unemployed adults at the time. One response was the setting up of adult access training centres attached to FECs. These were called Open Learning Centres and provided a combination of opportunities ranging from basic adult literacy and numeracy courses up to preparation courses for access to higher education. From this initiative emerged the concepts of open and flexible learning, that is, formalising the practice of drop in adult learning centres and providing flexible learning resources linked to open admissions via enrolment-on-demand. Such gateways to learning was seen as something that could reduce teenage and adult unemployment and also stem the tide of those being trapped into a poverty trap supported by the then Welfare State.

For school leavers the same ideas applied except the assumptions assumed that such people would be offered vocational education via a combination of industry and FEC run programmes, aptly named as the Youth Training Scheme (YTS). British teenagers progressing through school were once understood to have only one chance (around the age of 16) to be entered for their external public examinations, the then system called 'O' Levels, to be replaced by GCSEs in the late 1980s.

Most of these back-to-work or apprenticeship schemes were supported by new policies of flexible and open learning developed through the FECs and its applied curriculum development research arm then called the Further Education Unit (FEU) that had researched new forms of delivering education and training (FEU, 1983; 1987).

My own role was to engage in such curriculum development and support students as 'trainees' via the implementation of a policy of flexible learning for both school leavers and adult learners. I supported this as I could see how this enriched the lives of many people drawn from the local community and this rich experience became part of my own value system at that time as I could see this as contributing to the wider public good despite the politics of the various funding schemes. Without realising it I was engaged in a form of *leveraging living citizenship* in the local Cornish communities through my role as a FEC lecturer. I was thus living and working in Cornwall within the FE and HE sectors throughout the 1980s and 1990s and was involved in the setting up of open access resource centres as community workshops for educational inclusion across the digital, generational and gender divides. Digital, because in late 1983 onwards I was involved in the setting up of a new computer literacy open access workshop named 'The Microsuite' which intended to provide a flexible learning adult access curriculum in tune with current FEU thinking (FEU, 1984; 1984a). From this development the open learning computer workshop became an IT drop-in workshop available to many sectors of the community including those with special educational needs. I could see the value in this alternative method of delivering education and also the value that it represented to the local community. I noticed how school leavers that could not cope with formal schooling found a new pride, identity and motivation in attending this type of learning environment. I could see how women returners felt both safe and able to come back to education after a long break of child rearing. It made me reflect on the meaning of learning and the role of the community to service such learning opportunities. It sparked my own desire to re-engage in continuing professional development (CPD) to learn more about the systems of education and learning I had immersed my life within. I read about action research and could see that I was already engaged in something similar in my own day-to-day work, but in an informal manner. I became curious to find out more and understand the educational systems I had become immersed within as part of my living journey.

By 1990 this led up to my engagement in an action research doctoral project at the then Centre for the Study into Human Learning (CSHL) located at Brunel University in West London. My action research project (Coombs, 1995) involved the linking of reflective technology interfaces to Harri-Augstein and Thomas' Learning Conversation (1991) and the theory of self-organised learning (Thomas & Harri-Augstein, 1985). This led to my discoveries and theories of Knowledge Elicitation Systems (KES) based upon the systems thinking constructivist ideas of George Kelly (1955) and many others (e.g. Beer, 1974).

Later in 1997 I obtained a new post working abroad at Singapore's National Institute of Education engaged in integrating ICT and critical and creative thinking into the Singaporean teacher training curriculum (Coombs & Smith, 1999) and this also led to the development of an interesting project. This involved the bringing together of professional communities of practice, practicum students, head teachers etc., via the setting up of early systems of multi-point desktop videoconference (Sharpe, Coombs & Gopinathan, 1999) resources in Singapore at the end of the 1990s. Professional communities of practice benefit from working together as argued by Wenger (1998) and in this case technology was helping to form teacher identities and shared values of practice. I would now argue that such professional social networking that operates across national and cultural boundaries relates well to the notions and values of our Living Global Citizenship framework. Likewise, the development of authentic video clip sources (from real life teacher incidents) to support initial teacher education within the Californian State University as part of a large Preparing Tomorrow's Teachers to use Technology (PT3) (Fouché & Coombs, 2002) Federal grant also relates well to the framework of Living Citizenship and Living Educational Theories. The role of the authentic video case and video focus group to capture rich narrative and help scaffold teacher identities and elicit values can be related to the notions of a Living Case and therefore we can see the relevance of such a technology-assisted research methodology to support Living Global Citizenship projects.

4.4 Living out my values as a nurse across cultures – Je Kan Adler-Collins

This is Dr Je Kan Adler-Collins narrative as he demonstrates the value of living-global-citizenship in his work.

4.4.1 Background

My formative years were spent as a young soldier after joining the British Army to get out of a council run children's care home. At that time the British Army had an indoctrination process heavily clouded by the cold war and the expected military response by NATO and the United Kingdom, including the view that everything involving communism and the spread of communism throughout the free world was possibly going to be the cause of the next global conflict. The war in Vietnam was winding down with the loss of face to the American system and military in what was a very unpopular war. In my work as a Buddhist nursing monk in Japan, I had to very quickly identify and work to remove inappropriate conditioning from the Army and from my culture. I achieved this through sustained inquiries using the medium of living action research for my living theory masters dissertation and doctoral degree at the Department of Education in the University of Bath which provided me with a safe platform to critically analyse my values. The framework of scholarship that evolved from this process allowed me to take the best parts of my English higher education and leave what did not fit into my praxis to be held in tension as a known bias. The rigour of my training as an educator can partly be attributed to a unique system that the United Kingdom has in higher education, but the greater part was my contact with scholars in living action research under the leadership and guidance of Dr Jack Whitehead. After I moved away from the United Kingdom, I came to understand just how well I had been trained and what a gift I had been given as I lived my life with an ever increasing commitment and passion for building networks of global citizenship where our differences were valued and respected. I now explicitly include the value of living-global-citizenship in the evolution of my living-educational-theory.

4.4.2 The importance of values

The communication of meanings of relationally dynamics standards of judgement, that include the flows of energy and values across different cultural boundaries can transform what counts as educational knowledge in the academy. What is needed is the development of culturally sensitive listening skills and the ability to see differences as valuable aspects of learning new ways of doing things.

My interest in narrative and the embodied meanings within narratives has deepened as I have used them to describe and uphold my desire to create safe healing spaces which embrace all aspects of the classroom and practice. For my life choices have placed me outside of my culture of my birth and opened me up to the richness and diversity of different cultures and also the perils of colonisation. Values and how an individual lives them are important when holding to account our actions.

Buber, (1947) stated:

If this educator should ever believe that for the sake of education he has to practise selection and arrangement, then he will be guided by another criterion than that of inclination, however legitimate this may be in its own sphere; he will be guided by the recognition of values which is in his glance as an educator. But even then his selection remains suspended, under constant correction by the special humility of the educator for whom the life and particular being of all his pupils is the decisive factor to which his 'hierarchical' recognition is subordinated. (p. 122)

Buber's words, although dated are highly relevant in today's global communities. For in such communities the global citizen has to live, in their daily actions, values that have to transcend the cultural condition of individual race and religion, holding in compassionate care the often differing values, beliefs and cultural actions of others. A global citizen acts through a deep awareness of the responsibilities of their actions and how such actions can affect others. Global citizens live with a holistic sense of connectedness to the different neighbourhoods of self-hood and humanity. With the following link I invite you to engage with values that I used as a foundational framework for the basis of the cross-cultural co-creation of ideas and new values used in this *living-case* study.

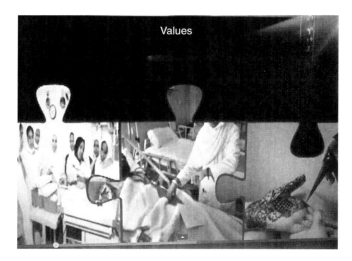

Figure 4.1   Values. http://www.youtube.com/watch?v=RpB78TVQ9-I

4.4.3 Neighbourhoods of self

Aspects of self-hood (Adler-Collins, 2007) are declared through my knowledge bias and filters of my Buddhist faith. Each is seen as an integral part of the (w)hole, distinct but not discrete (Rayner, 2003). My consciousness moves and weaves fabrics of understanding as it generates new knowledge of the lived aspect of the moment. I am feeling a sense of dis-ease at this point as I am required to separate out my holistic understandings grounded in different cultural biases and awareness into comprehensible strands. For without each of them I/we, as whole, cease to be. I live my life with the understanding I am a multidimensional being in the sense that I am a distinct but not discrete entity created as a temporary transient concept of self by the reflections of the neighbourhoods of the other. Very much like the African understanding of Ubuntu 'I am because we are' (Charles, 2007).

4.4.4 Work as a nurse in a hospice in Thailand

4.4.4.1 *Working in partnership*

I was fortunate to be invited as a keynote speaker to a conference of end of life care at Khon Kaen University in 2004 where I had the honour to meet another keynote speaker who was a Thai Buddhist monk and Abbot who had founded a volunteer hospice. Thai people hold Buddhist monks in very high respect and the values that the Abbot lived in his daily work inspired me. This gentle visionary monk had a history of nasal cancer and self-cured making a complete recovery from it through meditation and the taking of Thai herbs. This was another inspiration for, by Western thinking, he should have died. He and I were from very different types of Buddhism yet as he explained to me: 'the volunteer heart is not the property of any one person, organisation or culture. It is a Global thing, a Global heart, and a Global Love.' His words led to our sharing our ideas as we sought to reach out to the others knowing and from this a deep friendship evolved, one where we lived the Buddhist teaching of being each other's teacher and student.

4.4.4.2 *Intercultural learning*

Intercultural learning is not always easy and sometimes striving for global citizenship presents you with deep issues and conflicts. For example, one of the issues that caused the most dis-ease to me in my early association with Reverend Honourable Dr. Phrapaponpatchara Pibanpaknitee was the issue of pain in end of life care. My Western thinking could not get to grips with the suffering I would see in patients. The hospice had no drugs and the Abbot taught breathing into the pain and prayer as a technique to relieve pain. The use of narcotic drugs such as morphine, patient controlled analgesia etc., was not possible as there were no resources, nurses or doctors; just volunteers who visited as and when they could in an ad hoc manner. One of the social conditioning filters I quickly discovered in myself was that of a nurse who should bring about the relief of suffering of our patients. In Buddhist teaching, we suffer by ourselves through our fear. The mind needs to clear in the dying moments of life for enlightenment can come with the last breath. I suffered and still suffer from this thinking and asked for clarification from my teacher. The Abbott said that I think like a nurse and not a monk. That was my limitation. At first I was not able to understand this; however, as I worked with the problem I could see that I had become trapped in an identity of Western values that made up the complex values that I attached to nursing. As a Global citizen, I needed to be open to the wisdom, ideas and mistakes of others. Part of the wisdom given in this journey is that at times; we need to hold our core values closely but with flexibility. At times we need to bracket them and remove them from the equation until such time as they can be revisited and reassessed. I found that I was able to help relieve pain by developing a mind that focused on being alongside the dying individual bringing the only things I could, my humanity, compassion and love. This love helped me to evolve a system of touch that embraced many different ideas and teachings ranging from shamanism through to Chinese traditional medicine in the form of meridian lines and pressure points. The life affirming flow of human love and compassion was no longer just a theoretical concept to me. Rather it was a proven living entity, a workable tool that I saw bring about unexplained changes in conditions and degrees of pain. However, my scientific mind refused to accept the evidence and I looked for answers as to why this process worked. I collected samples of saliva and tested them for stress indicators and found that after only ten minutes of meditation significant changes occurred in stress release. In further research, I tested what happened after holistic oil massage and the results were even more surprising, showing that physical touch was extremely effective at reducing stress, fear and anxiety in the dying patient.

4.4.4.3 *The power of touch in caring for the dying*

Through working as a nurse in a hospice in Thailand I was privileged to be part of the dying process of many patients. In this next section I seek to show the flow of life affirming energy through the use of visual narrative images of my practice. Such images, I believe, offer evidence of the compassionate flow of love and healing energy between human beings. This short clip offers insights from the context of caring for the dying, in what can be sometimes trying circumstances as there are no full-time medical staff or nursing staff within the hospice. The context is that it is a volunteer hospice, serving the poor, with no state funding, relying solely on donations. It is my hope that you will be able to see what Whitehead (2008, p. 112) refers to as the life affirming flow of energy that I believe is a fundamental part of our humanity. All photographs were donated to me by the relatives of the patients with full permissions to be used in academic venues and publications as exemplars of what is known in Thailand as a good death.

YouTube: My work at; http://www.youtube.com/watch?v=23lPS2pnIYA.

The visual narrative I am presenting to you here clearly shows the process of teaching people to breathe and the process of holding and touching people as they die. I am aware that such thinking will be for some unacceptable and that in itself is okay because narratives are not just telling the story. The receiving individual decides on the value of the narratives for themselves. However, they must be conscious of the cultural lens with which they engage with the data.

4.4.5 The importance of cultural empathy

Working across cultures often requires the modification of the evolving story in relation to the circumstances that the narrator finds him or herself in at the time of the telling. By this, I mean that if the story has within it a moral value or a teaching approach that differs from the home culture I have to make the space safe for the mutual explorations. I (the storyteller) am responsible for using a language and items of belief and knowledge from within the home culture. If I am teaching on a particularly sensitive subject then I will use 'My life' as a medium of safety. Sometimes I describe my experiences from real life. Sometimes I present myself as an actor on a stage playing a part that has a meaning. Not only am I acting a part but also I have creative control of the design, the circumstances and the content. In such a manner, the actual content remains sound and understandable within the cultural context. An example is to use fairy stories which are very similar in different cultures, the morals and values transcending different aspects of socialisation. From within the profession of nursing, narratives of health and illness play an important role in cross cultural education. Nurse educators and practitioners at the point of care often use storytelling as a means of educating the patient or their families about the situation or condition they are facing. This is even more important within health promotion because health promotion is not just about health care, but must include politics, policy, education, history and environment.

4.4.6   Addressing cultural blind spots

Being a global citizen and seeing yourself living in a global community requires from an individual the constant focus on identify and making safe existing biases and inappropriate thinking or conditioning. I had such a revelation that I have shared in the following section.

Five Emirati nurses from Rashid Hospital, under the preceptorship and leadership of Dr Roxanne Nematollahi, PhD RN, an inspired and visionary scholar from Dubai Health Authority, shared their voices during the 25th International Council of Nurses Quadrennial Congress in Malta, in a symposium 'Giving New Emirati Nurses A Voice: Sharing Experiences Of Newly Graduated Emirati Nurses'. I was drawn to the very open and honest way the delegation presented their papers and the valuable insights that they presented to an international audience. I felt that the values they expressed were consistent with my own despite the fact that we are from very different cultural and religious backgrounds. Ms. Hind Mahmoud Abdulla Youne, one of the delegates, concluded her speech with a quote: 'The influence of each human being on others in this life is a kind of immortality'. These powerful words were further enhanced by the final speaker, Ms. Manal Essa Albaloshi (2011) who delicately explained the benefits of retaining new graduates based on evidence and detailed literature review. She concluded her talk with a beautiful quote of Sheikh Mohd Bin Rashid Al Maktoum, UAE Vice President, Prime Minister and Ruler of Dubai:

> UAE people are not living in a state of luxury disconnected from the world around us; we feel the pain and suffering of our fellow man around the world, and we make a positive and effective contribution to alleviate the suffering of others; we help the needy to combat poverty, hunger and disease around the globe.

Yet again I was reminded of the bias and incorrectness of a Western cultural heritage that gives no credit to the humanity of members of Arab nations. I could easily identify the causes of the hostility with our religious wars over the centuries and the colonisation of Arab culture. The oil crisis and the control that OPEC exercised on markets which reflected back to the winter of discontent in the United Kingdom were part of the building blocks of my images of Arab culture. Yet another wake up call to face, reflect and reduce my own bias and misconceptions.

4.5   Empowering communities and stories of activism in Tasmania

This is an account of the work of Phil Tattersall in developing community partnerships to tackle environmental issues of concern.

> The positivist worldview demands an objective and concrete, impersonal reality that is measurable and 'real'. The worldview tends to judge those views and opinions based upon local or experiential knowledge as lacking validity and credibility, seeing them as even unscientific. Thus 'everyday' common sense is always seen as just a very rough approximation of the real truth that only a select few can know. In similar fashion new or alternative paradigms or worldviews are usually not taken seriously. The resistance shown toward organic agriculture is just one example.
>
> (Tattersall, 2011, p. 1)

Tattersall has been involved in facilitating community involvement and empowerment in Tasmania, Australia, working with communities of interest across a range of issues from aerial overspray, pollution from heavy industry to water and forestry issues. He believes that a just and sustainable future is possible only through processes that encourage full participation and empowerment. The process of Community Based Auditing (CBA) is an attempt to engage the community as active players in the planning and management of their resources.

You can access Tattersall's doctoral enquiry 'How am I generating a living theory of environmental activism with inclusionality?' from:

http://www.actionresearch.net/living/tattersallphd/philtphd.pdf

Included in his thesis are his stories of activism, a series of brief narratives by participants in the partnerships that demonstrate how they have achieved social change through active participation in community partnerships.

CBA can be seen as an example of a Living Global Citizenship project in that it challenges predominant worldviews and encourages participants to find their own solutions to problems, based on dialogue within a community. The solutions emerge from the CBA process and are owned by the participants CBA serves as a good example of how community partnerships can bring about social change (see: http://www.actionresearch.net/writings/philtattersallcba3148.pdf).

4.6   The extent to which other community partnerships meet the specification for Living Global Citizenship projects that can be implemented through CPD fieldwork

Wider community partnerships can be seen as any social project or mission where overcoming cultural barriers can be understood as a useful goal, as well as developing a joint agenda for social change and meaningful impact. Such an applied research agenda for change benefits from adopting a 'social manifesto' (Coombs, 1995; Gardner & Coombs, 2010) approach, that links it to an 'improve' paradigm of social research and an *experiential research* methodology. A good example would be a CPD project embedded within an organisation seeking to change and transform itself. Such on-the-job CPD can benefit from adopting a Living Global Citizenship approach towards change management and cultural change. Given that much of CPD is regarded as providing *in-service* training courses for participants, maybe the activist work-based change agenda for Living Global Citizenship projects should be referred to as *living-service* CPD just so as to distinguish the nature of this type of professional community action. Evidence from living-service CPD projects would take the form of living-cases.

Learning organisations (Senge, 1990) generally seek to empower everyone through distributive leadership and shared task management of the processes levering change. Thus, shared task ownership is seen as a democratic form of leadership enabling all participants in the learning organisation to be mutual stakeholders; a kind of organisational active inclusionism. This social inclusion participant principle represents a core value of living-global-citizenship and would help to provide a powerful human resources policy for any organisation wishing to conduct and lead change through internal action research that is linked to authentic professional learning projects. Living-global-citizenship requires that participants' within any social organisation enter into dialogue about similarities and differences in values, recognise inequalities and why they exist, challenge existing hierarchies, mutually agree upon the common values and prior objectives in their context, and identify the agenda of the joint actions that flow from such cooperative joint ventures. In many ways the CPD paradigm shift towards a Living Global Citizenship agenda is a move from standard practices of continuing professional development towards what is now often referred to as critical professional development in the workplace. This idea is described by Coombs (Gardner & Coombs, 2010) who maintains:

> Thus, research, critical reflection and writing are all viewed as part of a 'symbiotic heuristic', or a mutually related process that encourages self-discovery of one's professional learning knowledge. Heuristic research operates in 'real-world' environments as a means of levering and articulating one's own practice as a form of positive change management and on-the-job CPD. (p. 141)

4.7   Data from living-theory research in South Africa, Japan, India, China, Canada, Australia, the Republic of Ireland and the United Kingdom, in relation to living global citizenship

Data from living-theory research from different national contexts is used to justify the claim that forms of living-global-citizenship are emerging from research by individuals into their own practice that involves living as fully as possible values that carry hope for the future of humanity.

4.7.1   South Africa

Data from South Africa includes living-theory research from the Transformative Education/al Studies project (TES, 2011–2014) funded by the National Research Foundation of South Africa. It includes data from Prof. Leslie Wood (2012) on the Transformative potential of action research. The African notion of Ubuntu (Charles, 2007; Phillips, 2011) will be used to relate this living-theory research to living-citizenship. The overarching research question of the TES project is 'How do I transform my educational practice as...?' The project includes an exploration of the South African concepts of Ubuntu in the Nguni languages and Botho in the Sotho and Tswana languages that view self or personhood in terms of ongoing and relational processes of becoming.

Professor Lesley Wood is one of the most influential action researchers in South Africa and has contributed to the establishment of the journal Educational Research for Social Change (ERSC). In her editorial for the first issue on 'Action Research: Its Transformative Potential', Wood (2012) points out that action research can support transformation on three levels:

Practical outcomes: transformation in social circumstances/ improvement in educational concern;

Epistemological outcomes: transformation in how people think about research, about knowledge creation and what counts as valid educational theory; and

Ontological outcomes: transformation of ways of living, how we interact with others, how we see our position in the world. (p. 2)

The ontological outcomes of transforming how we see our position in the world opens the possibility of including the value of living-global-citizenship in our way of being and in the values we use to account for what we are doing.

Eden Charles and Ian Phillips are two friends, colleagues and practitioner researchers I had the privilege of working with on the successful completion of their doctoral research programmes. Both acknowledged their African roots within their Afro-Caribbean heritages in Ubuntu ways of being. I identity with the values they clarified in the course of their emergence in their enquiries as those that distinguish living-global-citizenship and Charles (2007) brought Ubuntu, explicitly, as a living standard of judgement into the Western Academy.

4.7.2 Japan

Data from Japan includes the doctoral and post-doctoral research of Je Kan Adler-Collins (2007; 2013a; 2013b) on the implementation of a curriculum for the healing nurse in a Japanese university with the values of living global citizenship that can be related to the creation of a 'safe learning space' and Buddhist practices (see section 4.4).

Adler-Collins is a practicing nurse, a nurse educator, a Buddhist priest and a practitioner-researcher. His work includes supporting individuals and their families in a hospice in Thailand as well as contributing to the curriculum of the Chinese University of Chinese Medicine in Beijing. In his presentation to the British Educational Research Association (Adler-Collins, 2013b) he showed the openness of a Thai family culture to the public acknowledgement of death that surprised the mainly Western audience. This included images and video of individuals and families at the moment of death. As cultural boundaries become fluidised with greater understandings the work of Adler-Collins serves to bring into the value of living-global-citizenship a 'safe learning space' for the experience of a 'good' death.

4.7.3 India

Data from India includes the action research enquiries of Swaroop Rawal (2006; 2009) and her research to enhance the educational experiences of the most disadvantaged young people in Mumbai. Rawal's motivations include her Hindu values and these can be included in living-global-citizenship. The data includes the doctoral programme of Fr. Barnabe D' Souza (2008; 2012) with a question influenced by Professor Tony Ghaye (Whitehead, 1999, p. 90), 'How can we improve the educational experiences of the most vulnerable children in India?' D'Souza's motivations include his Christian values and help to explain his sustained commitment to supporting and working with some of the most vulnerable children in India and hence of the world. Hutchison (2013) writes about a living theory of care giving and a pooling of energy. Rawal and D'Souza demonstrate expressions of a pooling of life-affirming energy with values that carry hope for the future of humanity in their acts of living-global-citizenship.

4.7.4 China

Data from China includes accounts from researchers in China's Experimental Centre for Educational Action Research in Foreign Languages Teaching supported by Prof. Moira Laidlaw at Ningxia University. This includes an understanding of action research with Chinese characteristics (Laidlaw, 2008; Li & Laidlaw, 2006; Tian & Laidlaw, 2006) that can be related to notions of living-global-citizenship.

Before spending six years in China on Voluntary Service Overseas, during which time she received a Friend of China award from the Chinese Premier and was accredited as Professor for Life at Ningxia University, Moira Laidlaw (1994; 1996) received her doctorate from the University of Bath for her enquiry: How can I create my own living-educational-theory as I offer you an account of my educational development? Laidlaw demonstrated that, in the creation of a living-educational-theory, the researcher could not only clarify the meanings of her embodied values in the course of their emergence through practice, but could also show how the values were living and evolving in the course of the enquiry. Showing how insights from a Chinese culture, on the importance of working together within collaborative relationship, helped her understandings to transform and evolve into collaborative ways of being, acting and researching. Laidlaw contributes these understandings to the evolution of our understanding of the value of living-global-citizenship.

4.7.5 Canada

Data from Canada includes the research of Dr. Jacqueline Delong and the explanations of the living theory masters students she has supervised. These include the values of loving kindness (Delong et al., 2013, p. 13), a creation of a culture of enquiry and democratic processes of evaluation (Delong, 2002; 2013, p. 6). These have been clarified and evolved in her collaborations with students and colleagues. We are claiming that these values can be included in expressing as fully as possible the values of living-global-citizenship. We are thinking of the value of loving kindness that two practitioner-researchers supervised by Delong, acknowledged as being significant in their educational relationship with Delong (Delong et al., p. 13). We are thinking of the evidence that Delong (2009) presents in explaining how to build a culture of enquiry through the sharing of the embodied knowledge of teachers and teacher educators in aboriginal and non-aboriginal contexts. The building of this culture of enquiry required the fluidising of the boundaries that can sometime seem impermeable between aboriginal and non-aboriginal contexts. We see these values of loving kindness, the creation of a culture of enquiry and democratic processes of evaluation as included in our understandings of living-global-citizenship.

4.7.6 Republic of Ireland

Data from the Republic of Ireland includes the research and supervisions of Margaret Farren and Yvonne Crotty at Dublin City University (Crotty & Farren, 2013). It includes documentation from multimedia narratives to explain the importance of these narratives in expressing the embodied meanings of the values that we believe constitute living-global-citizenship. The explanations in the work of Farren and Crotty are informed by the relational values of Celtic spirituality.

Farren's (2006) doctoral enquiry is on the creation of a pedagogy of the unique through a web of betweenness. Farren's description of her thesis includes the following with her value of 'power-with' rather than 'power-over', which is something that we identify with the value of living-global-citizenship:

> This thesis examines the growth of my educational knowledge and development of my practice, as higher education educator, over six

years of self-study. The thesis sets out to report on this research and to explain the evolution of my educational influence in my own learning, the learning of others and in the education of social formations. By education of social formations I refer to Whitehead's (2005a) meaning of living values that carry hope for the future of humanity more fully in the rules and processes that govern its social organization...I clarify the meaning of my embodied values in the course of their emergence in my practice-based research. My values have been transformed into living standards of judgement that include a 'web of betweenness' and a 'pedagogy of the unique'. The 'web of betweenness' refers to how we learn in relation to one another and also how ICT can enable us to get closer to communicating the meanings of our embodied values. I see it as a way of expressing my understanding of education as 'power with', rather than 'power over', others. It is this 'power with' that I have tried to embrace as I attempt to create a learning environment in which I, and practitioner-researchers, can grow personally and professionally. A 'pedagogy of the unique' respects the unique constellation of values and standards of judgement that each practitioner-researcher contributes to a knowledge base of practice.

Farren explicitly embraces a Celtic spirituality in her way of being as she develops a pedagogy of the unique. As she expresses her spirituality in her relationships with students and colleagues we can appreciate how this spirituality can be included within living-global-citizenship. Farren has done much to spread the influence of living-educational-theories through her four years (2009–2013) as the Main Editor of the *Educational Journal of Living Theories*.

Crotty and Farren are friends and colleagues at Dublin City University. Farren supervised Crotty's doctoral research programme in a way that exemplified power-with rather than power-over. Crotty (2012) has brought an original meaning of 'an entrepreneurial spirit' into the Academy as a living standard of judgement. This meaning includes the values that carry hope for the future of humanity in a way that cannot reduce the meaning of 'entrepreneurial spirit' to an economic value. Crotty's work enables us to embrace a meaning of 'entrepreneurial spirit' in living-global-citizenship in a way that resists the damaging reduction of economic globalisation to forms of life that eliminate the values of humanity.

In a special issue of the *Educational Journal of Living Theories* Crotty (2011) gathered together collections of her masters' students multimedia writings and in a foreword, 'Through the enlightened eye and I – am I bringing creativity and visual literacy into Higher Level Education?' explained how visual literacy can be developed in multimedia narratives that enable the embodied values of practitioner-researchers to be clarified and evolved in the course of their emergence in practice.

4.7.7 United Kingdom

Data from the United Kingdom includes the archive of the living theory doctoral theses and masters dissertations accredited by various universities between 1996 and 2013. It documents the significance of changes in the regulations governing the submission of research degrees to universities, to permit the use of digital technologies in the submission of multimedia narratives that can be related to Living Global Citizenship (Whitehead, 2013).

This living theory archive from doctoral research programmes can be accessed at:

http://www.actionresearch.net/living/living.shtml

and the archive from masters' programmes can be accessed at:

http://www.actionresearch.net/writings/mastermod.shtml

It includes the resources for the international continuing professional development project on living values, improving practice cooperatively at:

http://www.spanglefish.com/livingvaluesimprovingpractice
cooperatively/

4.7.8 United States

Data from the United States includes the living theory research of Prof. Jill Farrell and Dr. William Barry of the Institute for Living Leadership. The data from Prof. Farrell's research includes her writings 'Transcending boundaries and borders: Constructing living theory through multidimensional inquiry' (Farrell, 2012). The data from Dr. Barry's research includes his writings on 'Challenging the Status Quo Meaning of Educational Quality: Introducing Transformational Quality (TQ) Theory' (Barry, 2012).

The significance of these writings from the United States in terms of living-global-citizenship can be appreciated in terms of the foci for the themes of the American Educational Research Association (AERA) for 2012, 2013 and 2014.

The theme of the 2012 conference was: 'Non Stis Scire: To Know Is Not Enough'

The theme of the 2013 conference was: 'Education and Poverty: Theory, Research, Policy and Praxis.'

The theme of the 2014 conference is: 'The Power of Education Research for Innovation in Practice and Policy.'

In the three calls for papers for these AERA conferences there is a slippage between education and educational research as if these two forms of research are identical. The slippage means that the calls for paper do not make a clear distinction between education research and educational research.

In living-global-citizenship we make a clear distinction between education and educational research. Education researchers make contributions to knowledge within the conceptual frameworks and methods of validation of disciplines and fields of education such as the philosophy, psychology, sociology, history, theology, economics, politics, leadership and administration of education. There is no responsibility within the research of education researchers to improve practice. Educational researchers make contributions to educational knowledge in their explanations of educational influences in learning of themselves in the learning of others and in the learning of the social formations in which we live and work. There is a responsibility within the educational enquiries of educational researchers to improve practice and to generate knowledge.

The writings of Farrell (2012) and Barry (2012) in the *Educational Journal of Living Theories* are clearly within the tradition of educational researchers while demonstrating a scholarly engagement with ideas generated by education researchers. We associate the responsibility of educational researchers to improve practice by living the values of humanity as fully as possible, with the values of living-global-citizenship and thereby serve the wider public good.

4.8   Living legacies

The above data from the descriptions and explanations of the influences of practitioner-researchers might be thought of as belonging to case-studies. However, there is a significant difference between a case study and a living-theory. The main difference is that a case study is a study of a bounded system while the explanatory principles of living theories such as living-global-citizenship are not constrained by a bounded system. Such an unbounded system project operating within a living-global-citizenship enquiry can be seen as contributing evidence as a living-case. In many ways such emergent living theories also fit into a grounded theory methodology (Glaser & Strauss, 1967), but we would also identify the living processes that generate such authentic evidence as leading to grounded knowledge from the living-case. Thus, we have a new form of living grounded theory as a methodology of Living Global Citizenship that leverages social evidence in the form of grounded knowledge that is derived from the living-case and leads to the generation of a unique living-educational-theory.

Such explanatory principles of an authentic Living Global Citizenship research paradigm are offered in terms of validating flows of life-affirming energy, values and understandings. If you are conducting an enquiry of the kind 'How do I improve what I am doing?' with the intention of improving your practice and generating knowledge in your living educational theory, we think that you will need to embrace Dadds' and Hart's (2001) idea of methodological inventiveness as you live your own unique value of living-global-citizenship as fully as possible (Whitehead, 2009). In creating and sharing your living-educational-theory we are claiming that you are providing your own Living Legacy (Forester, 2012), as a gift for others:

4.8.1   What is a living legacy?

Likewise, the story of 'living legacies' encapsulates another pivotal moment. It is the story of the moment I glimpsed my fate foretold in the lives of my contemporaries who, like me, without significant senior position or academic regard, were leaving the profession. Some left readily, time-served, fulfilled, looking towards new horizons but others left heads-low, hearts-broken, spirits depleted. However, what they all shared, beyond the brief handshake of thanks, was the absence of testimony to their professional, academic and personal journeys. Like hands removed from water, they left no lasting imprint that they had been there, experiencing a poverty of indifference and an absence of regard, rather than, celebrations of unique and reflective lives.

With the passing of time, and, in my case, the deterioration of health, there was a moment when 'they' became 'us'. This is a moment, at present, that few can avoid. Also, it is the moment where the knowledge game we have grown-up with and imparted to our students, starts to play us.

However, in describing the genesis of the idea, I would deny the very essence of 'living legacies' if I did not acknowledge those who's preceding work nourished the field in which it is seeded. They are legion; all part of the chain of 'flourishing humanity' that connects the loving, hope-filled values, aspirations and struggles across many disciplines and practices.

Some I have only met in reading their inspirational words and I hesitate from naming one over another. Nevertheless, there are three people without whom the idea of 'living legacies' would have been still-born. These are, Professor Jack Whitehead, whose work on 'living theory' parented the idea; Dr Joan Walton, whose work at Hope University Liverpool, guided and 'scaffold' its delivery; and, Dr Marie Huxtable, who adopted it at its public birth in May 2011 at York St. John's Conference on 'Values and Virtue in Practice' and has done so much to nourish its infancy. Their part in the birth and development of the idea highlights what is possible when the light from one candle is supported and strengthened by others.

Passionate teacher, reflective practitioner and lover of education for the best part of 30 years.

You can see a video of Catherine in conversation with Jack Whitehead see http://youtu.be/jCsuLoo33XA (Forester, 2012).

4.8.2 Creating your living legacy

The reason we are urging you to produce and share your living-theory of your influence as you explore the implications of living your value of global-citizenship as fully as possible is that you can offer as a gift for others your living legacy, of living a life that enhances the flow of values that carry hope for the future of humanity.

Questions may be asked about the social significance of making public these narratives of the lives and influences of individuals. Our response is that it is through the lives of individuals who are committed to holding themselves to account for living these values as fully as possible that creates a social movement that can contribute to transforming the world. We are not claiming that all individuals can have the social significance of a Gandhi, or a Mandela, or a Mother Teresa, but we are claiming that our living legacies in the form of our living-educational-theories of our influences in living-global-citizenship can make a significant contribution towards such social movements.

5
Designing a Living Global Citizenship Project

In the previous chapter we outlined several projects which continue to demonstrate the participants living out their values as global citizens through partnerships. We called these Living Cases. In this chapter we attempt to draw together the key elements in each of these projects, thereby identifying the key design features of a Living Global Citizenship project. The purpose of this is to provide a clear explanation for participants in partnerships as to how to establish a partnership based on the values of Living Global Citizenship and Cultural Empathy. We start by providing an explanation of the pedagogical protocols of a Living Global Citizenship project, followed by an analysis of the lessons that can be learnt from good and poor practice. There is a danger of what we call cultural blind spots within a partnership that can lead to inequitable power relationships and of development being 'done to people'. This leads to a lack of ownership and a lack of impact on people's lives and is therefore considered to be an unsustainable development. Finally, we consider alternative models for partnership development and offer a model for developing a sustainable community partnership for learning and development. It is this partnerships model that we believe will meet the UN's future agenda for international development as part of the post-2015 SDGs.

5.1   Partnerships and participants

By partnerships we mean a situated activity in which the citizens from at least two different communities enter into dialogue with a view to establishing an ongoing relationship; and with the express purpose of contributing to the improvement of their own lives and the lives of others. Thus, such a partnership might take many different forms. For example:

- an international partnership between two schools;
- an international partnership between two civic communities;
- a partnership between a NGO and a civic community;
- a partnership between a student or a group of students and a charity or a community group; or,
- a partnership between a group of individuals within a community.

We use the term 'participants' to mean the citizens who are engaged in the partnership that is being established or has already been established. Participants are assumed to be motivated to want to make a contribution to improving their own lives and the lives of others within the community and are considered by us as *active citizens*.

5.2   The pedagogical protocols of a Living Global Citizenship project

A key contribution of this book to the field of citizenship education is with the identification of a set of pedagogical protocols for Living Global Citizenship education based around a community partnership. This set of protocols provides a practical application of Sayers (2002) notion of citizenship education as touching the hearts of participants. They help to address the concerns of Martin and Griffiths (2012) about educational partnerships as a means of tackling negative prejudice and the concerns of postcolonial theorists (Andreotti, 2011; Bailee-Smith, 2011) about the hegemonic nature of the neo-liberal paradigm in the discourse about international development. Living Global Citizenship provides an alternative paradigm for international development, one that is contextualised, is based on dialogue between participants, is inclusive, recognises difference as well as similarity and leads to empowerment through common shared values underpinning the flow of action. The absence of a genuine pedagogy for citizenship education led to the question being posed by Gearon (2003): How do we learn to become good citizens? The proposed set of protocols that follows addresses this question, as well as the question posed by Zammit (2008) regarding what a partnership based on equality, mutual respect and understanding would look like. We also respond to Kerr (1999), who asks: what is effective citizenship education? The fact that these questions were posed illustrates evidence of a *curriculum deficit* and the need for pedagogical protocols in citizenship education and the need to integrate this within community partnerships. The protocols build on the work of Crick (1999) with an emphasis on citizenship education as a means of exploring and identifying values and developing human relationships. In a wider context the protocols we postulate provide a practical example of enabling Sachs (1999) notion of an *activist teaching profession* concerned with eliminating exploitation, inequality and oppression.

The pedagogical protocols for underpinning a Living Global Citizenship international partnership can be summarised as follows:

- Participants engage in dialogue about their values. These conversations about values are to explore what matters to the participants and what motivates them in the partnership. They should also encourage participants to recognise the limitations of their own knowledge, perspectives and values, opening their imagination to different viewpoints of the world while maintaining their right to contribute to the dialogue.
- Find ways of widening participation in the partnership and strengthening equality within it.
- Develop activities that touch the hearts of the participants and inspire them to live out their values more fully as citizens.
- Develop activities that tackle stereotypes and encourage a critical reflective and reflexive approach from the participants'. Participants must be challenged to assess their own prejudices and to reflect on their own views of each other so that a different perspective based on a shared Cultural Empathy can emerge.
- Develop activities that aim at nothing less than *meaningful social change;* identified and agreed by all partners as a joint *social manifesto* to govern the project.
- Develop desirable project activities that have the potential for long-term impact and will also sustain the community partnership. Build into the project an impact evaluation research methodology, which both leverages and regularly reports the changes being made in the partnership. This would operate as positive

feedback with in-project adjustments from regular reviews in order to achieve meaningful sustainable development.

- Provide a focus on the creativity of the individual participant. Living Global Citizenship values each participant operating as a Living Case with an individual contribution to make to the whole evidence base as an insider researcher. This policy of equanimity emphasises the status of each individual participant and the contribution that they can make to the wider development of the partnership.

- Encourage participants to construct personal living-case rich data in the form of multimedia narratives that are put freely into the public domain. This is to encourage both internal and external discussion and debate of the various project activities, thus raising the status of such community partnerships.

Each of these protocols is now examined in more detail.

5.2.1 Engaging in dialogue about values

This crucial first step is key to developing a Living Global Citizenship Project. Participants come to a partnership with their own values and perceptions. It is essential that they examine these values and perceptions and understand their origins and their implications prior to working together towards shared ideals. The process involves becoming open to learning from difference and relating to others as equals in the partnership, thus legitimising different ways of knowing and being (Andreotti, 2011). This is particularly important in partnerships involving participants operating across the Global North and the Global South *development divide*, where there has been a tendency historically for the North to see itself as the *norm* and to see its role as dominant; so as to enlighten, educate and civilize the South. There has been a tendency for the North to project its own ideals, desires and aspirations as a natural *universal culture* to be exported to all societies. Such a universal culture determines fixed policies and practices for designing and implementing international development projects and partnerships, often resulting in misguided 'policy borrowing' by unwitting development nations (Crossley, Bray & Packer, 2011). Living Global Citizenship partnerships aim is to avoid this cultural and policy 'trap' by moving towards an uncoercive relationship and mutual dialogue between participants. Andreotti (2011) considers how such partnership knowledge is conceptualised and suggests a negotiation of the frame of reference to include difference:

> This is enacted through a conceptualisation of knowledge as socially, culturally, and historically situated. As every knowledge is based on ontological and metaphysical choices that foreclose other choices, every knowledge is also an ignorance of other knowledges produced in different contexts. From this perspective knowledge is understood as a process (not a product) that is constantly renegotiated in encounters with difference and every knowledge snapshot is at the same time legitimate (in its context of production), provisional and insufficient. By exploring different knowledge systems and their limits, one can cast a fresh glance at one's own context of knowledge production and be in a better position to redefine the terms of knowledge construction. This redefinition is enabled by the expansion of one's frames of reference through the ethical imperative to work with the Other upholding the principles of mutuality, reciprocity and equality (which means keeping one's own learned epistemic arrogance in check and working without guarantees). (p. 6)

Such an agenda suggests that participants need to recognise the limitations of their own knowledge, perspectives and values, opening their imagination to different viewpoints of the world while maintaining their right to contribute to the dialogue. Through Other Eyes (ToE) (Andreotti & De Souza, 2008) is an educational resource for participants that encourages an openness and empathy (see also Skolnick, Dulberg & Maestre, 2004) to different cultures of the world. The free online version of the ToE resource focuses on engagements with indigenous/aboriginal perceptions of global issues. ToE focuses on indigenous knowledge systems as ways of knowing that offer different choices related to how we perceive the world compared to those of Western humanism (Andreotti, 2011). Tongan Professor Konai Thaman in the preface to the resource uses a Tongan proverb that makes reference to a metaphor of baskets to highlight the different ways that social groups perceive and relate to the world:

> In terms of North-South relationships it is common to witness the projection of one group's basket of knowledge as a universal

basket – one that is more valuable than the others and that should be imposed through strategies of human resource deployment, capacity building, enlightenment, cash employment, good governance, human rights, freedom, democracy and education. The expectation is that the recipient of these baskets of knowledge will change for the better. People who participate in these interventions rarely ask whether the values inherent in and propagated by their agendas are shared by the majority of the people whose lives are meant to be improved as a result of their interventions. Few realise the ideological and philosophical conflicts associated with differing perceptions of championed ideas, leaving many communities confused and, in some cases, angry.

(Thaman, 2008, p. 6)

Through Other Eyes seeks to engage participants in the examination of their own worldviews and to recognise the value of other knowledge systems. Thus, it starts with a component designed to promote 'learning to unlearn' whereby participants identify their own perspectives and relate these to dissenting perspectives in their social groups. This self reflective theme continues with consideration of the term 'development' and what it means from their own perspective. Subsequent sections present indigenous perspectives on development and encourage the participant to identify similarities and differences to their own perspective. Consequently, there is an emphasis on learning from difference as participants are challenged to reconsider their perspectives of community and development.

As a pedagogical framework ToE provides participants in a partnership with the opportunity to reflect on their own prejudices and learnt views of the world, opening up their minds to different perspectives and views on global development, thus learning from difference. This process encourages recognition of the equal contribution to be made by all participants in the partnership and provides an underpinning principle for the partnership. Once such a principle has been established then there is a firm foundation for exploring common ground in terms of shared values and agreeing the purposes that underpin the activities of the partnership. Discussion can then focus on how actions can be taken together that will move the partnership forward and enable participants to live out their shared values. The ToE resource therefore provides a useful pedagogical tool for the first pedagogical protocol of a Living Global Citizenship project, engagement in dialogue about values.

Another perspective on this protocol is provided by the idea of intercultural dialogue. Intercultural dialogue is defined by ERICarts (2013) as:

> A process that comprises an open and respectful exchange or interaction between individuals, groups and organisations with different cultural backgrounds or world views. Among its aims are: to develop a deeper understanding of diverse perspectives and practices; to increase participation and the freedom and ability to make choices; to foster equality; and to enhance creative processes.
>
> http://www.interculturaldialogue.eu/web/intercultural-dialogue.php

In this sense, intercultural dialogue processes, or encounters, can involve creative abilities that convert challenges and insights into innovation processes and new forms of expression, such as the ideas of Living Global Citizenship and Cultural Empathy.

In 2006 The Council of Europe initiated a consultation on intercultural dialogue, which was promoted with the following objectives:

- To share visions of the world, to understand and learn from those that do not see the world with the same perspective we do; and,
- To identify similarities and differences between different cultural traditions and perceptions.

In the Council of Europe White Paper published in 2008 in response to the consultation there are recommendations such as:

> Spaces for intercultural dialogue should be created and widened; and intercultural dialogue should be taken to the international level.
>
> (Council of Europe, 2008, p. 3)

> Civil-society organisations and education providers can contribute to intercultural dialogue in Europe and internationally,

for example through participation in European non-governmental structures, cross border partnerships and exchange schemes, particularly for young people.

(Council of Europe, 2008, p. 48)

These objectives and recommendations fit well with the pedagogical approach that we are suggesting for the development of a Living Global Citizenship project. We are promoting intercultural dialogue through the examination of participants' values and through the process of negotiation of values that underpin the partnership.

5.2.2   Widening participation and strengthening equality in the partnership

In order to engage as many people as possible in the intercultural dialogue and to promote exposure to different perspectives it is important that participation in the partnership is widened. Widening participation to others within the community/ies leads to greater inclusion and sustainability of the partnership and widens the social sphere of influence of the partnership. Increasing the number of community stakeholders provides more participants with the opportunity to live out and develop their values. The antithesis of such partnership inclusion and *not* promoting cultural-empathy of its participants contributes towards the general lack of social cohesion in society that sponsored the original calls for a citizenship education. It is through implementing an inclusive policy of *all* members of a proposed partnership that we have identified this approach towards the resolution of the thorny issues related to recognising *difference* and the potential problems linked to cultural imposition and policy borrowing via the typical North–South development divide.

As participation widens it is important to maintain the principle of equality in the partnership, allowing each participant the space to express their views and offer their perspectives on the way forward for the partnership. As more participants engage with the partnership all need to accept the principle that the partnership is based on equality. In order to do so, new participants, particularly from the dominant Western culture, may need to go through the process of 'learning to unlearn' (Andreotti, 2011). This is so that they move from an ethnocentric position to an idea of knowledge as located in culture and social/historical contexts. Thereby, moving from a deficit model of difference to an ethical relationship towards other participants based on the insufficiency of their own perspectives. This second pedagogical protocol of widening the partnership but maintaining equanimity of its membership relationships requires continued dialogue between all participants in order to strengthen the basis of the partnership with these core principles.

5.2.3   Developing activities which touch the hearts of participants

Building an awareness of one's role as a participant in the partnership and developing meaningful relationships with other participants based on negotiated shared values leads to agreed activities. The activities of the partnership are most effective when they *touch the hearts* of the participants and inspire them to discover and live out their values more fully. These types of activities give the partnership's participants authentic social meaning and engages them to become better citizens. We believe that the hearts of readers will be touched and inspired by Tattersall's (2011) generation of his living-theory of environmental activism over a period of 37 years, working and researching within the cultural context of a 6th generation Tasmanian. Tattersall has described the activities that can enable participants in a partnership to discover and live out their values more fully in a 'Community-Based-Audit' (Tattersall, 2007) – see the living-case in Chapter 4.

The living legacies provided in Chapter 4 show that the activities of these partnerships have touched the hearts of individuals to the extent that they have wanted to become active participants in developing and extending the partnerships. They have been galvanised to act and to live out their values more fully. There is evidence that their actions have in turn influenced others to act and to get involved and to live out their values more fully. This evidence provides a core rationale behind the concept of Living Global Citizenship and also helps to define the practical methodology of its approach and adoption by international education projects.

The legacies suggest that these are examples of Jack Whitehead's (2005) notion of personal actions influencing the education of others. The participants have facilitated the personal development of others through the design of opportunities for them to live out their values more fully. The response of the participants to the activities of the partnership shows that, as Chomsky (1971) suggested would be the case, the participant's brain, the rumination of their mind has led them to understanding, and then to actions, that further the values that they believe in. Their motivation to action has been influenced by the designing of opportunities for them to further their understanding of the injustices and inequalities that exist. It has then been left to them to ponder this and decide what actions to take to correct the situation. They have responded by taking action to create a more decent society. The evidence suggests that the activities of the partnership have stimulated participants souls and entered their very being as Chomsky (1971) suggested can be the case with moral actions that spring from free choice.

The influence of the partnerships can be seen as educative in the sense that Pring (2000) uses the term, in an evaluative sense to imply that the learning from the education is worthwhile. This approach contributes to personal well-being; providing the knowledge, understanding and values that enable people to think in a way that is considered worthwhile and so to live out their lives more fully.

Sayers (2002) comments about citizenship education being not just about teaching, but 'touching' something that is real and has meaning, living the life of a good citizen, teaching by example, provides a framework for this pedagogical protocol for the development of Living Global Citizenship. A successful living-global-citizenship project is not taught in the traditional sense, it is instead driven by the participants as they are motivated to develop activities that move the partnership forward. Thus, it is participant led, focused on their needs and is open and cooperative. The motivation derives from the 'touching of the hearts' of the participants, tapping into their values and emanating from a desire to be involved in activities that enable them to live out their values more fully.

5.2.4   Developing activities which tackle stereotypes and encourage critical reflection by participants

Martin's (2007) warning about the potential for reinforcement of negative prejudice and stereotypes arising from differences in ideology and culture among the participants in an international educational partnership is well heeded. Hence, the need as stated in the first pedagogical protocol (see 5.2.1 above) to focus on learning to unlearn through intercultural dialogue. This can be achieved through using frameworks such as Through Other Eyes, which engage participants in the process of reflecting on their own possible prejudices and opening their minds to alternative perspectives. This process helps to develop the value of Cultural Empathy. Understanding and articulating different cultural contexts and celebrating 'difference' is part of the essential design of any partnership project and this is what we refer to as Cultural Empathy. The ability of an emerging global citizen to appreciate other cultures and societies and to move towards a common set of shared values and understanding is a valuable goal. This global appreciation of other cultures, traditions and values is something we argue as Cultural Empathy and represents the paradigm shift and movement from Living Citizenship to Living Global Citizenship. A participant in a Living Global Citizenship project therefore needs to embody the value of cultural-empathy in their partnership activity.

In order to facilitate ongoing reflection it is important to establish a network of dialogues, similar to those shown in Chapter 2 (Figure 2.2) which are kept open over a sustained period of time. The constant reflection and discussion about the purpose of partnership activities and the encouragement of a reflective approach in the participants can lead to the articulation and development of shared values and a shared language to express those values, which are then in turn lived out through the related activities. The action reflection process is integral to this, which is why participant action research is a useful research methodology to adopt.

This model (Figure 5.1) originated in the Schools Council Mixed Ability Exercise (Whitehead, 1976) and in his classroom research in 1976 where he placed his 'I' as a 'living contradiction' within the action reflection cycles of expressing concerns, forming an action plan, acting and gathering data, evaluating actions, modifying concerns, plans and actions in the light of the evaluations.

These action reflection cycles can be seen to be within the pedagogical protocols listed above. The only addition, to the pedagogical protocols, offered by a living-educational-theory approach to living-global citizenship is the inclusion of the practitioner-researchers 'I'. This expresses a responsibility for living the value of global citizenship as fully as possible and for sharing evidence-based explanations of the individual's educational influence in learning within the partnership.

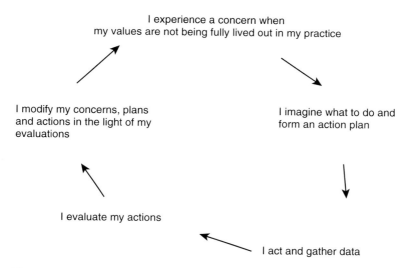

I experience a concern when
my values are not being fully lived out in my practice

I modify my concerns, plans
and actions in the light of my
evaluations

I imagine what to do and
form an action plan

I evaluate my actions

I act and gather data

Figure 5.1 The action reflection cycle (adapted from Whitehead, 1989; Elliott, 1991)

This active process of critical reflection therefore becomes a pedagogical protocol for participants who are engaging in a Living Global Citizenship Project.

5.2.5   Developing activities that bring about social change

The activities of the community partnership should aim at nothing less than *meaningful social change* identified and agreed by all partners. In a partnership where there is clear evidence of inequality and social injustice then correcting these injustices and imbalances through social change becomes a key motivational factor and useful direction for the participants. As outlined in the first protocol above (see section 5.2.1) there is a recognition that meaningful social change is needed in the North in terms of identifying a different perspective on development to the dominant Western discourse (Baillie Smith, 2011). Social change can be achieved by reaching agreement between participants on the need for change and then through the co-development of activities that meet this need. This gives participants in the partnership common ownership of the problem and the transformation.

The evidence suggests that the activities of the diverse partnerships and projects featured in Chapter 4 have challenged people's cultural perceptions and that this has led to challenging their values, which in turn has led to them changing their disposition. This repositioning of attitude and belief has then led to them wanting to take part in change-activities as a living-case. Such participants can then be said to have become change agents in the sense that Lewin (1948) and Yalom (1995) described them as part of social theory. This process mirrors the living theory action research change model (Whitehead, 1989), which sees the individual as motivated to change by the desire to live out his/her values more fully as she/he experiences a contradiction between his lived values and the values that she/he aspires to; a kind of creative tension. According to Whitehead (2005) this individual change can then influence the social formations in which we are living and working. So as individuals change their dispositions and act according to their new set of values they can bring about social change.

This can be seen in Laidlaw's influence in China in contributing to the establishment of China's Experimental Centre for Educational Action Research in Foreign Languages Teaching. Drawing insights from Laidlaw's living-theory doctoral research in a classroom within a secondary school in Bath, UK (Laidlaw, 1996), colleagues in China developed an action research approach with Chinese characteristics. As already highlighted in Chapter 4 Laidlaw received a Friendship of China Award, from the Premier, and was made Professor for Life at Ningxia Teachers University for her contributions to the centre (Laidlaw, 2006).

It can also be seen in South Africa in the Transformational Education/al Studies Project (TES, 2010) and in the Doctor of Education research of Mokhele Rampaola in a collaborative action research study to develop teaching and learning skills in a higher education institution (Rampaola, 2013) – see the full living-case in Chapter 4.

The generic question in the Transformational Education/al Studies Project is, 'How do I improve my educational practice as ...?' The practitioner-researchers are carrying out their self-studies within a cultural context influenced by Ubuntu as a relational way of being. They are explicitly committed to the processes of social change in post-apartheid South Africa. They are contributing to these processes through both their practice and their knowledge-creation.

Working and researching with the values of the Transformational Education/al Studies Project, Rampaola contributes to social changes in a collaborative action research study. The questions of individual researchers are focused on improving practice and generating knowledge within their particular social contexts. The influence of their knowledge creation can be seen, as Laidlaw has shown, in social contexts far removed in distance and culture from the original site of the self-study.

The activities of a Living Global Citizenship partnership would be regarded as successful educationally in Goodson's (2005) terms when they are built on personal experience and develop a personal narrative. Because of the deeply personal nature of the partnership the outcomes are not merely symbolic but are significant in terms of sustainability and of bringing about personal and social change and a new educational identity for the participants engaged in this process of change.

5.2.6 Developing activities that have impact and sustain the partnership

At the outset there should be a clear commitment to a long-term relationship between participants. It takes time for participants to engage with and question their own assumptions and values about global development through the processes described in sections 5.2.1 and 5.2.2 and for the underpinning values of the partnership to emerge. The ongoing action reflection cycle should be used to ensure that the focus remains on maximising social impact and that this key purpose contributes to the overall sustainability of the project.

In cases where external pump-priming funds are provided, for example British Council funding for international educational exchanges, this means developing activities that sustain the partnership beyond the provision of any time limited external funding. Activities need to be developed which have an impact and also widen participation in the partnership. Activities with useful social impact outcomes inspire and motivate participants to continue their involvement over a sustained period of time. Embedding the socio-educational values into the partnership activities leads to sustainability and to genuine permanent change. The adopted *values* become established in the partnership and this leads to a paradigm shift akin to that of Senge's (1990) learning organisation. When the partnership or the organisations involved in the partnership change towards new directions the values and participants (as internal stakeholders) also transfer with it. This illustrates the embedded nature of the partnership within the culture of the organisations it represents and that despite any radical change the participants remain to be the owners and beneficiaries of change, with the core shared values providing the stability of an agency in flux. Thus, the Living Case within a Living Global Citizenship organisational paradigm *becomes its agency*; whereupon, participants are enabled through distributed power and the ownership of useful tasks befitting the goal and social design of Senge's (1991) learning organisation.

Developing a partnership that can grow and be sustained over a long period of time so that it becomes embedded in organisational cultures and enables its participants as social agents to live out their values more fully is yet another pedagogical protocol for Living Global Citizenship education that can be derived from a learning community partnership. Indeed, the combination of a Living Global Citizenship approach with communities operating as learning organisations could be argued as one way to achieve a valid *learning community* as a means of creating a sustainable educational development social structure and agency.

At the heart of this sustainable educational development process for Living Global Citizenship is the requirement to leverage useful social impact within partnerships. If the applied research methodology is participant action research then we would expect to have Lewin's (1948) positive feedback cycles of reflective evaluation and review at regular intervals within the life of any project. From this idea we can see how a partnership project management approach would build in notions of Elliot's (1991) reflection in and on the action of the project as a means of critical evaluation. We suggest that this action research critical thinking and reflection framework is combined with the Living Global Citizenship purpose of leveraging social impact. Consequently, the overall project design would require an integrated applied research approach that we call an *impact evaluation research methodology* (IERM). The research agenda for this kind of sustainable applied educational research within a Living Global Citizenship international context would form the 'social manifesto' (Coombs, 1995; Gardner & Coombs, 2010) agenda for change. The social manifesto would identify the scope and range of project goals wanted by the partnership as a means of delivering and leveraging social improvements. The evaluation of the outcomes of these desired social improvements would be a review of the project's evidence base representing the overall nature of social impact. In conclusion, we argue that proffering an impact evaluation research methodology linked to the pedagogical protocols of Living Global Citizenship represents a sustainable educational development agenda. This would then go some way towards meeting the UN's aspiration of implementing SDGs (UN, 2013) as part of the post-2015 international development agenda.

5.2.7   Participants as living cases

Each participant within a Living Global Citizenship partnership project is seen as an insider researcher who is capable of developing a Living Case. Through participation in the partnership the individual's contribution as a living citizen who is living out their values more fully adds to the evidence base and contributes a living-case as a real life authentic professional learning activity. Integrating these living-cases generates a case study of the partnership. Such an approach to a partnership gives equal status to each individual participant and recognises their creativity and their potential to make an original contribution to the partnership and to the academy. Thus, each participant in a Living Global Citizenship project is seen as an active, critically reflective participant within a living context. This methodological inventiveness (Wright-Mills, 1959) recognises the creativity of each participant and enables them to engage in activities that impact on people's lives.

We make a clear distinction between the Living Cases that are produced within a Living Global Citizenship Project and the living-educational-theories that include the value of living-global-citizenship as an explanatory principle and living standard of judgement. The living-educational-theories of individuals include the value of living-global-citizenship within an open enquiry, 'How do I improve what I am doing?' A Living Case is produced within the boundaries of Living Global Citizenship Project. We are emphasising the importance of both.

In conclusion the insider researcher of a Living Global Citizenship partnership project is a participant operating as a living-case engaged in social change and transformation. Their living-case evidence can be constructed from recorded journals as narratives of their critical reflective experiences that both evaluate the change and feed new knowledge into the academy as described in the next section.

5.2.8   The construction of narratives that are put into the public domain

Participants should be encouraged to construct narratives from their living-cases that are then put freely into the public domain to encourage discussion and debate. Such acts raise the status of community partnerships as a means of empowering communities, levering social change and in educational terms raising standards; while providing participants with evidence of professionalism as part of an official continuing professional development (CPD) process.

We also emphasise the value of working with multimedia narratives and digital technologies to clarify and communicate embodied emotional expressions of meaning. We suggest using a process of 'empathetic resonance' in the narratives to communicate embodied expressions of meaning that are difficult to communicate through printed text alone (Huxtable, 2009). We first encountered the idea of empathetic resonance in the writings of Sardello (2008). For Sardello, writing from his theological perspective, *empathetic resonance*, is the resonance of the individual soul coming into resonance with the Soul of the World (p. 13). We are using *empathetic resonance* from a humanistic perspective to communicate a feeling of the immediate presence of the other in communicating the living values of the other's experiences as giving meaning and purpose to their life.

These reflective narratives should be put into the public domain for sharing, debating and contesting by others. This helps to create an activist identity (Sachs, 1999) for the participant. The democratic discourses around the narratives give rise to the development of *communities of practice* (Wenger, 1998) which can have a profound learning impact on participants' lives. These learning communities facilitate the values of Ubuntu (humanity), participation, collaboration and democracy.

Thus, a final pedagogical protocol is that participants in international educational partnerships ought to be encouraged to construct multimedia narratives about their experiences. This would represent a reflective, action based approach towards developing international CPD projects. This approach also encourages the embedding of values and creates an activist agency imperative within the partnership. Such proactivity generates additional status and identity to community partnerships.

5.2.9 The significance of the pedagogical protocols

As outlined in Chapter 2 and earlier in this chapter there are issues about how to deliver the goal of more informed citizens and how to address the question as put by the British Educational Research Association (BERA) in its professional user review of 2003: *How do we learn to become good citizens?* The transferable pedagogical protocols linked to the development of Living Global Citizenship have emerged from analysis of partnership projects such as those outlined in Chapter 4. These living-cases identified how participants can more fully live out their socio-educational values through participation in a *learning community* partnership. It is in this sense a pedagogical approach and strategy and is therefore an attempt to address the question about how we *learn* to become good citizens.

These protocols are transferable systems to all community partnerships and can help to provide a pedagogical framework for the delivery of citizenship education in a way that enables participants to become Living Global Citizens. Such an activist approach towards engaging in citizenship projects enables participants to take responsibility for their own contribution to civic society and gives them *social agency* in the form of ownership of the process and priorities for development.

The living-global-citizenship approach of recognising social and cultural similarities and differences can be applied just as much to local intra-national community partnerships as well as international global community partnerships. However, global community partnerships allow participants to discover their own national identities through experiencing and understanding different national identities and cultures, thereby enabling greater tolerance and appreciation of different cultures within nationally bound multicultural environments. This opportunity to engage in global community partnerships enables individuals to develop personal skills in cultural-empathy as a form of *cultural agency* and learning within a Living Global Citizenship community of practice (Wenger, 1998).

Bridging cultural divides through the personal development of cultural-empathy and understanding is a key part of living-global-citizenship.

5.3   An outline of minimum standards and criteria for the projects

Our research indicates certain standards that need to be met in order for a Living Global Citizenship project to be successful. These standards are suggested by the authors. They are subject to further development and amendment through dialogue. They are provided for guidance to help underpin the quality of any proposed partnership project.

The minimum standards of any Living Global Citizenship project relate to the pedagogical protocols outlined above and as such they provide the criteria by which Living Global Citizenship learning community partnerships can be evaluated:

- The establishment of effective and regular channels for dialogue between the participants in the partnership. Dialogue is to initially focus on exploring values; recognising the limitations and validity of contributions; and, participants examining their own worldviews. Once Rogerian congruence and trust (Rogers, 1961) has been established and there is recognition of the equal value of contributions from participants then there is a move towards co-constructing the aims and purposes of the partnership and agreeing upon the shared principles.
- The partnership activities to be identified and agreed through a democratic and inclusive process within the generated Rogerian 'climate of trust'. This inclusive process to critically identify and reflect upon the agreed purposes and aims of the partnership.
- All participants to feel that they can have their viewpoint heard and their opinions considered within the context of the agreed aims and purposes of the partnership. Participants each become a living-case actor, leveraged through their social and cultural agency.
- The inclusion of an *impact evaluation research methodology* from the start of the project so that space is provided for the action reflection process. The values of the participants in the partnership and the related activities that are agreed upon are regularly evaluated for their impact; and these are positively fed back to influence the ongoing outcomes and future direction of the partnership.

- Efforts are made to widen participation in the partnership across any diverse community participants through encouraging personal cultural-empathy, thereby overcoming any initial social boundaries.
- The development of activities that tackle stereotypes and lead to critical engagement with negative prejudice, leading to the participants embodying the value of Cultural Empathy.
- Through the establishment of Cultural Empathy and understanding there is the development of friendships between participants.
- The development of activities that lead to meaningful social change.
- Participants engage with the partnership over an extended period of time. The partnership is sustained through ongoing activities that are designed to continue for several or more years.
- Each participant in the partnership is given status and is valued for the contribution that they can make as a creative individual in the form of a living-case.
- Participants are encouraged to elicit and put their multimedia narrative about their experiences of the partnership into the public domain. This policy adds to the knowledge base regarding effective community partnerships and leverages effective citizenship education in the process.

5.4   Measuring the pig, not fattening the pig – lessons learnt from partnerships that have limited impact

5.4.1   The new agenda for sustainable development partnerships

There is no doubt that the ideas, assumptions and practice of international development is changing. In recent times we have seen the UN engaged in the development of the MDGs and the follow-up Education for All (EFA) initiative at the World Education Forum in 2000 (UNESCO, 2000). These have now been re-examined and the post-2015 agenda (ECOSOC, 2013) is moving towards what are being referred to as SDGs, whereupon a UN open working group (United Nations Sustainable Development Knowledge Platform, 2013) is consulting all stakeholders on the definition of these protocols for future implementation as actions. From these ideas we also have the notion of education for sustainable development (ESD). The main differences in this new development agenda is that their needs to be both impact and relevance at the local level for any development project to benefit local communities. The key issue here is that a new paradigm of educational research is now required to deliver sustainable educational development projects. Indeed, a new methodology that can be applied to understanding, articulating, leveraging, developing and evaluating local and complex cultural contexts so as to allow for genuine long-term sustainable impact on local community partnerships linked to such projects.

One explanation in the change of thinking surrounding educational research applied to international educational development has been amusingly characterised by some agency workers as the 'pig metaphor'. In the pig metaphor we have an analogy where measurement based research has managed to solve all the issues around how to size up the *pig* but has made little or no impact on how to fatten it up. In a similar fashion one might criticise much of international research that is supposed to be engaged with reducing poverty as only having solved the problem of measuring and assessing poverty issues; which has had little impact upon resolving poverty itself. We may know all the reasons, scope and scale of poverty, but few projects are designed to impact upon its resolution. Clearly, an improve paradigm of educational and international development research linked to the goals and objectives of Living Global Citizenship has the potential to make a real impact within the international educational development arena.

The new emerging global emphasis is now focusing efforts upon funding capacity-building applied research projects that are designed to leverage and evaluate educational impacts as part of the new sustainable agenda. Such an educational research capacity-building agenda is also argued by Crossley (2011) who argues that the role and assistance of international collaboration can usefully serve as a way of leveraging meaningful educational development in small states (Barrett, Crossley & Dachi, 2011). Identifying and developing a new 'impact evaluation' educational research methodology that takes into account local needs and contexts is therefore both an innovation and important priority that a Living Global Citizenship approach seeks to implement. Projects in the past have included many well intended initiatives in regions such as the South Pacific, and served by a range of well meaning agencies. Initiatives have included trying to improve literacy rates for small island nation states that have to cope with having English as a Second Language (ESL) as well as the local mother tongue(s). Unfortunately, there has been little impact upon ESL literacy rates and in many cases matters have got worse. Many projects now fund development aid (Cassity, 2008) more effectively through the ministries of developing countries, but it has been reported by UNESCO (2011) that many such educational development plans still suffer from poor implementation and therefore have little impact upon communities. Clearly, a paradigm shift in both the thinking and approach towards international development projects is required if the post-2015 UN SDGs and Sustainable Economic Development Goals (SEDs) (ECOSOC, 2013) are to be ever achieved. We therefore argue that international educational development projects, indeed, any type of international development project, need to adopt the set of earlier defined pedagogical protocols and criteria for creating Living Global Citizenship partnerships – see sections 5.2 and 5.3.

In our terms partnerships don't have a significant impact when they fail to challenge the dominant Western discourse of development and are consequently unable to provide the means for social change. They also fail to have impact when they reinforce negative stereotypes and prejudices and Western notions of development providing an unquestioning acquiescence to dominant power structures. They have little impact if the participants do not engage in and develop Cultural Empathy and genuine mutual understanding. Such failures are usually the result of uncritical policy borrowing from Western donor contexts, resulting in automatic transfer of such systems that are also compounded with an inability to analyse the development context.

Consequently, the focus of a Living Global Citizenship community partnership is not only on knowledge. It is an opportunity to both apply and create knowledge. The emphasis is on values-based action and critical reflection on action leading to further useful activity. Thus, it is not about achieving results that, for example, lead to passive forms of citizenship education, like the extant Life in the United Kingdom test. Such static forms of citizenship education can lead to impersonal embedding of national values as cultural stereotypes. We would therefore recommend that we avoid the trap of simplistic testing of predetermined citizenship knowledge. The alternative focus needs to concentrate on values, action, reflection and participation, that is, our call for a more balanced and socially inclusive 'Living in the UK' examination, achieved via a new form of living-global-citizenship assignment, whereby an individual can demonstrate a living-case through positive feedback of their genuine engagement in community partnership activity (see section 6.2).

5.4.2   The dangers of international educational partnerships

The potential dangers and pitfalls of international educational partnerships are well documented (Bourn & Cara, 2013; Disney, 2004; Gaine, 2005; Martin, 2005; 2007; 2012; Scott, 2005). Martin (2005) suggests that 'teachers' willingness to engage with and question their own assumptions and values about global development issues is fundamental to good practice in school linking' (pp. 47–54). Some international educational partnerships do not allow time for this to happen and as a result they can reinforce negative prejudice and stereotypical views of development. The partnership therefore needs to be sustained over a long period of time and the activities of the partnership needs to encourage the participants: students, parents, governors and teachers to question their assumptions about development issues and consider how the two communities can live out their shared values more fully. Scott (2005) suggests that learning from partnerships can be poor if it is not successfully managed. Good learning will not automatically happen. Living-global-citizenship activities need to be designed to encourage effective learning to take place so that the participants reassess their worldviews, develop Cultural Empathy and understanding and live out their shared values more fully. Gaine (1995) argues that cross-cultural contact that focuses on differences between people can foster a negative attitude by embedding prejudice and stereotypes. However, Disney (2004) warns against adopting a focus on only the similarities, as it may lead to the opportunity being missed to become critically aware of the social and political structures that support inequality and social injustice and to decide on actions to tackle these issues. A living-global-citizenship approach encourages critical reflection on differences and discussion of the social and political structures that support inequality and injustice and supports mutual agreement upon appropriate action to tackle them.

Martin (2007) suggests that there are three reasons why schools establish a partnership: educational context, political context and teacher dispositions. The educational context is identified as the need for meaningful citizenship education in schools. The political context is the push from government to develop international partnerships as characterised by various government papers and strategy documents, such as the former UK Department for Education and Schools (DfES, 2004) paper 'Putting the World into World Class Education'. The teacher dispositions are to do with teachers' views of school partnership, including 'personal experience of other countries, friendship and world views of how to respond to economic disparity' (Martin, 2007, slide 6). Teacher dispositions are shaped by the educational and political context they are embedded within, but also are developed through individual experience. Martin warns that if the schools do not agree on the purposes of the partnership then it will fail to produce effective learning for the participants. Establishing a partnership for educational and/or government reasons alone without proper teacher commitment is inadequate. In order to lead to effective learning the partnership needs a personal values-based approach from participants, teachers or others, and ideally should include participants who are all committed to developing cultural-empathy, and understanding, tackling negative prejudice, stereotypes and economic disparity.

Bourn and Cara (2013) suggest that most school international partnerships:

> despite good intentions, tend to have a Northern driven agenda. Also, there is an underlying assumption that mutual learning and co-operation is not only desirable but feasible. Yet few programmes address the fact that power relations can and do play an important role in what and how pupils learn, in terms of who sets the framework and content of any educational programme, and who influences the pedagogy. (p. 16)

They suggest that any review of a school partnership should cover the following questions:

- To what extent does the link go beyond fundraising, fasting and having fun?
- To what extent does the partnership encourage critical self-reflection, learning 'through other eyes', challenging

stereotypes and moving from a charitable mentality to one concerned with social justice?

- To what extent is there a respect for difference as well as similarity, for valuing a range of perspectives?
- To what extent does the link encourage learning that addresses global perspectives and the value of mutual learning?

(pp. 16–17)

Questions such as these should form part of the reflective process that participants engaged in a living-global-citizenship project consider on a regular basis (see section 5.2.4).

5.4.3   Building partnerships that challenge existing hierarchies

Building a partnership based on hierarchy which leads to dependency is damaging and in terms of international partnerships could be construed as another kind of colonisation. Slater and Bell (2002) assert that the association of aid with dependence raises issues concerning the desirability, effectiveness and long-term value of aid for the societies of the South. Partnership should not be built on self-gratifying and indulgent philanthropy. Maxwell and Riddell (1998) say potential partners may interpret this idea of partnership to mean:

> We know how best to achieve development...we know how you should alleviate poverty...either you accept the approaches which we think are right for you or you will not qualify for a long-term partnership with us...if you do not accept our view of development, then we will not provide you with aid. (p. 264)

This authoritarian view of 'development' or 'progress' is rooted in Western imperialism (Andreotti, 2011; Nederveen Pieterse, 2000; Rahnema & Bawtree, 1997) and can have negative connotations. Partnerships which adopt this approach are doomed to failure as they will reproduce existing unequal power relationships. In a Living Global Citizenship partnership participants have engaged in dialogue and identified and agreed upon a way forward. Some of their activities may be aimed at raising funds as a means of furthering social justice and embedding social change and thus carrying out a perceived moral duty; thus emphasising the idea of partnership in the donor–recipient relationship and representing an attempt to move away from relationships based on hierarchy.

5.4.4   Building partnerships that challenge a deficit model of development

Adopting an unquestioning approach to the term 'development' is not desirable. It is important to ask the question: what does development mean and is it desirable? According to Manji and O'Coill (2002) the distinction by the US government and international agencies between half of the world being developed and the other half being underdeveloped has led to the idea of development as a universal goal. This discourse of development and the labelling of Africans and Asians as 'underdeveloped' underpinned the more overt racist discourses of the past. It gave the 'civilised' or 'developed' European a role in 'civilising' or 'developing' Africa. The inhabitants of the developing world are described in terms of what they are not instead of what they are. This deficit model leads to a desire among Europeans to improve the lot of Africans. Esteva (1996) argues that development is a term that has been used to extend American hegemony through free market economics and maintains: 'The term offers an image of the future that is a mere continuation of the past' (p. 23). Esteva sees development as a conservative myth and makes a plea for people to develop their own ways of living by disengaging from the assumed economic logic of the free market or the economic plan and defining their own needs. At the same time a vast array of development non-governmental organisations (NGO's) have been involved in providing aid and support to the developing world, for example, Voluntary Service Overseas (VSO) from the United Kingdom. Manji and Coill (2002) suggest that they have contributed marginally to the relief of poverty, but significantly to undermining the struggle of African people to emancipate themselves from oppression. The programme of welfare provision by NGOs is a 'social initiative that can be described as a programme of social control' (Manji & Coill, 2002, p. 578). Given the neo-liberal economic rhetoric of retreat from state provision in many African countries the NGOs have replaced the state as providers of a 'safety net' of social services for the most vulnerable (Edwards & Hulme, 1995). Bailee Smith suggests that the social change that needs to take place is not in the South but in the North and the nature of that transformation is a change in attitudes towards development and aid, a transformation in worldviews. Being aware of this type of critical view of the notion of development and the role of charities and aid brings a new perspective to the work of community partnerships and informs the notion of Living Global Citizenship. It is important that the participants in the partnership engage with these ideas and consult on the nature of the activities so that they are clear about their purposes and how they fit in with their shared values.

Insufficient consideration of the impact of activities can lead to misguided thinking about partnership activities based on a perspective of education that sees the Western model as superior and one to be copied. It is easy to accept a view of development which sees it as a one-way flow whereby the poor have to wait for the benefits of access to Western knowledge and technology as if they have no independent sources of knowledge and relevant ideas.

The language of developed and developing countries has an ontological assumption that developing countries aspire and wish to model those that are developed. This may be partially true but it also sets up an unequal power relationship and potential imposition of the developed nation's culture and external values. Slater and Bell (2002) remind us:

> Genuine dialogue clearly implies, if it is to be effective, recognition that there are other sites of enunciation and other agents of knowledge, located in the South, whose vision and priorities might be different from those of the donor community. The recognition of other voices requires political will, but it is also crucially linked to the presence or absence of a genuine belief in partnership and reciprocity. (p. 353)

5.4.5 Building partnerships for postcolonial development

Andreotti (2011) quotes Chakrabarty (1995) who puts the postcolonial perspective as follows:

> Postcolonial theory is an examination of the hostility to difference embedded in the normative teleological project of Western/Enlightenment humanism, which is the basis of dominant Western epistemologies. From this perspective the investment of Western/Enlightenment humanism in rational unanimity (i.e., universal consensus through rational thought) in regard to conceptualisations of humanity, human nature, progress and justice only produces opportunities for relationships and dialogue

that are 'structured from the very beginning, in favour of certain outcomes' (Chakrabarty, 1995, 757).

(Andreotti, 2011, pp. 1–2)

This perspective indicates how partnerships can fail if they do not include an acceptance of difference of opinions about issues such as progress and justice. This analysis gives rise to the criteria for Living Global Citizenship projects concerned with giving the voices of all participants in the partnership weight in determining the purposes, direction and activities of the partnership, and as a means of redressing the imbalance of power relations between them. This is why participants should be encouraged to engage with activities such as those in the Through Other Eyes project (see section 5.2.1) which encourages participants to examine their own worldviews and to recognise the value of other knowledge systems. Participants are challenged to re-consider their own perspectives of community and the meaning of the term 'development' by considering other perspectives, thus learning from difference.

This should lead to participants driving the partnership forward to realise their own vision of progress and development. We therefore argue that the term 'development' is reconceptualised and interpreted as a means of giving power to participants within partnerships to determine their own future. This key assumption is what distinguishes the meanings of living-global-citizenship from other forms of citizenship. Living-global-citizenship focuses attention on a process of social accountability that engages with issues of power and privilege within society and across nation States. Only in this way can the dominant Western discourse be challenged and alternative outcomes be achieved.

5.4.6   Building dynamic, values-led partnerships

Poor communication between participants can lead to the failure of a partnership. It is important to set up channels of communication for regular dialogue. This is essential in terms of building relationships between participants and in terms of negotiating shared values and activities. Enabling an action research ongoing process of reflection upon action, review, reflective evaluation and then further action requires channels of communication between participants to be open. It is important for participants to over-come any barriers to communication that may exist. This may mean, for example, overcoming any deficits of common resource platforms, that is, setting up and funding appropriate Internet access.

Over-reliance on one person to lead the partnership can lead to failure in two ways. Firstly, there is a danger that the person has too much power within the partnership and dominates the decision-making process. Decision making should be shared and leadership of the partnership should be distributed in order to facilitate dialogue and to embed democratic values. Each participant has status and generates evidence as an active living-citizen as they contribute to the partnership. Secondly, there is the issue of sustainability of the partnership. While this person is there he/she keeps the energy flowing, however if this person leaves the organisation the partnership may wither. The partnership needs to engage a wide range of participants to ensure sustainability. A living-global-citizenship approach does not keep partnership activity small or low key. If the partnership is narrow in terms of participation and private in terms of scope then it will not fulfil the requirements of living-global-citizenship as a form of community engagement and empowerment. There is a danger that a small, low key partnership will become self-serving for the few people involved in it and be regarded with suspicion by those not involved. It is vitally important that the participants seek to broaden participation and involve others who can question the aims and purposes of the partnership and bring their own critical voices and contributions to bear. This is what leads to reflection and then action, and drives the partnership forward. The shared values need to be questioned and reviewed on a regular basis, that is, values are also dynamic and 'living' and subject to renegotiation by participants. Each participant in the partnership is given the opportunity to put their work into the public domain so that they can be held accountable for the work that they do and the activities that they undertake in explaining their influences in learning. An ethos of critical enquiry needs to pervade the partnership so that participants generate evidence in the form of a living-case of their contribution as living-global-citizens. Claims and achievements of the partnership need to be made public through whatever means possible to increase their validity and wider impact upon society, e.g.

findings and knowledge disseminated on the internet via a Creative Commons License and archive.

5.5 A model for developing a sustainable community partnership for learning and development

5.5.1 An analysis of some existing models for partnership development

5.5.1.1 *The United Kingdom One World Linking Association model*

The UK One World Linking Association (UKOWLA) is an organisation that seeks to inspire and support partnerships between communities through friendship, equality and solidarity. They produce a Toolkit for Linking which has a great deal to commend it and provides guidance for the development of a partnership based on Living Global Citizenship principles in the following ways:

- The need for consideration by participants of why the link is being established and the motives behind it.
- The importance of relationships and the building of friendships in developing the link.
- The need for regular review of the activities and relationships to be built in to the planning of the partnership.
- A commitment by participants to work to a set of negotiated and agreed values.
- Emphasis to be put on broadening the partnership to involve more participants from the communities.
- The importance of genuine dialogue which explores difference and leads to critical reflection on participants' own perceptions and values.
- The need for participants to challenge colonialism and the dominance of Western discourse.
- The importance of collecting evidence and using it to share findings, to review progress made in the partnership and to change plans as necessary.
- The emphasis on learning from the partnership and the key role that it can play in delivering global education in schools.
- The encouragement of active participation and the motivation of participants to be agents for change.

We would agree that all of the points above are important ingredients in building a successful partnership. In addition we would argue that the Toolkit could be strengthened by the following:

1. More guidance for users on how to encourage participants to engage critically with their perspectives and values and on how to develop Cultural Empathy. There is recognition in the Toolkit of the need to focus on learning to unlearn through intercultural dialogue and there could be reference to frameworks such as Through Other Eyes, which engage participants in the process of reflecting on their own possible prejudices and opening their minds to alternative perspectives. This process helps to develop the value of Cultural Empathy.

2. While the Toolkit emphasises the collection of evidence from a range of possible sources, there could be increased emphasis on participants within a partnership as insider researchers who are capable of developing a Living Case. Participants should be encouraged to collect and analyse the evidence generated by the partnership activities in a systematic way. Through participation in the partnership the individual's contribution as a living citizen who is living out their values more fully adds to the evidence base and contributes a living-case as a real life authentic professional learning activity. In this way each individual participant is given status and their creativity and potential to make an original contribution to the partnership is recognised.

3. The Toolkit suggests a range of ways for participants to collect evidence using various media. It does not however, emphasise sufficiently the construction of narratives from their living-cases that are put freely into the public domain to encourage discussion and debate. Putting such narratives into the public domain raises the status of community partnerships as a means of empowering communities. It levers social change and in educational terms raises standards and provides participants with evidence of professionalism as part of an official continuing professional development (CPD) process. There is a great deal of potential for professional development learning in participation in a partnership and this is an opportunity that should not be missed.

The UKOWLA Toolkit for Linking is an excellent resource for those who wish to develop partnerships based on the principles of Living Global Citizenship.

5.5.1.2   *Connecting classrooms*

The Connecting Classrooms website run by the British Council offers a number of resources for teachers to use with partners in other schools. It also offers a professional learning programme for teachers who wish to establish and develop a partnership to: 'gain a deeper understanding of school partnership objectives, such as increased global citizenship, and international themes that can be explored with students'. (http://schoolsonline.britishcouncil.org/your-journey/stage-three)

The British Council presents a six-stage model for partnership development. In Table 5.1 we outline the model and link it with the criteria for a Living Global Citizenship (LGC) Project as outlined in Section 5.3.

Table 5.1   British Council model for partnership development

Stage	Title	Description	Links with LGC Criteria
Stage 1	Make a start	Discovering how international learning can benefit the teacher and the school.	The brochures provided encourage teachers to engage in international educational partnership work. There is a focus on a range of benefits including coverage of the curriculum, enhancing teaching and learning, providing pupils with the skills of global citizenship and preparation for playing a positive role in society, professional development, collaborative learning, friendship and fun.
Stage 2	Connect with the world	How to find a suitable partner school.	There is a database of teachers and schools in 180 countries providing a wide ranging source of potential partnerships. There is also advice on how to find the right partner with participants filling in a profile which identifies their aims. This could be used to start a discussion about values. Teacher forums provide a means of communication that can enhance dialogue and develop reflective practice.

Table 5.1 (Continued)

Stage	Title	Description	Links with LGC Criteria
Stage 3	Explore the possibilities	Resources for participants to use with the partner school.	A range of resources are provided that support activities for participants to challenge stereotypes, tackle negative prejudice and learn from difference. There are also professional learning opportunities open to all participants where their contributions as creative individuals are valued and they can develop their living-case.
Stage 4	Get together	Funding opportunities to meet with other participants face to face.	Guidance is provided on how to manage a successful visit. This includes useful suggestions that fit in with a LGC approach such as, having a shared focus for the visit, building relationships, working collaboratively with participants and organising follow up sessions which review and evaluate the activities of the partnership.
Stage 5	Discover another dimension	Ideas on how to expand the partnership.	In a supporting document entitled *"How to Build Sustainable Partnerships"*, there is emphasis on the importance to sustainability of establishing shared values, learning from difference, developing activities that challenge stereotypes, valuing the contributions of all participants as creative individuals, continuing dialogue, extending participation in the partnership and the development of professional practice through partnership activity. These elements are very consistent with good LGC practice.
Stage 6	Become a British council ambassador	Working with the council to convince other teachers of the value of engaging in an international partnership.	Partnership participants are encouraged to share their experiences with teachers who are embarking on an international partnership. The opportunity to share their expertise encourages the development of their narrative of their living-global-citizenship project as a living-case which others can learn from.

This six-stage model has considerable merit in terms of encouraging successful living-global-citizenship partnerships. The principles behind the stages and the resources available to support the various stages of development of the partnership are laudable. However, there are some aspects of the model that could be strengthened to make it more consistent with a Living Global Citizenship approach.

1. A Living Global Citizenship approach would emphasise the importance of all participants being involved in the formation of the aims of the partnership. This strengthens the democratic accountability and inclusiveness of the partnership from the beginning. This is not emphasised sufficiently in stage 2 of the model.

2. Although there is mention of the importance of follow up sessions which review and evaluate the activities of the partnership in stage 4 of the model, this process of reflection should start much earlier and be part of the ongoing dialogue between the participants. Once the aims of the partnership have been agreed and appropriate activities developed there should be constant review of the activities to ensure that they continue to meet the aims of the partnership and there should also be review of the aims themselves to ensure they continue to reflect the shared values of the participants. A Living Global Citizenship approach would emphasise the action reflection process far more than is suggested in the model and the associated supporting materials.

3. In promoting engagement in international educational partnerships there is insufficient emphasis on the potential of international educational partnerships to provide life changing opportunities for learning and on the potential for creating social change. Providing opportunities for participants to live out their values as citizens can be a truly life-changing experience, bringing about personal and social transformations as highlighted in this book.

4. Participants are encouraged to use resources that have already been developed by teachers for use in their partnership. While recognising that this may be useful in terms of saving time, participants should be encouraged to develop their own projects that fit their agreed aims and their particular contexts. This provides

opportunities for participants to make a contribution as creative individuals, emphasising their ability to create new knowledge which can be put into the public domain. Developing their own projects will lead to greater ownership and the sharing of the narratives from participants will add to the resources available to the wider community.

Thus, the Connecting Classrooms model and the supporting resources provide a very useful starting point for the development of an international educational partnership but there is insufficient emphasis on the inclusiveness of the process, the action reflection aspects, the potential for transforming lives and society and the creativity of the participants as knowledge producers.

5.5.1.3 The development education association – stages towards participative and experiential learning

In seeking to develop a pedagogical approach for the delivery of citizenship education through the establishment of international educational partnerships the framework of stages towards participative and experiential learning designed by the Development Education Association (D.E.A., 2001) provides a useful starting point (Table 5.2).

The D.E.A. model is attractive in that it emphasises the importance of experience, participation and action. It has merit in emphasising that ultimately it is important for students to be active citizens and to simply put the issues before them and get them to think them through is not enough. In order for them to become active citizens, activities that touch them and engage them need to be provided so that they see their actions as meaningful and as having impact. The model refers to emotions and this is an important element of the pedagogy. The students need to feel in order to engage with the issues. Through the partnership activities the intention is to influence the participants to take action, the fifth and final stage in this continuum. It will be assumed that they will have reached a level of understanding and developed their own views and opinions sufficiently to urge them to act. Through partnership activities the aim is to have helped to inform their opinions and helped them to develop the confidence to take a stand.

Table 5.2 Five stages towards participative and experiential learning

Stage	Title	Description	Links with LGC Criteria
Stage 1	Pupils become aware	Teachers provide opportunities for pupils to identify issues that interest them through reading/watching and discussing news items. Pupils are given a safe and secure environment to discuss issues that concern them.	This awareness raising can generate discussion about values and what motivates participants to establish partnerships. It can encourage learners to recognise the limitations of their own knowledge, perspectives and values, opening their imagination to different views of the world whilst maintaining their right to contribute to the dialogue. Such activities can also be used to widen participation in a partnership.
Stage 2	Pupils become more informed	Pupils develop the skills to research information about global issues for themselves, to seek explanations as to why things are as they are and the range of opinions that exist. They express their emotions about the issues that are raised.	Developing autonomy in participants is important and pupils finding information about global issues can provide the basis for discussion about different perspectives, power relations, the limitations of knowledge and values. Encouraging participants to express their emotions about the issues raised means that they are more likely to be engaged by it and to be motivated to act.
Stage 3	Pupils develop their under-standing	Ways are found that enable pupils to engage with someone who lives in a different environment or culture, to explore issues with their peers, to address real issues and to tackle and question their own attitudes.	If the pupils have been prepared to question their own perspectives and values and explore different perspectives then they will be ready to engage in LGC partnership projects which address real issues

Table 5.2 (Continued)

Stage	Title	Description	Links with LGC Criteria
Stage 4	Pupils develop their own opinions	Pupils develop the skills to recognise bias and to support their views with evidence. Their opinions are more informed and considered and they have the confidence to take a stand once they have formed an opinion.	This supports participants in a LGC project in making a contribution to the dialogue about the values that underpin the partnership and the activities that should be developed to achieve the aims of the partnership. Well informed and confident participants will make a creative contribution to the partnership and build their own living-case as they live out their values more fully as a citizen.
Stage 5	Pupils take action	Pupils are given the knowledge and skills that will enable them to take appropriate action. Who do they need to talk to? How can they persuade the people they want to influence? Action can be contacting the local press, putting on a performance, writing to an MP or local councillor, exploring the policy and practice in your own school, making decisions about whether to buy certain products and telling others why.	This emphasises the importance of action. Action could also be engaging in a partnership with others to bring about social change and to engage with others in activities that enable the participants to live out their values more fully. It can be about developing activities that touch the hearts of others and motivate them to act.

Our Living Global Citizenship pedagogical protocols for citizenship education can strengthen the model in several ways as follows.

1. At stages 1 and 2 during the awareness raising it is important that participant's perspectives are challenged and that different world-views are represented in the news items. Otherwise, there is a danger

that stereotypes and negative prejudice will remain unchallenged. Teachers need more guidance on how to manage this process successfully and using materials such as those produced by the Through Others Eyes (ToE) project (see section 5.2.1) should be encouraged. As students do their own research they should be encouraged to find different perspectives to their own and to question their own assumptions leading to an understanding of the origins and limitations of their own knowledge and value systems. Again, this needs skilful management by the teacher.

2. This model implies that action is the final stage in the learning process. We would suggest that learning is more of a cyclical process with reflection on action leading to further actions. We regard reflection within action research cycles as an essential part of evaluation which should be ongoing throughout the learning process. Any activities that are agreed in the final phase should be subject to constant review against the agreed values of the partnership. In addition, awareness raising and research does not stop once action is undertaken, indeed it is vital that research continues to enable participants to continuously review the aims of the action or the values of the partnership.

3. It is important to recognise that the learning will be not only for pupils/students but also for the adult participants. Much of the literature on citizenship education ignores the adult learning dimension, referring to the adult only as the teacher. We prefer to talk about the 'participants' in a partnership to cover all ages and positions. It is important to recognise the influence that the activities are having on the learning of all of the participants. The teacher needs to play a lead role here in modelling to the pupils how to recognise the limitations of his/her own knowledge, perspectives and values. They should show their openness to different perspectives and worldviews and their willingness to challenge stereotypes and negative prejudice.

4. We emphasise the value of working with multimedia narratives and digital technologies to clarify and communicate embodied emotional expressions of meaning. This can be built into the work carried out by the participants as they explore their own and others' perspectives to strengthen their accounts of how they live out their own values as citizens.

5.5.2 A Living Global Citizenship Model for sustainable education development

Having reviewed some of the models for partnership development that are currently available, we would like to conclude this chapter by restating the need for a Living Global Citizenship approach to help deliver a long term and therefore sustainable educational development programme and by providing our own model for such an approach. The sustainable development goals post-2015 have been described by a key online forum[1] as:

> In June 2012, governments agreed at the UN Conference on Sustainable Development (also known as Rio+20 or Earth Summit 2012) to launch a UN led process to create a set of universal sustainable development goals (SDGs). The SDGs are envisaged to be an international framework that will enable countries to better target and monitor progress across all three dimensions of sustainable development (social, environmental and economic) in a coordinated and holistic way. The goals will be applicable to all countries, regardless of their level of development.

The SDGs post-2015 are, as yet, not defined. However, it is clear that designing a partnership project that is sustainable and has impact on people's lives would fulfil the core purposes of this global agenda. Sustainability requires inclusion of an impact evaluation research methodology. We therefore propose a new argument and proposition for leveraging a sustainable education development goal and would suggest that this is linked to a Living Global Citizenship approach.

Building on the core partnership protocols and criteria of the earlier sections 5.2.6.and 5.2.7 and the ideas of *values* being connected to a *social manifesto* of useful activities, we propose an action research model for sustainable educational development given in Figure 5.2.

This model assumes that participants can operate as reflective *Living Cases*, evaluating and feeding back project outcomes into new and ongoing sustainable cycles of future development. It is also to be noted that the emergent evidence from such a grounded theory living-case approach produces unique evidence in the form of *grounded knowledge* as a consequence of the living-global-citizenship activities undertaken by all the participants.

The living global citizenship impact evaluation research methodology

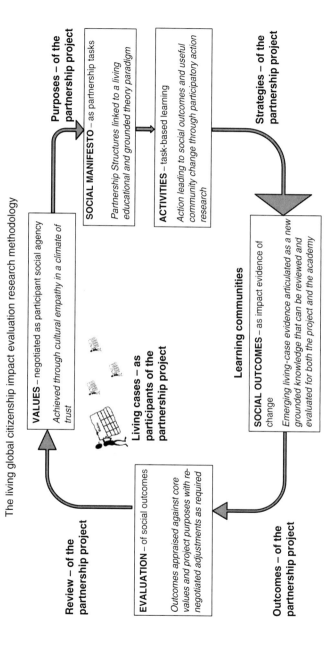

Purposes – of the partnership project

SOCIAL MANIFESTO – as partnership tasks

Partnership Structures linked to a living educational and grounded theory paradigm

ACTIVITIES – task-based learning

Action leading to social outcomes and useful community change through participatory action research

Strategies – of the partnership project

VALUES – negotiated as participant social agency

Achieved through cultural empathy in a climate of trust

Living cases – as participants of the partnership project

Learning communities

SOCIAL OUTCOMES – as impact evidence of change

Emerging living-case evidence articulated as a new grounded knowledge that can be reviewed and evaluated for both the project and the academy

Review – of the partnership project

EVALUATION – of social outcomes

Outcomes appraised against core values and project purposes with re-negotiated adjustments as required

Outcomes – of the partnership project

Figure 5.2 A Living Global Citizenship action research model for sustainable educational development

The positive feedback model also builds upon the conversational learning paradigm and systems theory of Harri-Augstein and Thomas (1991) and Coombs (1995). This approach uses a Purposes-Strategy-Outcomes-Review (P-S-O-R) critical thinking scaffold that has been used as a knowledge elicitation system (Coombs, 2001) to articulate the above Living Global Citizenship action research model for proposing any international or national sustainable educational development partnership project.

6

Propositions for Living Global Citizenship Projects

6.1 Reporting a Living Global Citizenship project

In Chapter 4 we gave some examples as Living Legacies of Living Global Citizenship partnerships. In the same way that we have presented these multimedia narratives concerning participation in the partnership, we want to encourage others to do the same. These should be multimedia accounts and should be put into the public domain for sharing, debating and contesting by others. This helps to create an activist identity (Sachs, 1999) for the participant. The democratic discourses around the narratives give rise to the development of communities of practice (Wenger, 1998) which can have a profound impact on participants' lives. Teacher participants can use such narratives to evidence professional standards. Values are part of the professional attributes for teachers as indicated in the Professional Standards for Teachers in England (2007) by the phrase: 'Demonstrate the positive values, attitudes and behaviour they expect from children and young people'. There is a clear expectation that teachers model the values that the students are to adopt. The evidence shows that a Living Global Citizenship partnership with emphasis on the exploration of values provides many opportunities for participants to form and demonstrate positive values. In providing opportunities for the living out of values as a form of living-global-citizenship, educational partnerships can deliver improved educational standards.

Thus, participants in educational partnerships ought to be encouraged to construct multimedia narratives about their experiences. This would represent a reflective, action-based approach to CPD that will encourage the embedding of values and an activist approach. Multimedia narratives therefore give additional status and value to educational partnerships. We see this process of reporting through narrative as a transition structure within the continuous process of transformation. Next we make some suggestions as to how a Living Global Citizenship project could fit a variety of contexts where evidence of good citizenship is required.

6.2 A Living Global Citizenship Life in the United Kingdom test

We reviewed in section 2.4 that more passive notions of citizenship seek merely to embed national identity. We also reviewed the processes and assumptions behind the current 'Life in the United Kingdom' test as a requirement for anyone seeking to naturalise as a British citizen. The current test is designed to prove that the applicant has a sufficient knowledge of British life and sufficient proficiency in the English language. The test is a requirement under the United Kingdom's Nationality, Immigration and Asylum Act, 2002 consisting of 24 questions covering topics such as British society, government, everyday life and employment. We noted that the current test had been widely criticised (Glendinning, 2006; Hasan, 2012) and made the argument that it was largely irrelevant in determining who might become a good citizen. This led to the conclusion that such forms of citizenship education lead to impersonal embedding of national values as cultural stereotypes and that this in turn creates potential myth-making and passive misconstruing of the 'citizenship' construct.

We now ask the question what would a Living Global Citizenship interpretation of the 'Life in the United Kingdom' test look like? How could the examination process be reconceptualised? Given the core values of Living Global Citizenship we argue for a paradigm shift from the passive assumption of 'life' reported second hand to 'living' reported personally by the would-be citizen. This would change the reporting emphasis from researching facts about others' *life* in the United Kingdom to instead accumulating evidence of constructive engagement through *living* in the United Kingdom. In Living Global Citizenship terms the applicant would prepare evidence of their *life-case* justification of wanting to become a British citizen, obviously with suitable guidance provided.

In conclusion, a personally constructed and authenticated 'living in the United Kingdom' presentation portfolio could be produced by prospective British citizenship 'applicants'. Such a life-case portfolio would be put together so as to demonstrate a genuine attempt by the applicant to become actively included within society and this evidence could also be examined for authenticity through a brief oral examination that could demonstrate language proficiency. In this way various examples of personal experience of understanding and adapting to British culture combined with a personal proficiency of language could be embedded within such a proposed 'Living in the United Kingdom' test.

6.3 Reconceptualising the notion of the UN passport as a demonstration of Living Global Citizenship

In Chapter 2 we contrasted and compared three notions of citizenship: in the United Kingdom, United States and internationally. In this section we wish to speculate on the notion of a UN-sponsored universal right to a global citizenship passport and international identity.

From the UN perspective on citizenship we reviewed UNESCO's (1995) policy regarding the Declaration and Integrated Framework of Action on Education for Peace, Human Rights and Democracy. From this declaration UNESCO in 1995 recognised the importance of including an international dimension to citizenship education, arguing that people needed to become more aware of other cultures in order to promote general peace and understanding linked to human rights and freedom. We would also argue that freedom of passage across nations and national boundaries might also be a good idea. Currently the UN has provision for a special UN passport for some world citizens. This, however, applies mainly to stateless refugees seeking travel and asylum from a host country that refuses to issue them with their own national passport. The other type of UN passport is known as a United Nations Laissez-Passer (UNLP) and is a travel document that accredits the identity and the affiliation of the individual bearer to one of the UNLP-issuing United Nations organisations: United Nations, World Bank Group, International Monetary Fund, World Health Organization etc.

Apart from certain refugees and officials working for UN-recognised international organisations no one else is entitled to such a document. We would like to suggest that this scheme should be opened up as a new universal human right to any global citizen that seeks international freedom of movement beyond the constraints of their own nation state. While some might argue that this represents a form of global anarchy and lack of national control on humanity, we would counter this by saying that such an international passport fulfils the aspirations of Living Global Citizenship. And that access to such a document might be by means of a new 'Living Global Citizenship' test based upon an individual applicant's *life-case* demonstrating evidence of *cultural-empathy* in accordance with UNESCO's 1995 declaration and values relating to international citizenship.

6.4   A Living Global Citizenship project in a 16–19 context

In the United Kingdom there has been a particular interest in developing citizenship education post 16. Since 2002 citizenship has been a statutory requirement within the National Curriculum at key stages 3 and 4 (11–16 year olds). Post-16 citizenship aims to build on pre-16 learning with a particular emphasis on active involvement in learners' own communities (Association for Citizenship Teaching (ACT), 2013).

According to the ACT, active citizenship (taking part in the process of social change, working with others, making decisions and taking action) should be at the centre of all post-16 citizenship activities. They also argue that young people should have time to reflect on and review the activities that they have undertaken and to identify the citizenship knowledge, skills and understanding they have developed. The now defunct Qualifications and Curriculum Authority (QCA) (2004) provided guidance to UK teachers for post-16 citizenship saying that effective citizenship education aims to give young people the confidence and conviction that they can act with others, have influence and make a difference in their communities (locally, nationally and globally). They also suggested that young people should carry out an extended personal research project and wider activities that reflect their personal interests and enrich their lives by engaging them as active citizens in their communities.

Accordingly, in 2011 the National Citizen Service (NCS) programme was established by the government. The Department for Education (2013) says that the purpose of the NCS is for it to act as a gateway to the Big Society by supporting young people to develop the skills and attitudes they need to become more engaged with their communities. Resources have been developed by the ACT to support the programme.

The NCS programme provides an excellent opportunity for students to engage in a Living Global Citizenship project. Implementing the pedagogical protocols explained in section 5.2 of the book would help to motivate post-16 students to become living-global-citizens. Thus, we make the following suggestion to strengthen the NCS programme.

Initially, the students need to be stimulated to engage in dialogue about their values. This stimulation may come from the students themselves if they have strong feelings about particular issues. It may come out of their previous involvement in partnership work, for example, an international educational partnership that their school has established. They may have engaged in community-based work at a younger age. These conversations about values are to explore what matters to the participants and what motivates them to act. They should take part in activities using resources such as those produced by Through Others Eyes (ToE) and ask the following questions about their values:

- What are my values?
- To what extent am I living out those values?
- What are the values of the other participants?
- To what extent are our values the same and different?
- Which values do we believe are crucial to the partnership?
- How can we develop partnership activities which reflect those values?

These activities encourage openness to different views of the world leading them to recognise the limitations of their own knowledge, perspectives and values. The ACT and NCS can build partnerships with post-16 students in other countries who can provide alternative perspectives that challenge the UK students in order to develop Cultural Empathy. Developing Cultural Empathy should be seen as a core element in the NCS programme. Technology should be used to facilitate this process – see section 6.6. Putting young people in touch with each other allows friendships and trust to grow; essential ingredients in developing their value of cultural-empathy and for young people as living-global-citizens.

Once these discussions have come to fruition and the students have had an opportunity to explore their values and different perspectives they will be ready to take action. At this point it is important to help the students to develop project activities that are consistent with their values by making sure an impact evaluation research methodology is built in from the start (see Figure 5.2) so that there is constant review with questions such as:

- What are we trying to achieve by taking this action?
- How are these actions bringing about meaningful social change?
- Are our values changing, and if so, how do our actions change to reflect this?

This ongoing impact evaluation as part of the action reflection cycle is an essential ingredient in a Living Global Citizenship project and should be built into the NCS programme. By keeping the activities and the values under constant review there can be fine tuning or wholesale change as necessary[1] and this will lead to improved outcomes for the partnership project. If done successfully students will continue the partnership that is established as part of the NCS programme beyond the eight weeks of the programme so that it becomes a sustained commitment. Students may need support beyond the eight weeks to continue their participation.

Another recommendation for the NCS is that from the very beginning of the programme, students should be supported to construct multimedia accounts of their participation. Each student should be valued for the creative contribution that they can make to the development of the project. The aim from the outset should be for each participant to see themselves as an insider researcher developing their own living-case as a contribution to the community. This gives each student status within the programme and enables them to demonstrate how they are living out of the values of cultural-empathy and living-global-citizenship. The multimedia accounts should be shared publicly and added to the Living Legacies available for use by the community. In this way the new knowledge developed enables a learning community to emerge as a sustainable educational development – see Figure 5.2.

The NCS is an excellent opportunity to establish meaningful learning community partnerships that young people can engage with over a sustained period of time and to enable them to generate evidence of themselves as living-global-citizens.

6.5   The significance for a citizen of becoming a Living Global Citizen

We like the idea of being citizens in the sense of accepting a responsibility for participating in democratic processes of governance and of living as fully as possible the values that contribute to the well-being and prosperity of the country within which we live. However, with the extension of our cognitive range and concerns through our experiences of different cultural contexts and international partnerships, we have come to recognise the importance of understanding ourselves and our influences within such global contexts.

Our collective experiences have involved work, lectures, keynote and workshops in South Africa, Europe, Asia, North and South America and the South Pacific. We recognise tensions within the living boundaries (Huxtable, 2012) between different cultures which must be acknowledged and faced in becoming a global citizen and engaging in acts of living-global-citizenship.

To illustrate our own commitment to developing ourselves with others as living-global-citizens we participate in partnerships that can be distinguished by the following engagements:

- Examining the reasons why we want to participate in the partnership.
- Reflecting on our personal values, asking the question: What is it that really matters to me/us?
- Discussing with other participants in the partnership what their values are.
- Considering which values we share and which ones we do not.
- Discussing how we can take actions together that will move the partnership forward and enable us to live out our shared values.
- Reflecting together on the actions and the extent to which they enable us to live out our values more fully.
- Continuing the dialogue about values and considering further actions, followed by reflection. This is an ongoing process.

- Providing an evidence-based narrative of our influences in the partnership as a Living Global Citizenship project and reporting it in the public domain.

In extending our cognitive range and concerns we have learnt much from our work in different cultures. For example, our commitment to Ubuntu ways of being has evolved from our understanding of the relational ways of knowing and being from Africa. From Asian cultures (Inoue, 2012) we have learnt to focus on the importance of flows of energy (Chi) in the embodied expressions of the meanings of values. From reflecting on our Western culture we now explicitly value the Western epistemology of valuing evidence-based explanations of influence and the emphasis on the validity of explanations. From these reflections and our evolving awareness of Islamic cultures that are influenced by Sharia Law we have come to understand that our Western view of democracy is not a universal value. This recognition has heightened our awareness of the importance of developing a socio-historical and socio-cultural understanding of the constraints and opportunities in the cultures we are working within, as we share our understandings of Living Global Citizenship and support ourselves and others in creating our living-educational-theories with our unique values of living-global-citizenship.

6.6   The potential of technology to support Living Global Citizenship partnerships

Our concept of Living Global Citizenship puts partnerships and communication across groups of diverse people and cultures at its heart. It is therefore very fortunate, indeed serendipitous one might say, that we have mobile technologies and other platforms in the form of the worldwide web/Internet to help individuals easily communicate across international boundaries both quickly and cheaply. Information and Communication Technology (ICT) has seen a revolution in connecting people across the globe, whether using tools such as mobile phones, email or Skype®. Gaining access to different people across different cultures to promote greater understanding is one of the major goals and core values of Living Global Citizenship, namely 'Cultural Empathy'. However, we recognise that closing the gap to enable benefits to such digital resources may not be easy for all and hence the need to overcome any 'digital divide' by making available adequate resources to support living global citizenship partnerships. The social nature of a digital divide has been defined by the Digital Divide Institute (DDI website, 2013), who maintain that:

> 'Digital Divide' refers to the gap between those who can benefit from digital technology and those who cannot. 'Closing the Digital Divide' therefore means more than just giving the poor the same technologies already received by the rich. Closing the Divide involves restructuring the telecommunications sectors in each nation so that broadband's benefits can flow to the masses, not just the elite urban sectors of emerging markets. It took digital-divide researchers a whole decade to figure out that the real issue is not so much about access to digital technology but about the benefits *derived from access.*

Clearly, access to online digital resources is a major social issue and creating a level playing field in this respect will prove to be a major challenge in many developing nations. Living Global Citizenship projects will take this into account as part of any prior preparations to mitigate this uneven access issue. One example of this problem might be assumed access to online services such as e-commerce. Such services are well established in developed countries but in parts of the world where most people don't even have a bank account, assumptions around e-banking and e-commerce need to be taken into account for any global project that relies upon participants to use such technology. The same arguments also surround access to online resources such as e-books and other taken-for-granted educational services.

Digital resources (Crotty & Farren, 2013) to enable living-global-citizenship activities range from access to the Internet to the use of video cameras to capture 'visual narratives' of any ensuing partnership project. Visual narratives can provide useful authentic case study evidence for educational action research projects and contribute to an epistemological transformation in what counts as educational knowledge (Whitehead, 2013). The role and purpose of such technology can be socially empowering and such visual evidence produced in a Living Global Citizenship project becomes part of the participant's living-case action research data. This living-case personal knowledge is visual data that is grounded from social experience and can be evaluated as part of the project's outcome as impact evidence – see the living global citizenship action research process illustrated in Figure 5.2. Such visual data linked to the living-case evidence of a Living Global Citizenship project can also be described as a videocase (Coombs & Potts, 2013). Coombs and Potts (2013) maintain:

> Video case studies (or videocases) are becoming increasingly popular as a way of bridging the gap between theory and practice in pre-service education (Cannings and Talley, 2003: Stigler and Hiebert, 1999). The videocase allows not only the demonstration of practice, but also helps the development of reflective practice for learning (Cannings and Talley, 2003). . . . (and) enable(s) the researcher to critically analyse the qualitative video data and elicit findings from it in a systematic way . . . (p. 432)

The role of using such technology to support action research living-case data acquisition is especially important for times when captured visual narratives can be posted online to promote team-based sharing and greater subsequent reflection of any partnership activity. Any Living Global Citizenship partnership project is therefore likely to contain a digital technology 'target' within any negotiated 'social manifesto' of project tasks and activities in general. Indeed, where such projects are operating across national boundaries with limited funds for international travel the adoption of ICT can be both empowering and essential to breaking down what might otherwise be a 'cultural divide' and thereby achieve cultural-empathy through such technology assisted activities. A good example of where this is being achieved in transnational education initiatives is the 'World Ecitizens' project administered by the education charity 'Mirandanet'.[2]

From such global activities we can see the sophisticated role that technology can play in bringing different peoples and cultures together. Another important global role is the development of international databases and knowledge exchange portals for enabling regional context-based knowledge bases. This is an important international paradigm shift towards creating and validating the context-driven academy that integrates cultural difference and locally created knowledge. The key mission is to enable the development of such regional *knowledge bases* that can democratically capture, archive and share the locally produced and context-driven knowledge and culture (Thaman, 2004). In this way the local 'voice' and cultural differences can be both celebrated as well recognised and shared through implementing such diverse regional academy portals.

In conclusion we proffer the use of new digital technologies as a tool to enable greater Cultural Empathy across diverse peoples as a means of breaking down both digital and cultural divides, which we also argue is at the heart of the Living Global Citizenship mission that we wish to develop.

7
Living Global Citizenship: Lessons for Humanity

7.1 The significance of Living Global Citizenship as a concept and as a means of improving humanity through the embodied expression of living-global-citizenship

Embodied living-global-citizenship is a significant and original contribution to both knowledge and knowledge production and operates as a standard of judgement for evaluating the validity of the contributions to knowledge. The notions of living-global-citizenship emerge as a synthesis of the research approach adopted and the actions of the participants in an educational partnership. Embodied meanings of living-global-citizenship can be expressed in descriptions of the way that participants in educational partnerships identify, negotiate and then live out their values in a practical way, through their joint actions and engagement in cultural-empathy.

This notion has epistemological significance for the nature of educational knowledge (Whitehead, 2012). The idea of using living-global-citizenship approaches and schema in the creation of one's own living-educational-theory focuses attention on a process of accountability that engages with issues of power and privilege in society. This can be seen as a response to Ball and Tyson's (2011) claim that educational researchers have fulfilled the American Educational Research Association mission to advance knowledge about education and to encourage scholarly enquiry related to education, but have only weakly fulfilled the mission to promote research to improve practice and serve the wider public good. Living Global Citizenship projects are grounded in a commitment to both improve practice and to generate knowledge that serves the public good, through the expression of each individual's living standard of judgement of living-global-citizenship.

In relation to living-global-citizenship we are accepting Habermas' (1998) point that 'The private autonomy of equally entitled citizens can only be secured insofar as citizens actively exercise their civic autonomy' (p. 264). Participants who are living their values of living-global-citizenship in a practical way are exercising civic autonomy and as a consequence they are securing the private autonomy of equally entitled citizens.

Living-global-citizenship is a creative act. It can be linked to the values and aspirations of the $5 \times 5 \times 5 = $Creativity project (John & Pound, 2011). Living-global-citizenship is about the development of human relationships to unlock participants' creativity within the personal framework of cultural-empathy. This is enacted within participants' responses to situations where they see the need to live out their values as citizens more fully. It therefore supports the development of a democratic and inclusive society in the sense that

> a democratic society only exists when each of us feels we belong and are seen as uniquely creative, capable and self-determining individuals.
>
> (John & Pound, 2011, p. 2)

Living-global-citizenship rejects the misguided and dominant Western-led discourse around development and progress. Through challenging this discourse and the power relations behind it and providing a space for learning through dialogue, *all* participants as mutual stakeholders come to a new understanding of their own priorities for development and progress. Such inclusiveness of all participant stakeholders ensures a process to underpin sustainable development and the recommended protocols for establishing Living Global Citizenship are a potential solution towards the UN's post-2015 mission of securing a working definition for SDGs.

Research into living-global-citizenship enables individuals to create their own living-educational-theories that advance knowledge, encourage scholarly enquiry and improve practice for the public good. Clarifying and communicating the meanings of living-global-citizenship, as one engages in a continuing educational professional development project and creates one's own living-educational-theory, makes an original and significant contribution to the field of Living Educational Theory.

Living-global-citizenship carries a message of hope for humanity. Such hope is achieved through participants operating within *learning community* partnerships that are actively engaged in negotiating, discovering and then living out their shared values more fully. And in so doing cultural divisions are transcended, cultural-empathy is developed, real lives are improved and the applied research social manifesto achieved. In this way living-global-citizenship can become *normalised* as an authentic socio-educational research process that seeks wider community engagement through enabling a living consensus agenda as an act of society. From this engagement with living-global-citizenship the participant community transforms itself into becoming a *learning community* that can carry forward its own momentum and enthusiasm for future sustainable development. Within educational contexts we now offer a working plan, indeed blueprint,[1] for establishing educational sustainable development projects.

7.2   How Living Global Citizenship makes sense of sustainability and inclusion

Living Global Citizenship has been defined by key pedagogical protocols and criteria that help to define a sustainable educational development agenda. In Chapter 5, section 5.3 we outlined minimum standards and criteria for any project that meets the standards for Living Global Citizenship. These include developing project partnerships that are inclusive of a wide and diverse range of participants that also operate over the long term making them sustainable. We determined that Living Global Citizenship learning community partnerships can be evaluated through a number of criteria whereupon participant inclusion is generated through the necessary application of Rogerian congruence and trust (Rogers, 1961). Developing Rogers' 'climate of trust' within a frame of cultural-empathy between all participants in a Living Global Citizenship partnership defines what we regard as social inclusion and democratic inclusivity. This inclusion policy establishes recognition of the equal value of contributions from *all* participants and also forms the basis of social ethics within the applied research methodology. The partnership activities are therefore identified and agreed through a democratic and inclusive process within the generated Rogerian climate of trust. This trust among participants results in a move towards co-constructing the aims and purposes of the partnership and agreeing upon the shared principles.

Sustainability is achieved through developing activities that have impact and maintain the long-term nature of the partnership resulting in the formation of a leaning community. We argue that implementing an impact evaluation research methodology linked to the pedagogical protocols of Living Global Citizenship represents a sustainable educational development agenda. This process is underpinned by a continuous improvement cycle of action research as illustrated in Figure 5.2. In conclusion, a key beneficiary of a Living Global Citizenship sustainable educational development partnership is the emergent learning community and its *development* of a local knowledge base of resources that has been put into the public domain for the wider good of society.

7.3   How Living Global Citizenship addresses the question: How do we become living global citizens?

There is widespread agreement that effective citizenship education is about more than knowledge transmission and that what is required is to engage people in meaningful learning experiences and to use active teaching strategies to facilitate their development as politically and socially responsible individuals. Living Global Citizenship seeks a paradigm shift from a passive knowledge transmission learning environment to one that is experiential and in which knowledge is elicited from the activities that are participated in.

Compulsory citizenship education for students in the United Kingdom and elsewhere will not, on its own, produce good citizens. Nor will a compulsory 'Life in the United Kingdom' test. These do, however, provide an opportunity for participants to explore their personal values, to question existing power relations and to develop the value of cultural-empathy. It is important to engage the participants in the work that they do and make it worth their while. Turning it into a Living Global Citizenship project with attendant publication of one's own multimedia narrative is a way of making it worthwhile.

The intention of citizenship education, according to the United Kingdom's QCDA in 2008, is to equip people to play an active role in wider society as global citizens. As QCDA was discontinued by the

UK government in 2010, there is an even greater need to fill the vacuum left for the citizenship curriculum; with projects that can deliver effective citizenship education and where citizens are playing an active role as global citizens. The Citizenship Education Longitudinal Study conducted by the National Foundation for Educational Research (NFER) (2010) showed that schools still require help to embed citizenship education, not just in the curriculum, but also in the school culture and wider community. Kerr (1999) identified growing concern in many countries about the attitudes of young people and, in particular, with the signs of their increasing lack of interest and non-participation in public and political life. Effective citizenship education in schools was seen as crucial towards addressing this social concern and deficit. However, there remained considerable debate as to what was meant by the term 'effective' and how it could best be measured.

The notion of living-global-citizenship with its associated projects as presented in this book through educational partnerships can help to address the questions put by Kerr (1999): 'What is effective citizenship education?' and by Gearon (2003) in the British Educational Research Association publication: 'How do we learn to become good citizens?' It can fulfil the requirement of UNESCO (1974) for projects that encourage participation by students to link education and action to solve problems at the local, national and international level. More recently it resonates with the findings of the international study of citizenship education by Schulz, Ainley et al. (2010) which indicated that the participating countries increasingly were seeing civic and citizenship education as activities that promote civic attitudes and values alongside opportunities for students to participate in activities in and beyond the school (Eurydice, 2005; Torney-Purta, Schwille & Amadeo, 1999).

The Living Legacies narrated in Chapter 4 not only show participants playing an active role as global citizens, but they also illustrate all three of the conceptions of the 'good' citizen as outlined by Westheimer and Kahne (2004), 'personally responsible, participatory and justice orientated'. The participants have taken personal responsibility in engaging in activities to further social justice. The response of the participants has not been an uncritical one resulting in the reinforcement of stereotypes and negative prejudice as feared by Martin (2007) and Disney (2004). Rather, the evidence suggests that the participants have adopted a critical approach and have made a considered response to circumstances and one that promotes the fulfilment of potential within both communities. As has been shown, the participants have shown a willingness to engage with and question their own assumptions and values about development issues and as Martin (2005) says, this is fundamental to good practice in partnership.

The evidence presented in this book demonstrates that educational partnerships have the potential to embed citizenship education in the community by raising awareness of international issues, challenging existing cultural perspectives, promoting discussion about values and encouraging more active citizens who live out their values with a view to making a difference to their own lives and the lives of others. Thus, participants can become living-global-citizens and in so doing they promote greater community cohesion. Therefore, traditional, locally delivered and *passive* citizenship education in the United Kingdom, the United States and in other countries can be reconceptualised using educational partnerships as a vehicle for the development of activities that touch the hearts of participants and mobilise them to act, to identify and live out their values more fully. These 'citizenship' values should be negotiated and agreed by the participants in the partnership so that they become authenticated, shared and thereby underpin the activities that are carried out. This emancipatory process gives rise to the notion of Living Global Citizenship and explicates how and why it delivers benefits for both the participants and wider society.

At the heart of our understanding of 'Living Global Citizenship' and of the unique meanings of each individual's value of living-global-citizenship is the experience of 'cultural empathy'. In our experience, 'cultural empathy' emerged after many years of professional practice in the United Kingdom, teaching individuals from diverse ethnic origins and heritages and from working visits to a range of other cultures and countries. One of our clearest illustrations of the development of cultural empathy has been described by Potts in his responses to the lack of opportunity to benefit from higher education by a 16-year old student in South Africa. Potts expressed his empathetic resonance with the personal constraints experienced by this particular student. He also developed his cultural empathy in his understanding of the socio-historical and socio-cultural conditions that influenced both the constraints and opportunities within this particular cultural context. We are suggesting that a priority is given to the development of cultural-empathy in both the general idea of Living Global Citizenship and in the unique expressions of living-global-citizenship within the life of each individual as they create and share their own living-educational-theories.

7.4 Some limitations in Living Global Citizenship

One of the major limitations in living-global-citizenship is the individual's understanding of differences between cultures in the expressions of cultural empathy. For instance, Inoue (2012) points out in a section on wisdom development:

> The direction that this book is pointing to is the horizon of wide and open possibilities of wisdom development. This book has offered a variety of opportunities for you to develop important wisdoms and insights as an educator. If you would like, you can always go back to earlier sections and go through some of the reflective journeys again. However, no matter how many times you read this book and learn about the key concepts, please remember that you could still fail in your practice improvement. It is always the case that educational practice involves numerous personal, social, cultural and historical factors that make things happen or stop from happening against your expectations. (p. 171)

We agree with Inoue that educational practice involves a number of personal, social, cultural and historical factors. In living-global-citizenship it is important to continuously evolve one's understanding of these factors while perhaps bearing in mind Lather's point about ironic validity:

> Contrary to dominant validity practices where the rhetorical nature of scientific claims is masked with methodological assurances, a strategy of ironic validity proliferates forms, recognizing that they are rhetorical and without foundation, post epistemic, lacking in epistemological support. The text is resituated as a representation of its 'failure to represent what it points toward but can never reach . . . (Lather, 1994, pp. 40–41)'.
>
> (Donmoyer, 1996, p. 21)

The idea that we will never fully reach cultural empathy but that we can continuously evolve our understandings points to an important limitation of living-global-citizenship. Inoue advocates the integration of insights from East Asian Epistemologies into research that is predominantly influenced by a Western Epistemology. We imagine that you may not have encountered all the ideas of Ba, Kizuki, Omoi, Takumi, Kizuna and Chi (Inoue, 2012, pp. 135–136) from an East Asian Epistemology. We say this to emphasise the importance of learning about the ways of knowledge from different cultural traditions.

In the generation of our living-educational-theories we use validation groups to help strengthen the validity of our accounts. One of Habermas' (1976) criteria of social validity is that we should demonstrate our understandings of normative influences in our communications. We focus on the importance of extending our understandings of the socio-historical and socio-cultural influences in our thinking, writings and practice. Hence, we look for the evidence that we are extending these understandings in our expressions of cultural-empathy in living-global-citizenship and in the creation of our living-educational-theories. Finally, we hope that this book has informed your cultural wisdom and developed a greater understanding of what we mean by Living Global Citizenship and inspired you to want to take part in this journey with us.

Videoarchive Appendices: Interviews with the authors

The urls are as follows:

Coombs: http://www.youtube.com/watch?v=EvORnWK2gu0
Potts: http://www.youtube.com/watch?v=4cqp0UpIQfQ
Whitehead: http://www.youtube.com/watch?v=2GA3pzd9gHc

How to get in touch with the authors of this book?

The notion of Living Global Citizenship is a developing concept and the authors of this book welcome your contributions as we come to understand it more fully. Please visit the website: http://www.livingcitizenship.uwclub.net/ and do get in touch that way.

Visit the website.

Notes

1 Transforming International Educational Development through Living Global Citizenship

1. The original MDGs came from the UN 2000 Millennium declaration. For an update see the 2010 progress report at: http://www.un.org/en/mdg/summit2010/pdf/MDG%20Report%202010%20En%20r15%20-low%20res%2020100615%20-.pdf (accessed: 27 January 2014). Linked to the MDGs was the 2000 World Education Forum at Dakar, providing the Dakar Framework for Action: Education for All agenda and targets. See: http://unesdoc.unesco.org/images/0012/001211/121147e.pdf (accessed: 27 January 2014). For the link between the Education related MDGs and the EFA targets see the UNESCO website: http://www.unesco.org/new/en/education/themes/leading-the-international-agenda/education-for-all/education-and-the-mdgs/ (accessed: 27 January 2014).

    In the last few years a post-2015 development agenda has been considered, and it is proposed to replace the current MDGs with a set of new SDGs – for a work in progress on SDGs see: United Nations Sustainable Development Knowledge Platform (2013) Sustainable Development Goals. Open Working Group Platform. Available online from: http://sustainabledevelopment.un.org/index.php?menu=1300 (accessed: 2 October 2013).
2. In many ways this was a forerunner of what international educationalists now refer to as the sustainable development agenda and links education to the emerging post-2015 UN SDGs.
3. The North-South development construct is a crude assumption as we realise that there are also developed nations in the south as well as developing nations in the north. But we use this term for convenience to refer to the wider literature where it originates and understand that it is in fact a broad-based stereotype.
4. We realise that this in practice is a difficult task to achieve, which is why we later on provide a set of pedagogical protocols and guidance in general to assist the setting up of Living Global Citizenship educational partnership projects.
5. For a deeper theory of the conversational learning paradigm, see Harri-Augstein and Thomas' (1991) seminal work 'Learning Conversations'.

2 Pedagogy for Effective Citizenship Education

1. This is a pedagogical trap that many teachers fall into when delivering any curriculum subject, citizenship being no exception.

2. Coombs (1995) described this learning environment as being one of Rogerian 'equanimity' of all those persons involved. Steve Coombs further described this deliberate attempt at equalling of the power relationships as implementing a policy of social parity, developing a Rogerian climate of trust, congruence and the ideal living conditions for building Senge's (1990) learning organisation.
3. See a press release on this at: http://www.ed.gov/news/press-releases/ us-department-education-calls-action-develop-21st-century-citizens-strengthen-de.
4. See the UK's Department for International Development (DfID) Research website at: https://www.gov.uk/government/organisations/department-for-international-development/about/research.
5. See also the article 'Impact evaluation: how to measure what matters' in the *Guardian* (2013) on their Global Development Professionals Network at: http://www.theguardian.com/global-development-professionals-network/2013/may/02/impact-evaluation-global-development-live-chat.
6. See this document entitled Building the Big Society at: https://www.gov. uk/government/publications/building-the-big-society.
7. The *Sunday Observer* online article featuring Edward Said on culture and imperialism is available at: http://www.sundayobserver.lk/2011/02/13/ mon05.asp.
8. This UK government policy paper is available at: https://www.gov.uk/ government/publications/cultural-education.
9. This UK government document is available at: https://www.gov.uk/ government/uploads/system/uploads/attachment_data/file/226569/ Cultural-Education.pdf.
10. The FEdMM comes under the Pacific Islands Forum Secretariat and their reports can be accessed at: http://www.forumsec.org/pages.cfm/strategic-partnerships-coordination/education/forum-education-ministers-meeting-fedmm/fedmm-2012-2.html (accessed on 4 February 2014).
11. For more details on the UTP see the story at the USP website: http://www. usp.ac.fj/news/story.php?id=1036 (accessed on 4 February 2014).

3 Living Theory Transformed into Living Global Citizenship

1. These ideas clash with notions of power and control of the 'academy' over accepted knowledge in society. A classic example of this power over knowledge production was the Catholic Church's pre-Renaissance view of the world and people such as Galileo. His 'peers' arrested him and forced him to withdraw his observed version of written 'knowledge' by consuming it! The European Renaissance was meant to be about freedom of thought and expression from tyranny. Living educational theories is very much the grandchild of the original Renaissance as it validates the individual to develop and share their theories of the world as they emerge from personal experiences.

2. Instead it could be argued that a living educational-theory is derived out of personal experiences derived from real life contexts. This viewpoint of personal knowledge production from living experiences is supported by George Kelly (1955) with his personal construct theory. Kelly argues that all humans operate as 'personal scientists' generating new knowledge from their lived experiences via personal reflection and construing. Kelly also developed tools as learning aids to help people to elicit personal meaning from their prior experiences and called them repertory grids.

3. The difference between ethics-based principles and values-based principles and their philosophical understanding could be distinguished between the collective viewpoints versus the personal. Consequently, ethics may be already shared and collectively accepted, whereas values are emergent from the individual's experience and being with the potential for sharing with others. There is therefore a complex and dynamic relationship between wider ethics and personal values. Ethics is generally accepted as informing one's practice, but it is also possible that new and emergent values can challenge and change ethics.

4. Each individual possesses their own experiential slant of the world they live in and this affects the personal construction of common language and meaning. This is why learning within oneself and externally with others is a form of experiential negotiation and exchange of meanings that ultimately leads to the formation of personal knowledge and values. Thomas and Harri-Augstein's (1985) definition of human learning recognises this personal need to make sense of the world through lived experiences and they maintain it is 'the construction and reconstruction, exchange and negotiation of significant, relevant and viable meanings' (p. 2). This academic framework of human learning fits well with the concept of living educational theories.

5. Living theories therefore provide a narrative around an individual's reflection upon their own and others educational practice and the personal influences engaged within that authentic realm and the resultant learning outcomes. It could also be argued that such narrative is actually experiential data and that the living educational methodology is in fact closer to an experiential research paradigm drawing upon such personal data as critical episodes of practice. Shared experiences, however, could be understood as co-experiential data, linking a phenomenological outcome with the group's individual living educational theories and explanations.

5   Designing a Living Global Citizenship Project

1. See sustainable development website at: http://www.sustainable development2015.org/index.php/uncsd-official-docs/sdgs-an-introduction and also the UN conference at Rio 2012: http://www.uncsd2012.org/ (Both last accessed: February 2014).

6 Propositions for Living Global Citizenship Projects

1. See the whole cycle of P-S-O-R for a Living Global Citizenship action research project illustrated in Figure 5.2.
2. See the Mirandanet website at: http://www.mirandanet.ac.uk/worlde citizens/ (Accessed: September 2013).

7 Living Global Citizenship: Lessons for Humanity

1. The epistemological and methodological model for this blueprint is illustrated in Figure 5.2.

Bibliography

Adichie, C.N. (2009) The Danger of a Single Story. *Paper Presented at the TED Global Conference*, Oxford. Retrieved 17 July 2013 from: www.ted.com/talks/chimamanda_adichie_the_danger_of_a_single_story.html.

Adler-Collins, J. (2000) *A Scholarship of Enquiry.* MA Dissertation, University of Bath. Retrieved 28 August 2013 from: http://www.actionresearch.net/writings/values/jekanma.pdf.

Adler-Collins, J. (2007) *Developing an Inclusional Pedagogy of the Unique: How do I Clarify, Live and Explain my Educational Influences in my Learning as I Pedagogise my Healing Nurse Curriculum in a Japanese University?* Ph.D Thesis, University of Bath. Retrieved 30 September 2013 from: http://www.actionresearch.net/living/jekan.shtml.

Adler-Collins, J. (2013a) Engaging with Emotional Poverty across Cultural Boundaries and Differences? *BERA Paper 2013.* Retrieved 10 September 2013 from: http://www.actionresearch.net/writings/bera13/jekanbera13sym.pdf.

Adler-Collins, J. (2013b) Inclusive Education Across Borders: How do we Prevent Educational Design of Nursing Curriculum Design from Colonising Indigenous Forms of Knowing? Paper presented at the *British Educational Research Association* Conference, University of Sussex. Retrieved 5 September 2013 from: http://article.wn.com/view/2013/11/26/Varsity_registrar_removed_OUR_SPECIAL_CORRESPONDENT_Rampada_/

Allender, J. S. (1991) *Imagery in Teaching and Learning: An Autobiography of Research in Four World Views.* New York: Praeger.

Albaloshi (2011) Giving new Emirati Nurses a Voice: Sharing Experience of Newly Graduated Emirati Nurses. Paper presented *at the International Nursing Council, Nursing Driving Access, Quality and Health General Conference 2011,* Malta.

Andreotti, V. (2008) Development vs Poverty: Notions of Cultural Supremacyin Development Education Policy. In D. Bourn (Ed.) *Development Education: Debates and Dialogues.* London: Bedford Way Papers, pp. 45–64

Andreotti, V. (2011) *Actionable Postcolonial Theory in Education.* New York: Palgrave Macmillan.

Andreotti, V. & De Souza, L. (2008) Learning to Read the World Through Others Eyes (ToE). Retrieved 13th October 2013 from: http://www.academia.edu/575387/Learning_to_Read_the_World_Through_Other_Eyes_2008_.

Association for Citizenship Teaching. (2013) Post-16 Citizenship. Retrieved December 2013 from: http://www.teachingcitizenship.org.uk/about-citizenship/citizenship/citizenship-curriculum/post-16-citizenship.

Bailee Smith, M. (2011) *European Development Days: Beyond 2015.* Retrieved 13 March 2013 from: http://www.youtube.com/watch?v=9x0YLfcDlFI.

Baker, J. (2000) *Evaluating the Impact of Development Projects on Poverty: A Handbook for Practitioners.* Washington, DC: LCSPR/PRMPO, The World Bank. Retrieved 1 February 2014 from: http://web.worldbank.org/

WBSITE/EXTERNAL/TOPICS/EXTPOVERTY/EXTISPMA/0,,contentMDK: 20194198~pagePK:148956~piPK:216618~theSitePK:384329,00.html.

Ball, F. & Tyson, C. (2011) *American Educational Research Association 2012 Annual Meeting Call for Submissions*. Vancouver, BC, Canada. Retrieved December 2013 from: http://www.aera.net/uploadedFiles/Publications/Journals/Educational_Researcher/4004/198-220_05EDR11.pdf.

Barber, M., Donnelly, K. and Rizvi, S. (2012) *Oceans of Innovation: The Atlantic, the Pacific, Global Leadership and the Future of Education*. Retrieved 14 June 2013 from: http://www.ippr.org/publication/55/9543/oceans-of-innovation-the-atlantic-the-pacific-global-leadership-and-the-future-of-education.

Barrett, A., Crossley, M. & Dachi, H.A. (2011) International Collaboration and Research Capacity Building: Learning from the EdQUal Experience, *Comparative Education* 47(1), pp. 67–77.

Barry, B. (2012) Challenging the Status Quo Meaning of Educational Quality: Introducing Transformational Quality (TQ) Theory©, *Educational Journal of Living Theories* 5(1), pp. 1–26. Retrieved 30 September 2013 from: http://ejolts.net/node/191.

Beer, S. (1974) *Designing Freedom*. New York: Wiley.

Beveridge, W. (1942) *Report of the Inter-Departmental Committee on Social Insurance and Allied Services*. London: HMSO.

Bhabha, H. (1994) *The Location of Culture*. London: Routledge.

Bloom, B. (Ed.) (1956) *Taxonomy of Educational Objectives: Book 1 Cognitive Domain*. London: Longman.

Bourdieu, P. (1990) *The Logic of Practice*. Stanford, CA: Stanford University Press.

Bourn, D. & Cara, O. (2013) School Linking – Where Next? Partnership Models Between Schools in Europe and Africa. Development Education Research Centre Research Paper No.10. Institute of Education, University of London. Retrieved 27 November 2013 from: http://www.ukowla.org.uk/publications/other-publications.

Brighouse, T. (2005) Values in Society and Education Conference, *CSCS Journal* 16(3), p. 2 Summer 2005.

British Council Connecting Classrooms. Managing a Successful Visit. Retrieved 27 November 2013 from: http://schoolsonline.britishcouncil.org/sites/default/files/files/Managing%20a%20successful%20visit.pdf.

British Council Connecting Classrooms. How to Build Sustainable Partnerships. Retrieved 27 November 2013 from: http://schoolsonline.britishcouncil.org/sites/default/files/files/Sustainability%20Toolkit.pdf.

British Council Schools Online. Bring the World Into Your Classroom. Retrieved 27 November from: http://schoolsonline.britishcouncil.org/your-journey.

Broudy, H.S. (1981) *Truth and Credibility*. New York: Longman.

Buber, M. (1947) *Between Man and Man*. Fontana Library. Retrieved 13 September 2013 from: http://deakinphilosophicalsociety.com/texts/buber/betweenmanandman.pdf.

Cassity, E. (2008) More Effective Aid Policy? AusAID and the Global Development Agenda, *IEJ: Comparative Perspectives* 9(2). Retrieved 21 April 2012 from: http://files.eric.ed.gov/fulltext/EJ894344.pdf, pp. 2–17.

Cavanagh, M. (2003) *Against Equality of Opportunity*. Oxford: Clarendon Press.

Chakrabarty, D. (1995) Radical Histories and Question of Enlightenment Rationalism. *Economic and Political Weekly*, 30(14), pp. 751–759.

Charles, E. (2007) *How Can I bring Ubuntu as a Living Standard of Judgment into the Academy? Moving Beyond Decolonisation through Societal Reidentification and Guiltless Recognition*. Ph.D. Thesis, University of Bath. Retrieved 30 September 2013 from: http://www.actionresearch.net/living/edenphd.shtml.

Chomsky, N. (1971) *Problems of Knowledge and Freedom*. New York: Pantheon.

Chomsky, N. (1976) On the Nature of Language. In S.R. Harnad, H.D. Steklis & J. Lancaster (Eds.) *Origins and Evolution of Language and Speech. Annals of the New York Academy of Sciences*, New York: Wiley, pp. 46–57.

Chomsky, N. (2003) *On Democracy and Education*. New York: Routledge Falmer.

Coombs, S. (1995) *Design and Conversational Evaluation of an IT Learning Environment Based on Self-Organised Learning*. PhD thesis, 2 Volumes. London: CSHL, Brunel University, p. 315.

Coombs, S. (2001) Knowledge Elicitation Systems (accepted for proceedings). Paper presented at th.322255e *EdMedia 2001 Conference in Tampere*, Finland, 25–30 June 2001.

Coombs, S. (2007) Developing a CPD Framework for PPD Impact: The Southwest ESCalate project. *IPDA Conference*, Ramada Hotel, Belfast, 30th November–1st December 2007.

Coombs, S. & Harris, C. (2006) *An Integrated Approach Towards Impact-led Research and CPD for the Teaching Profession*. Paper presented at the IPDA, University of Stirling, Scotland, 1st–2nd December 2006.

Coombs, S. & Potts, M. (2012) Bringing Living Citizenship as a Living Standard of Judgment into the Academy. A paper presented at the *2012 BERA Conference*, University of Manchester, 4–6 September 2012.

Coombs, S. & Potts, M. (2013) Living Citizenship: Transcending the Cultural Divide, *Educational Action Research* 21(3), pp. 429–443.

Coombs, S. & Smith, I. (1999) Integration of Critical and Creative Thinking Skills into an Instructional Technology Module of the Post-graduate Teacher Training Programme at Singapore's NIE. In Margit Waas (Ed.) *Enhancing Learning: Challenge of Integrating Thinking and Information Technology into the Curriculum*, Vol. 1 & 2 Ch.6: Creativity and Thinking. Singapore: NIE, pp. 670–679.

Coombs, S. & Smith, I. (2003) The Hawthorne Effect: Is it a Help or Hindrance in Social Science Research? *Change: Transformations in Education* 6(1), pp. 97–111.

Coombs, S., Lewis, M. & Denning, A. (2007) *Designing and Evaluating Impact Evidences for the TDA's PPD: A Southwest Perspective*. Paper presented at the *BERA Conference at the Institute of Education*, London, UK. Retrieved 5–8 September 2007 from: http://www.leeds.ac.uk/educol/documents/166148.pdf.

Council of Europe. (2008) White Paper on Intercultural Dialogue: Living Together as Equals in Dignity. Retrieved 13th October from: http://www.coe.int/t/dg4/intercultural/Source/Pub_White_Paper/White%20Paper_final_revised_EN.pdf.

Council of Europe. (2013) *Intercultural Dialogue*. Retrieved 13th October 2013 from: http://www.coe.int/t/dg4/intercultural/concept_EN.asp.

Council for Industry and Higher Education (CIHE). (2011) *Global Graduates into Global Leaders*. Retrieved 23 June 2013 from: http://www.cihe.co.uk/global-graduates-into-global-leaders/.

Cresswell, J. (2007) *Qualitative Inquiry & Research Design: Choosing Among Five Approaches*. California, London, New Dehli: Sage.

Crick, B. (1999) In *The National Curriculum, Handbook for Secondary Teachers in England* (QCA). London: DfES and QCA.

Crier, C. (21 May 2006) A Degree in Citizenship. *Huffington Post*. Retrieved 19 June 2013 from: http://www.huffingtonpost.com/catherine-crier/a-degree-in-citizenship_b_21404.html.

Crompton, T. (2010) *Common Cause: The Case for Working with our Cultural Values*. Retrieved 18th December 2012 from: http://www.wwforg.uk/change.

Crossley, M. (2011) Strengthening the Development of Educational Research Capacity in Small States. In M. Martin & M. Bray (Eds.) *Tertiary Education in Small States: Planning in the Context of Globalisation*. UNESCO/IIEP: Paris.

Crossley, M., Bray, M. & Packer, S. (2011) *Education in Small States: Policies and Priorities*. London: Commonwealth Secretariat.

Crotty, Y. (2011) An Introduction to the Special Issue on Digital Creativity and Video in the Workplace, *Educational Journal of Living Theories* 4(1), pp. i–xxxvi. Retrieved 30 September 2013 from: http://ejolts.net/node/184.

Crotty, Y. (2012) *Thesis, How am I Bringing an Educationally Entrepreneurial Spirit into Higher Education?* Ph.D. Thesis, Dublin City University, 2012. Retrieved 30 September 2013 from: http://www.actionresearch.net/living/yvonnecrotty.shtml.

Crotty, Y. & Farren, M. (2013) *Digital Literacies in Education: Creative, Multimodal and Innovative Practices*. Oxford: Peter Lang.

Dadds, M. & Hart, S. (2001) *Doing Practitioner Research Differently*. London: Routledge Falmer, p. 166.

Damen, L. (1987) *Culture Learning: The Fifth Dimension on the Language Classroom*. Reading, MA: Addison-Wesley.

De Coster, I., Forsthuber, B., Kosinska, R., Steinberger, M. (2005) *Citizenship Education at School in Europe*. Brussels: Belgium.

Delong, J. (2002) How Can I Improve My Practice As A Superintendent Of Schools And Create My Own Living Educational Theory? Ph.D. Thesis, University of Bath. Retrieved 9 May 2014 from http://www.actionresearch.net/living/delong.shtml

Delong, J. (2009) Building a Culture of Inquiry through the Embodied Knowledge of Teachers and Teacher Educators in Aboriginal and Non-aboriginal

Contexts. Paper presented at the 2009 Conference of the *American Educational Research Association*. Retrieved 30 September 2013 from: http://www.jackwhitehead.com/delong/jdAERA09Paperfinal.pdf.

Delong, J. (2013) *Lesson Improvement and School Reform through Action Research in Canada*. A workshop at Mejiro Campus at Japan's Women's University in Tokyo on 9 November 2013.

Delong, J., Campbell, E., Whitehead, J. & Griffin, C. (2013) How are we Creating Cultures of Inquiry with Self-Studies That Transcend Constraints of Poverty on Empathetic Learning? Paper presented at the 2013 *American Educational Research Association* Conference in San Francisco. Retrieved 30 September 2013 from: http://www.actionresearch.net/writings/aera13/jdlcjwaera13cgopt.pdf.

Department for Education (DfE). (2013) National Citizen Service. Retrieved December 2013 from: http://www.education.gov.uk/childrenandyoungpeople/youngpeople/nationalcitizenservice.

Department for Education. (2013) Cultural Education: A Summary of Programmes and Opportunities. Retrieved 26 June 2013: https://www.gov.uk/government/uploads/system/uploads/attachment_data/file/226569/Cultural-Education.pdf.

Dewey, J. (1915) *Schools of Tomorrow*. New York: Dutton.

Dewey, J. (1933) *How We Think: A Restatement of the Relation of Reflective Thinking to the Educative Process*. Boston: D.C. Heath.

Dfe (2012) *Study Programmes for 16 to 19 Year Olds: Government response to consultation and plans for implementation*. Retrieved on 30 January 2013 from: https://www.education.gov.uk/consultations/downloadableDocs/1.%20Government%20response%20to%20consultation%20on%20study%20programmes%20for%2016-%20to%2019-year-olds%20for%20publication%20july%202012.pdf

Dfes (2004) *Putting the World into World Class Education*. Nottingham: Dfes Publications.

DfES/DfID. (2005) Developing the Global Dimension in the School Curriculum. Retrieved 13 June 2013 from: www.education.gov.uk/publications/.../1409-2005DOC-EN-02.docý.

Digital Divide Institute. (2013) Online website. Retrieved September 2013 from: http://www.digitaldivide.org/digital-divide/digitaldividedefined/digitaldivide.html.

Disney, A. (2004) Children's Developing Images and Representations of the School Link Environment. In S. Catling & F. Martin (Eds.) *Researching Primary Geography*. London: Register of Research in Primary Geography, pp. 139–147.

Dixon, K. (1987) *Implementing Open Learning in Local Authority Institutions*. FEU/MSC: (Crown©).

Donmoyer, R. (1996) Educational Research in an Era of Paradigm Proliferation: What's a Journal Editor to Do? *Educational Researcher* 25(2), pp. 19–25.

D'Souza, D. (2000) *The Virtue of Prosperity: Finding Values in an Age of Techno-Affluence*. New York: The Free Press.

D'Souza, B. (2008) *Changing Mindsets? Evaluation of a Rehabilitation Programme for Chemically Dependent Male Street Adolescents in a Major Indian City.* Ph.D. Thesis, Coventry University in collaboration with the University of Worcester, April.

D'Souza, B. (2012) *From Ecstasy to Agony and Back. Journeying with Adolescents on the Street.* London: Sage.

Dworkin, R. (2000) *Sovereign Virtue.* Cambridge: Harvard University Press.

ECOSOC. (2013) Millennium Development Goals and post-2015 Development Agenda. United Nations Economic and Social Council. Retrieved October 2013 from: http://www.un.org/en/ecosoc/about/mdg.shtml.

Edwards, M. & Hulme, D. (Eds.) (1995) *Non-Governmental Organisations: Performance and Accountability, Beyond the Magic Bullet.* London: Earthscan.

Elliott, J. (1991) *Action Research for Educational Change.* Buckingham: Open University Press.

Ellis, C. & Bochner, A. (2000) Autoethnography, Personal Narrative, Reflexivity: Researcher As Subject. In N. Denzin & Y. Lincoln (Eds.) *The Handbook of Qualitative Research* (2nd Edition). Thousand Oaks, CA: Sage, pp. 733–768.

Esping-Anderson, G. (1990) *The Three Worlds of Welfare Capitalism.* Princeton, New Jersey: Princeton University Press.

Esteva, G. (1996) Development. In W. Sachs (Ed) *The Development Dictionary.* London and New Jersey: Zed Books. pp. 12–24.

European Institute for Comparative Cultural Research (ERICArts). (2013) What is Intercultural Dialogue? Retrieved October 2013 from: http://www.interculturaldialogue.eu/web/intercultural-dialogue.php.

Eyler, J., Giles Jr., D., Gray, C., Stenson, C. (2001) *At A Glance: What We Know About the Effects of Service-Learning on College Students, Faculty, Institutions and Communities, 1993–2000*: Third Edition. Retrieved 24 June 2013: from: http://www.compact.org/wp-content/uploads/resources/downloads/aag.pdf.

Farrell, J. (2012) Transcending Boundaries and Borders: Constructing Living Theory Through Multidimensional Inquiry, *Educational Journal of Living Theories* 5(1), pp. 27–48. Retrieved 30 September 2013 from: http://ejolts.net/node/192.

Farren, M. (2006) How Can I Create a Pedagogy of the Unique Through a Web of Betweenness. Ph.D. Thesis, University of Bath. Retrieved 9 May 2014 from http://www.actionresearch.net/living/farren.shtml

Finley, A. (2011) A Brief Review of the Evidence on Civic Learning in Higher Education. Retrieved 21 June 2013: from: http://www.aacu.org/civic_learning/crucible/documents/CivicOutcomesBrief.pdf.

Flecknoe, M. (2003) Measuring the Impact of Teacher Professional Development: Can it be done? *European Journal of Teacher Education* 25(2&3), pp. 119–134.

Forester, C. (2012) What is a Living Legacy? In A. Henon (Ed.) *APEX Living Legacies: Stories Creating Futures.* Keynsham: Bath and North East Somerset.

Fouché, J. & Coombs, S. (2002) Developing and Integrating Internet-2 video Content into Teacher Education Programs. In D. Willis et al. (Eds.)

Proceedings of Society for Information Technology & Teacher Education International Conference 2002. Chesapeake, VA: AACE, pp. 1560–1561. Retrieved 13 December 2013 from: http://www.editlib.org/p/6793.

Fountain, S. (1995) *Education for Development, A Teacher's Resource for Global Learning*. London: Hodder and Stoughton.

Fromm, E. (1960) *The Fear of Freedom*. London: Routledge & Kegan Paul.

Further Education Unit. (1983) *Flexible Learning Opportunities*. London: FEU.

Further Education Unit. (1984) *Computer Literacy, Four Units*, LLoyd, Taylor & West Eds, 2nd. ed. London: FEU.

Further Education Unit. (1984a) *IT in FE: A Framework for Action in IT*. London: FEU.

Further Education Unit. (1987) *Supporting Adult Learning: A Curriculum Strategy for the Development of Continuing Education & Training for Adults*. London: FEU.

Gaine, C. (1995) *Still No Problem Here*. Stoke-On-Trent: Trentham Books.

Gardner, J. (1984) *Excellence: Can we be Equal and Excellent too?* New York: Norton.

Gardner, F. & Coombs, S. (Eds.) (2010) *Researching, Reflecting and Writing About Work: Guidance on Training Course Assignments and Research for Psychotherapists and Counsellors*. London: Routledge.

Garratt, Dean & Piper, Heather. (2010) Heterotopian Cosmopolitan Citizenship Education? *Education, Citizenship and Social Justice* 5(1), pp. 43–55.

Gearon, L. (2003) How Do We Learn to Become Good Citizens? *A Professional User Review of UK Research Undertaken for the British Educational Research Association*. Notts: BERA Retrieved 6 May 2014 from: http://www.bera.ac.uk/wp-content/uploads/2014/01/citpur1.pdf.

Ginnott, H. (1972) *Teacher and Child: A Book for Parents and Teachers*. New York: Macmillan.

Glaser, B. & Strauss, A. (1967) *The Discovery of Grounded Theory: Strategies for Qualitative Research*. New York: Aldine.

Glendinning, Lee. (29 April 2006) Citizenship Guide Fails its History Exam. *The Guardian*, London. Retrieved 15 June 2013 from: http://www.theguardian.com/uk/2006/apr/29/immigration.immigrationpolicy.

Goleman, D. (1998) *Working with Emotional Intelligence*. London: Bloomsbury Publishing.

Goodson, I. (2005) *Learning, Curriculum and Life Politics: The Selected Works of Ivor F. Goodson*. Oxon: Routledge.

Govinnage, S. (2011) *Edward Said on Culture and Imperialism*. Retrieved 25 June 2013 from: http://www.sundayobserver.lk/2011/02/13/mon05.asp.

Habermas, J. (1975) *Legitimation Crisis*. Boston, MA: Beacon Press.

Habermas, J. (1976) *Communication and the Evolution of Society*. London: Heinemann.

Habermas, J. (1998) *The Inclusion of the Other: Studies in Political Theory*, C. Cronin & P. De Greif (Eds.). Cambridge, MA: MIT Press, pp. 165–202.

Habermas, J. (2002) *The Inclusion of the Other: Studies in Political Theory*. Oxford: Polity.

Halstead, J.M. (1996) Values and Values Education in Schools. In J.M. Halstead & M.J. Taylor (Eds.) *Values in Education and Education in Values*. London: The Falmer Press.

Harri-Augstein, E. & Thomas, L. (1991) *Learning Conversations: The Self-organized Learning Way to Personal and Organizational Growth*. London: Routledge & Kegan Paul.

Hasan, M. (2012) Testing Makes a Mockery of Britishness. *New Statesman*. Retrieved 12 October 2013 from: http://www.newstatesman.com/blogs/politics/2012/07/testing-makes-mockery-britishness.

Hasan, Mehdi. (4 July 2012) Testing Makes a Mockery of Britishness. *New Statesman*. Retrieved 14 June 2013 from: http://www.newstatesman.com/blogs/politics/2012/07/testing-makes-mockery-britishness.

Henley, D. (2011) *Cultural Education in England*. Retrieved 29 June 2013 from: https://www.gov.uk/government/uploads/system/uploads/attachment_data/file/77941/Cultural_Education_report.pdf.

Hirst, P. (Ed.) (1983) *Educational Theory and its Foundation Disciplines*. London: RKP.

Hutchison, S. (2013) A Living Theory of Care-Giving. *Educational Journal of Living Theories*, 6(1), pp. 40–56. Retrieved 9 May 2014 from: http://ejolts.net/node/203

Huxtable, M. (2009) How do we Contribute to an Educational Knowledge Base? A Response to Whitehead and a Challenge to BERJ. *Research Intelligence* 107, pp. 25–26. Retrieved 11 January 2008 from: http://www.actionresearch.net/writings/huxtable/mh2009beraRI107.pdf.

Huxtable, M. (2012) Thesis, How do I Evolve Living-Educational-Theory Praxis in Living-Boundaries? Ph.D. Thesis, University of Bath. Retrieved November 2013 from: http://www.actionresearch.net/living/mariehuxtable.shtml.

Huxtable, M. & Whitehead, J. (2013) Living-Educational-Theories as Transformational Continuing Professional Development. A paper presented at the *2013 Conference of the British Educational Research Association* at the University of Sussex.

Ilyenkov, E. (1977) *Dialectical Logic, Essays on its History and Theory*. Moscow: Progress Publishers.

Inoue, N. (2012) *Mirrors of the Mind: Introduction to Mindful Ways of Thinking Education*. New York: Peter Lang.

International Association for the Evaluation of Educational Achievement (IEA). (2010) *Initial Findings from the IEA International Civic and Citizenship Education Study*. Retrieved 18 June 2013 from: http://www.nfer.ac.uk/nfer/publications/ICCX01/ICCX01_home.cfm.

Jefferess, D. (2008) Global Citizenship and the Cultural Politics of Benevolence, *Critical Literacy: Theories and Practices* 2(1), pp. 27–36.

John, K. & Pound, R. (2011) 5x5x5 = creativity, Events and Publications. Retrieved 16 September 2012 from: http://www.5x5x5creativity.org.uk/?id=129.

Kekes, J. (2001) Dangerous Egalitarian Dreams, *City Journal*. Retrieved 23rd December 2012 from http://www.city-journal.org/html/11_4_urbanities-dangerous.html.

Kelly, G. (1955) *The Psychology of Personal Constructs*, Vols. 1 & 2. New York: Norton.

Kerr, D. (1999) *Citizenship Education: An International Comparison.* Retrieved 12 June 2013 from: http://www.inca.org.uk/pdf/citizenship_no_intro.pdf.

Kezar, A. (2002) Becoming a Pluralistic Leader: Using Case Studies to Transform Beliefs, *Metropolitan Universities Journal* 13(2), pp. 95–104.

Khoza, R. (1994) *African Humanism.* Ekhaya Promotions: Diepkloof Extension SA.

Krugman, P. (2011) More Thoughts on Equality of Opportunity. *The New York Times.* Retrieved 23rd December 2011 from: http://krugman.blogs.nytimes.com/2011/01/11/more-thoughts-on-equality-of-opportunity/.

Kuhn, T. (1962) *The Structure of Scientific Revolutions* (1st ed.). University of Chicago Press.

KuhnThomas, S. (2012) *The Structure of Scientific Revolutions: 50th Anniversary.* Ian Hacking (intro.) (4th ed.). University of Chicago Press.

Laidlaw, M. (1994) The Democratising Potential of Dialogical Focus in an Action Enquiry, *Educational Action Research* 2(2), pp. 223–241.

Laidlaw, M. (1996) *How Can I Create my own Living Educational Theory as I Offer you an Account of my Educational Development?* Ph.D. University of Bath. Retrieved 30 September 2013 from http://www.actionresearch.net/living/moira2.shtml.

Laidlaw, M. (2006) *How Might We Enhance the Educational Value of our Researchbase at the New University in Guyuan? Researching Stories for the Social Good* (Inaugural Professorial Lecture). Retrieved 30 September 2013 from: http://www.jackwhitehead.com/china/mlinaugural.htm.

Laidlaw, M. (2006) Action Research in China's Experimental Centre for Educational Action Research in Foreign Languages Teaching at Ningxia Teachers University. Retrieved 16 October 2013 from: http://www.actionresearch.net/writings/moira.shtml.

Laidlaw, M. (2008) In Pursuit of Counterpoint: An Educational Journal, *Educational Journal of Living Theories* 1(1), pp. 69–102.

Lather, P. (1994) Textual Strategies and the Politics of Interpretation in Educational Research, *Australian Educational Researcher*, 21(1), pp. 41–63.

Lederach, J.P. (1995) *Preparing for Peace: Conflict Transformation Across Cultures.* Syracuse, NY: Syracuse University Press.

Lee, C.D. & Rochon, R. (2009) *2010 AERA Annual Meeting Theme:Understanding Complex Ecologies in a Changing World.* Retrieved on 12 December 2012 from: www.spanglefish.com/.../lee-and-rochon-09-complex-ecologies.doc

Lewin, K. (1948) *Resolving Social Conflicts: Selected Papers on Group Dynamics.* Gertrude W. Lewin (Ed.). New York: Harper & Row.

Lewin, R. (1993) *Complexity: Life on the Edge of Chaos.* London: Phoenix.

Li, P. & Laidlaw, M. (2006) Collaborative Enquiry, Action Research, and Curriculum Development in Rural China: How can we Facilitate a Process of Educational Change? *Action Research* 4(3), pp. 333–350.

Linton, R. (1945) *The Cultural Background of Personality.* New York: Appleton.

Liverpool Hope University (2011) Faculty of Education Strategic Map 2011–2012. Retrieved 9 May 2014 from: http://www.actionresearch.net/writings/lhu/lhusm11-12.pdf

Lord Goldsmith. (2008) *Citizenship: Our Common Bond*. Lord Goldsmith's Report. Retrieved 17 June 2013 from: http://www.natecla.org.uk/news/302/Citizenship-Our-Common-Bond-Report.

Louw, D. (1998) Ubuntu: An African Assessment of the Religious Other. *Twentieth World Congress of Philosophy*. Massachusetts: University of Boston. Retrieved on 7 April 2012 from: http://www.bu.edu/wcp/Papers/Afri/AfriLouw.htm

Manji, F. & O'Coill, C. (2002) The Missionary Position: NGO's and Development in Africa. In *International Affairs* 78(3), pp. 567–583.

Marcuse, H. (1964) *One Dimensional Man*, London: Routledge and Kegan Paul.

Marshall, G. (1998) Social Justice. Encyclopedia.com. Retrieved 23 December 2011 from: http://www.encyclopedia.com/topic/Social_justice.aspx#1.

Martin, F. (2005) North-South Linking as a Controversial Issue, *Prospero* 14(4), pp. 47–54.

Martin, F. (2007) School Linking as a Controversial Issue. In H. Claire & C. Holden (Eds.) *The Challenge of Teaching Controversial Issues*. Stoke-on-Trent: Trentham Books Ltd.

Martin, F. & Griffiths, H. (2012) Power and Representation: A Postcolonial Reading of Global Partnerships and Teacher Development Through North-South Study Visits, *British Educational Research Journal* 38(6), pp. 907–927.

Maxwell, S. & Riddell, R. (1998) Conditionality or Contract: Perspectives on Partnership for Development, *Journal of International Development*, 10, pp. 257–268.

McNiff, J. (2006) My Story is my Living Educational Theory. In J. Clandinin (Ed.) *Handbook of Narrative Inquiry*. London & New York: Sage.

McTaggart, R. (1992) Reductionism and Action Research: Technology Versus Convivial Forms of Life. In C.S. Bruce & A.L. Russell (Eds.) *Transforming Tomorrow Today*. University of Queensland, Australia: Brisbane, pp. 47–61.

Mezirow, J. (2011) *Fostering Critical Reflection in Adulthood A Guide to Transformative and Emancipatory Learning 'How Critical Reflection Triggers Transformative Learning'*. Retrieved 12 September 2013 from: http://wwwprod.ln.edu.hk/osl/conference2011/output/breakout/4.4%20%5Bref%5DHow%20Critical%20Reflection%20triggers%20Transformative%20Learning%20-%20Mezirow.pdf

Mitroff, I. & Kilman, R. (1978). *Methodological Approaches to Social Science*. San Francisco: Jossey-Bass.

Murray, M. & Kujundzic, N. (2005) *Critical Reflection: A Textbook For Critical Thinking*. Québec, Canada: McGill-Queen's University Press.

National Citizen Service (NCS). (2013) Welcome to NCS. Retrieved December 2013 from: http://www.ncsyes.co.uk/.

Nationality, Immigration and Asylum Act UK. (2002) Retrieved 13 June 2013 from: http://www.legislation.gov.uk/ukpga/2002/41/contents.

National Service-Learning Clearing House. Retrieved 11 December 2012 from: http://www.servicelearning.org/.

Ndaba, W.J. (1994) *Ubuntu in Comparison to Western Philosophies*. Pretoria: Ubuntu School of Philosophy.

Nederveen Pieterse, J. (2000) 'After Post-Development', *Third World Quarterly*, 22(4), pp. 479–489.

New Economics Foundation (NEF). (2010) *Ten Big Questions about the Big Society and Ten Ways to Make the Best of it*. Retrieved 22 June 2013 from: http://dnwssx4l7gl7s.cloudfront.net/nefoundation/default/page/-/files/Ten_Big_Questions_about_the_Big_Society.pdf.

NFER. (2010) CELS: The Citizenship Education Longitudinal Study. *National Foundation for Educational Research (NFER)*. Retrieved 3 July 2013 from: http://www.nfer.ac.uk/research/projects/cels/.

Nozick, R. (1974) *Anarchy State and Utopia*. New York: Basic Books.

Nussbaum, M. (1997) *Cultivating Humanity: A Classical Defense of Reform in Liberal Education*. Massachusetts and London: Harvard University Press.

OFSTED. (2004) *Making a Difference: The Impact of Award-Bearing INSET on School Improvement*. HMI1765. Retrieved on 24 September 2012 from: http://www.ofsted.gov.uk/resources/making-difference-impact-of-award-bearing-service-training-school-improvement

OFSTED. (2010) *Citizenship Established? Citizenship in Schools 2006/09*. Retrieved 18 June 2013 from: http://www.ofsted.gov.uk/resources/citizenship-established-citizenship-schools-200609.

Parekh, B. (2000) *Rethinking Multiculturalism. Cultural Diversity and Political Theory*. London: Macmillan Press.

Patel, E. (18 March 2010) The Faith Divide. *Newsweek*. Retrieved 19 June 2013 from: http://newsweek.washingtonpost.com/onfaith/eboo_patel/2010/03/obama_and_his_council.html.

Paton, G. (2012) Voluntary Work to Form Part of A-levels. *Daily Telegraph* 17 October 2012. Retrieved 16 June 2013 from: http://www.telegraph.co.uk/education/educationnews/9613859/Voluntary-work-to-form-part-of-A-levels.html.

Peters, R.S. (1966) *Ethics and Education*. London: Allen and Unwin.

Phillips, I. (2011) *My Emergent African Great Story 'Living I' as Naturally Including Neighbourhood, Embodying an Audacious Valuing Social Living Pedagogy and Imagining the Universe Luminously, as an Energetic Inclusion of Darkness Throughout Light and Light in Darkness*. Ph.D. Thesis, University of Bath. Retrieved 30 September 2013 from http://www.actionresearch.net/writings/phillips.shtml.

Pickerel, W. (2006) *Center for Communication and Civic Engagement*. Retrieved 13 June 2013 from: http://depts.washington.edu/ccce/research/UndergradResearch.htm.

Popper, K. (1963) *Conjectures and Refutations: The Growth of Scientific Knowledge*. London: Routledge.

Porter, N. (2004) *CMA Methodology: Autoethnography. Computer Mediated Anthropology. An Online Resource Centre of the University of South Florida*. Retrieved 7 August 2013 from: http://anthropology.usf.edu/cma/CMAmethodology-ae.htm.

Potts, M. (2012) *How Can I Reconceptualise International Educational Partnerships as a Form of 'Living Citizenship'?* Ph.D. Thesis, Bath Spa University. Retrieved 8 August 2013 from: http://www.actionresearch.net/living/markpotts.shtml.

Pring, R. (2000) *Philosophy of Educational Research*. London and New York: Continuum.

QCA. (1999) *National Curriculum. Handbook for Secondary Teachers in England*. London: DFES and QCA.

QCDA. (2008) *Citizenship Key Stage 4*. Retrieved February 2011 from: http://curriculum.qcda.gov.uk/key-stages-3-and-4/subjects/key-stage-4/citizenship/programme-of-study/index.aspx?tab=3.

Qualifications and Curriculum Authority (QCA). (2004) Play Your Part Post-16 Citizenship. Retrieved November 2013 from: http://www.zinestudio.co.uk/activecitizens/images//QCAGuidance.pdf

Rahnema, M. and Bawtree, V. (Eds) (1997) *The Post-develpment Reader*. New Jersey: Zed Books.

Rampaola, M.P. (2013) *Developing Teaching And Learning Skills At A Higher Education Institution: A Collaborative Action Research Study*. D.Ed. Thesis, Walter Sisulu University.

Rawal, S. (2006) *The Role of Drama in Enhancing Life Skills in Children with Specific Learning Difficulties in a Mumbai School: My Reflective Account*. Ph.D. Thesis, Coventry University in Collaboration with the University of Worcester. Retrieved 30 September 2013 from: http://www.actionresearch.net/living/rawal.shtml.

Rawal, S. (2009) ... as I Engaged in Reflection: A Play in Three Acts, *Reflective Practice* 10(1), pp. 27–32.

Rawls, J. (1971) *A Theory of Justice*. Cambridge, MA: Harvard University Press.

Rayner, A. (2003) *Rationality and Inclusionality. The "Outs" and "Ins" of Biological and Other Science*. Retrieved 12 September 2013 from: http://people.bath.ac.uk/bssadmr/inclusionality/cultureandbelief.htm.

Roberts, M. (2005) *Launch of Black Dust at Ottakars Bookshop in Salisbury*, 2005 (DVD). Salisbury: Roberts, M.

Roemer, J. (1998) *Equality of Opportunity*. Cambridge, MA: Harvard College.

Rogers, C. (1961) *On Becoming a Person: A Therapist's View of Psychotherapy*. London: Constable.

Rothstein, B. (1998) *Just Institutions Matter: The Moral and Political Logic of the Universal Welfare State (Theories of Institutional Design)*. Cambridge.

Ryan, M. *Service-Learning After Learn and Serve America: How Five States Are Moving Forward*. Denver: Education Commission of the States. Retrieved on 8 August 2013 from: http://www.nylc.org/sites/nylc.org/files/09-ECS%20NCLC%20Report%20-%20Service-Learning%20After%20LSA.pdf

Sachs, J. (1999) Teacher Professional Identity: Competing Discourses, Competing Outcomes. Paper Presented at AARE Conference Melbourne, November 1999. Retrieved 15th October 2013 from: http://www.aare.edu.au/99pap/sac99611.htm.

Said, E. (1993) *Culture and Imperialism*. London: Vintage Books.

Said, E.W. (1997) *Beginnings: Intention and Method*. London: Granta.

Sardello, R. (2008) *Silence: The Mystery of Wholeness*. Berkeley: Goldenstone Press.

Sayers, H. (2002) Citizenship in the School Curriculum, *CSCS Journal* 13(2), pp. 14–15.

Scott, W. (2005) *Education for Sustainable Development (ESD): What Sort of Decade?* Keynote address at the UK Launch of the UNESCO. Decade for ESD, December 13th.

Schön, D. (1995) The New Scholarship Requires a New Epistemology, *Change*, 27(6), pp. 27–34.

Schulz, W., Ainley, J. Fraillon, J. Kerr, D. Losito, B. & Schulz, W. (2010) *Initial Findings from the IEA International Civic and Citizenship Education Study*. Retrieved December 2013 from: http://www.iea.nl/fileadmin/user_upload/Publications/Electronic_versions/ICCS_2009_Initial_Findings.pdf.

Senge, P. (1990) *The Fifth Discipline: The Art and Practice of the Learning Organization*. New York: Doubleday/Currency.

Sharp, J. (2009) *Geographies of Postcolonialism*. London: Sage.

Sharpe, L., Coombs, S. & Gopinathan, S. (1999) Computer Communications Discourse for Singapore's Practicum Students. In Margit Waas (Ed.) *Enhancing Learning: Challenge of Integrating Thinking and Information Technology into the Curriculum*, Vol. 1 & 2, Ch.2: Information Technology. Singapore: NIE, pp. 216–222.

Shaver, J.P. & Strong, W. (1976) *Facing Value Decisions: Rationale Building for Teachers*. Belmont, CA: Wadsworth.

Shutte, A. (1993) *Philosophy for Africa*. Rondebosch. South Africa: UCT Press.

Simon, A. (2005) *Citizenship Education and Multiculturalism: The Needs of Educators within the Contemporary Multicultural Context*. Retrieved 29 August 2013 from: http://www.ece.salford.ac.uk/proceedings/papers/14_07.pdf.

Simon, B. (1991) *Education and the Social Order, 1940–1990*. New York: St Martin's Press.

Skolnick, J., Dulberg, N. & Maestre, T. (2004) *Through Other Eyes: Developing Empathy and Multicultural Perspectives in the Social Studies* (2nd ed.). Pippin Teacher's Library (Book 43). Toronto: Pippen Publishing Corporation.

Slater, P. (1976) *The Measurement of Intrapersonal Space by Grid Technique*. Oxford, England: J. Wiley & Sons.

Slater, D. and Bell, M. (2002) Aid and the Geopolitics of the Post-Colonial: Critical Reflections on New Labour's Overseas Development Strategy. *Development and Change*, 33(2), pp. 335–360.

Stake, R. (1995) *The Art of Case Study Research*. Thousand Oaks. CA: Sage Publications.

Tattersall, P. (2007) What is Community Based Auditing and How Does it Work? *J. Tas. Comm. Res. Auditors Inc* 4(2), pp. 31–48.

Tattersall, P. (2011) How am I Generating a Living Theory of Environmental Activism with Inclusionality. Ph.D. Thesis, The University of Western

Sydney. Retrieved 16 October 2013 from: http://www.actionresearch.net/living/tattersallphd/philtphd.pdf.

TES. (2010) Transformative Education/al Studies Project. Retrieved 16 October 2013 from: http://www.actionresearch.net/writings/southafrica/TESproposalopt.pdf.

TES. (2011–2014) *The Successful Proposal: Transformative Education/al Studies*. Retrieved 30 September 2013 from: http://www.actionresearch.net/writings/southafrica/TESproposalopt.pdf.

Thaman, K. (2008) Preface to Learning to Read the World Through Others Eyes. Retrieved 13th October 2013 from: http://www.academia.edu/575387/Learning_to_Read_the_World_Through_Other_Eyes_2008_ (p6).

Thaman, K.H. (2004) Whose Values and What Responsibility? Cultural and Cognitive Democracy in Education, Keynote address, *Pacific Circle Consortium Conference*, Hong Kong, SAR, 21–23 April 2004.

The Center for Information & Research on Civic Learning and Engagement. (2003) *Special Report: The Civic Mission of Schools*. Retrieved 13 June 2013 from: http://www.civicyouth.org/special-report-the-civic-mission-of-schools/.

The Guardian. (2013) Impact Evaluation: How to Measure What Matters, online article published in *the Guardian* on their *Global Development Professionals Network*. Retrieved 1 February 2014 from: http://www.theguardian.com/global-development-professionals-network/2013/may/02/impact-evaluation-global-development-live-chat.

The Parliamentary Assembly Council of Europe. (2008) *Cultural Education: The Promotion of Cultural Knowledge, Creativity and Intercultural Understanding Through Education*. Retrieved 26 June 2013 from: http://www.dieangewandte.at/jart/prj3/angewandte/resources/dbcon_def/uploads/Universitaet/Berichte%20und%20Leistungsvereinbahrungen/EreportBparis0812.pdf.

Thomas, L. & Harri-Augstein, E. (1985) *Self-organized Learning: Foundations of a Conversational Science for Psychology*. London: Routledge & Kegan Paul.

Tian, F. & Laidlaw, M. (2006) *Action Research and the New Curriculum in China: Case-studies and Reports in the Teaching of English*. Xi'an: Shanxi Tourism Press.

Tillich, P. (1962) *The Courage to be*. London: Fontana.

Tisch, J. (27 April 2010) Active Citizenship: A New Approach to Volunteering. *Huffington Post*. Retrieved 19 June 2013 from: http://www.huffingtonpost.com/jonathan-tisch/active-citizenship-a-new_b_553417.html.

Tocqueville (1835) *Democracy in America: Translated by Henry Reeve*. Adelaide: The University of Adelaide. Retrieved on 12 August 2013 from: http://ebooks.adelaide.edu.au/t/tocqueville/alexis/democracy/complete.html

Tocqueville, A. (2000) *Democracy in America*. Chicago: The University of Chicago Press.

Todd, S. (2008) *Toward an Imperfect Education: Facing Humanity, Rethinking Cosmopolitanism*. Boulder, CO: Paradigm. Toronto District School Board (TDSB).

Torney-Purta, J., Schwille, J. & Amadeo, J.A. (Eds.). (1999) *Civic Education Across Countries: Twenty-four Case Studies from the IEA Civic Education Project*. Amsterdam, The Netherlands: International Association for the Evaluation of Educational Achievement (IEA).

UK Government. Retrieved 21 June 2013 from: https://www.gov.uk/government/uploads/system/uploads/attachment_data/file/78979/building-big-society_0.pdf.

UNESCO. (1974) Recommendation Concerning Education for International Understanding, Cooperation and Peace and Education Relating to Human Rights and Fundamental Freedoms. Retrieved December 2013 from: http://www.unesco.org/education/tlsf/mods/theme_b/mod07.html.

UNESCO. (1995) *Declaration and Integrated Framework of Action on Education for Peace, Human Rights and Democracy*. Retrieved 21 June 2013 from: http://www.unesco.org/education/tlsf/mods/theme_b/mod07.html.

UNESCO. (2000) *World Education Forum: Final Report*. Paris: UNESCO. Retrieved February 2014 from: http://www.unesco.org/education/efa/wef_2000/.

UNESCO. (2011) *Feasibility Study on Establishing a Regional Mechanism (or institute) to Provide Sustainable and Ongoing Training in the Pacific on Educational Policy and Planning*. Feasibility Study Conducted by Kingfisher Consultancy and Commissioned by the UNESCO Pacific Office. Retrieved February 2014 from: http://www.forumsec.org/resources/uploads/attachments/documents/2012FEdMM.05_Attach1.pdf.

United Kingdom One World Linking Association (UKOWLA). (2011) *Welcome to the UKOWLA*. Retrieved 18 June 2013 from: http://www.ukowla.org.uk/.

United Nations Sustainable Development Knowledge Platform. (2013) *Sustainable Development Goals*. Open Working Group Platform. Retrieved October 2013 from: http://sustainabledevelopment.un.org/index.php?menu=1300.

U.S. Department of Education. (2012) *U.S. Department Of Education Calls For Action To Develop 21st Century Citizens, Strengthen Democracy*. Retrieved 23 June 2013 from: http://www.ed.gov/news/press-releases/us-department-education-calls-action-develop-21st-century-citizens-strengthen-de.

Useem, J. & Useem, R. (1963) Men in the middle of the third culture, *Human Organizations*, 22(3), pp. 169–179.

Van De Merwe, W. (1996) Philosophy and the Multi-cultural Context of (Post) Apartheid South Africa, *Ethical Perspectives* 3(2), pp. 1–15.

Vybiral, M. (2005) Values: Ideals and Reality, *CSCS Journal* 16(3), Summer 2005, pp. 2–3.

Wallace, B. & Erickson, G. Eds. (2006) *Diversity in Gifted Education: International Perspective on Global Issues*. Abingdon: Routledge, pp. 45–55.

Wenger, E. (1998) *Communities of Practice: Learning, Meaning, and Identity*. Cambridge: Cambridge University Press.

West Burnham J. (2006) Understanding learning: creating a shared vocabulary. In: B. Wallace and G. Erickson (Eds). *Diversity in Gifted Education: International Persepective on Global Issues*. Abingdon: Routledge, pp. 45–55.

Westheimer, J. & Kahne, J. (2004) What Kind of Citizen? The Politics of Educating for Democracy, *Published In the American Educational Research Journal* 41(2), pp. 237–269.

Whitehead, J. (1976) *Improving Learning for 11–14 Year Olds in Mixed Ability Science Groups*. Swindon: Wiltshire Curriculum Development Centre. Retrieved 16 October 2013 from: http://www.actionresearch.net/writings/ilmagall.pdf.

Whitehead, J. (1989) Creating a Living Educational Theory From Questions of the Kind, 'How Do I Improve my Practice?' *Cambridge Journal of Education* 19(1), pp. 41–52.

Whitehead, J. (1993) *The Growth of Educational Knowledge: Creating Your own Living Educational Theories*. Bournemouth: Hyde Publications. Retrieved 8 August 2013 from: http://www.actionresearch.net/writings/jwgek93.htm.

Whitehead, J. (1999) Educative Relations in a New Era, *Pedagogy Culture and Society* 7(1), pp. 73–90.

Whitehead, J. (1999) *How Do I Improve My Practice? Creating A Discipline Of Education Through Educational Enquiry*. Ph.D. Thesis, University of Bath. Retrieved 8 August 2013 from: http://www.actionresearch.net/living/jackwhitehead2.shtml.

Whitehead, J. (2005) How can we Improve the Educational Influences of Our Teacher-Researcher Quests? Keynote Presentation to the *12th International Conference of Teacher Research* at McGill University, 16 April 2005. Retrieved 8 June 2013 from: http://www.actionresearch.net/writings/ictr05/jwictr05key.htm.

Whitehead, J. (2008) Using A Living Theory Methodology in Improving Practice And Generating Educational Knowledge in Living Theories, *Educational Journal of Living Theories* 1(1), pp. 103–126. Retrieved 2 September 2013 from: http://ejolts.net/node/80.

Whitehead, J. (2009) *Justifying the Use of a Living Theory Methodology in the Creation of Your Living Educational Theory. Responding to Cresswell.* Retrieved 12 October 2013 from: http://www.actionresearch.net/writings/arsup/Cresswellqualitativemethods.pdf.

Whitehead, J. (2009) How do I Influence the Generation of Living Educational Theories for Personal and Social Accountability in Improving Practice? Using a Living Theory Methodology in Improving Educational Practice. In D.L. Tidwell, M.L. Heston & L.M. Fitzgerald (Eds.) (2009) *Research Methods for the Self-Study of Practice*. Chicago: Springer, pp. 173–194.

Whitehead, J. (2011) *Notes for Jack Whitehead's 2011 Mandela Day Lecture at Durban University of Technology* on the 18th July 2011 with the Video of the Lecture. Retrieved 8 August 2013 from: http://www.actionresearch.net/writings/jack/jwmandeladay2011.pdf.

Whitehead, J. (2012) Living Educational Theories for Action Research in a Turbulent World, in *Action Research for Sustainable Development in a Turbulent World*. Emerald Group Publishing Ltd, pp. 67–84.

Whitehead, J. (2013) A Living Logic for Educational Research., A paper presented at the *British Educational Research Association* Conference at the

University of Sussex and the 4th September 2013. Retrieved 30 September from: http://www.actionresearch.net/writings/bera13/jwbera13phil010913. pdf.

Whitehead, J. (2013) An Epistemological Transformation in Educational Knowledge from S-STEP Research. In Y. Crotty & M. Farren (Eds.) (2013) *Digital Literacies in Education: Creative, Multimodal and Innovative Practices.* Oxford: Peter Lang. Retrieved 26 November 2013 from: http://www. actionresearch.net/writings/jack/jwsstep130409sandiego.pdf.

Whitehead, J. & Huxtable, M. (2013) Living Educational Theory Research as Transformational Continuing Professional Development, *Gifted Education International* 29(3), pp. 221–226.

Wood, L. (2012) Action Research: Its Transformative Potential, *Educational Research for Social Change* 1(1), pp. 1–4.

Wright-Mills, C. (1959) *The Sociological Imagination.* Oxford: Oxford University Press.

Yalom, I.D. (1995) *The Theory and Practice of Group Psychotherapy.* New York: Basic Books.

Zammit, J. (2008) Global Learning and School Partnerships, Thinking it Through Retrieved 15th October 2013 from: http://www.tidec.org/Tidetalk/ articles/GL%20and%20Sch%20part.html.

Zuniga, X., Nagda, B. A., Chesler, M. & Cytron-Walker, A. (2006) Intergroup Dialogue in Higher Education: Meaningful Learning About Social Justice, *ASHE Higher Education Report* 32(4).

Index

Printed and bound by CPI Group (UK) Ltd, Croydon, CR0 4YY